A. ROSS MCCORMACK ~~~~~~~~~~~~~~~ ~~~~~~~~~ ry at the
University of Winnipeg.

Reformers, Rebels, and Revolutionaries in examining the roots of the radical movement in western Canada explores the constituencies, ideologies, and development of early reformist, syndicalist, and socialist organizations from the 1880s up to the Winnipeg General Strike in 1~~~~~~~~~~~~~~~~~~~~~~~~~~~ three types of radicals – reformers, rebels, an with each other to fashion a general western

The reformers wanted to change society f but both their aims and methods were mode philosophy and tactics of the British labour . The rebels, militant industrial unionists, periodically battled the Trades and Labor Congress in order to establish unions strong enough to defeat the employers and, if necessary, the state. The revolutionary Marxists were committed to the destruction of industrial capitalism and the establishment of a society controlled by the workers.

The book describes the origins of radicalism, traces the histories of the various organizations that expressed its ideals, and discusses the impact of the first world war on the labour movement.

Using previously unexplored sources, McCormack has produced the first comprehensive examination of the early history of the radical movement in western Canada, adding an important dimension to our knowledge and understanding of Canadian labour history.

A. ROSS McCORMACK

Reformers, Rebels, and Revolutionaries: The Western Canadian Radical Movement 1899–1919

UNIVERSITY OF TORONTO PRESS
Toronto Buffalo London

© University of Toronto Press 1977
Toronto Buffalo London
Reprinted 1979
Printed in Canada

Library of Congress Cataloging in Publication Data

McCormack, Andrew Ross, 1943–
  Reformers, rebels, and revolutionaries.

  Bibliography: p.
  Includes index.
  1. Socialism in Canada – History. 2. Radicalism – Canada – History.
  3. Trade-unions – Canada – Political activity – History. I. Title.
  HX109.M3   320.5′315′0971   77-4338
  ISBN 0-8020-5385-8
  ISBN 0-8020-6316-6 pbk.

For Carolyn

Contents

9
Epilogue 165

Preface

By entitling this study *Reformers, Rebels, and Revolutionaries*, I intended to convey the tension that was the principal characteristic of the early western Canadian radical movement. To elaborate that tension, the study focuses on the social and economic circumstances that fostered the movement's growth, the external doctrinal influences that inspired it, and, principally, the nature of its institutional and ideological development. By radicalism I mean a commitment to social change and a design for modifying society which were based ultimately on a Marxian analysis of capitalism.

Certainly the materialistic and predatory society that the prewar Boom produced was in need of modification. Many western workers were brutally exploited under the industrial capitalism which emerged with phenomenal rapidity after the mid-1890s. The process of industrialization had resulted in the growth of radical movements in Britain, the United States, and Europe. Because industrial capitalism was not peculiar in Canada, radical doctrines, which were part of the immigrants' cultural baggage, were relevant to the workers' experience in the West.

Radical doctrines had a constituency. Support was concentrated in the coal fields of Vancouver Island, Victoria, Vancouver, the hardrock mining camps of the Kootenays, the Crow's Nest Pass of southeastern British Columbia and southwestern Alberta, and Winnipeg, places where the transition to pure industrial capitalism was most complete. These were virtually the only places in western Canada where trade unions demonstrated vitality. Here workers persistently elected radicals to union offices. Because radicals played an influential, if not predominant, role in the labour movement where it was most vital, they gave a special character to western unionism. More important in the long run, workers in these places elected radicals to municipal councils, provincial legislatures, and the federal Parliament and thus firmly laid the foundations of the region's continuing tradition of working class political action. A vigorous radical movement, then, emerged in western Canada during the first two decades of the century.

Because of the diversity of the workers' experience and because of the variety of doctrinal influences, the radical movement could not be monolithic. It contained three attitudinal tendencies - reformers, rebels, and revolutionaries. Labourites were essentially reformers who transferred, virtually without modification, the philosophy and tactics of the British Labour party to the West; they appealed primarily to trade unionists in prairie cities. Militant industrial unionists, whose tactics were based on Marxism and experience, periodically rebelled against the Trades and Labor Congress in order to found unions sufficiently powerful to beat employers and if necessary the state; their principal constituency was among low-status workers in isolated camps. And socialists were revolutionary Marxists committed to the destruction of industrial capitalism through political action; their propaganda achieved its greatest following among coal miners and eastern European immigrants. To demonstrate the diversity of the tendencies and the variations in their patterns of development, I have discussed each separately during the prewar period. This emphasis should not obscure the clear similarities between them, similarities which, as the study shows, were important. Nonetheless, during the early years of the movement's development, common attitudes and inspiration were obscured by social and political factors and, thus, largely ignored by radicals.

In the years before 1919 the three radical tendencies competed with each other to fashion a general western constituency. At different times and in different places a party or union won ascendancy over its rivals. Labourism dominated the movement in Winnipeg. Revolutionary doctrines flourished in the class-polarized mining and construction camps of British Columbia. But western hegemony appeared impossible. In that most extraordinary of times, the chaotic months following the end of the Great War, the revolutionary tendency achieved an ephemeral ascendancy in the labour movement. The victory ended in disaster, ensuring the decline of ideological tension. As a result labourism dominated the radical movement in the postwar years and eventually became the basis of the Co-operative Commonwealth Federation.

In the eight years since this study began as a doctoral dissertation, I have received generous assistance from a great many people; it is a pleasure to acknowledge my gratitude. Librarians and archivists from Ottawa to Victoria have been courteous and energetic in meeting my requests, some of which were confused or unreasonable. I am especially indebted to Jay Atherton of the Public Archives of Canada, J.P. Whitridge of the Canada Department of Labour Library, Shirley Payment, Louise Sloane, and Sandra Zuk of the University of Winnipeg Library, George Brandak of the University of British Columbia Special Collections Division, and J.G. Mitchell of the BC Provincial Library. During two busy and often hectic summers, my research was made more easy by the assistance of Walter Enns and Marlene Toews. The manuscript benefited from the criticism of R.I.K. Davidson and Patricia Lagace of the University of Toronto Press. Much of the credit for any worth which this book may have should go to friends and colleagues: Irving Abella and Ramsay Cook of York University, David Bercuson of the University of Calgary, and Garin Burbank, Vincent Rutherford, and Walter Stein of the University of Winnipeg gave me encouragement and advice for which I will always be grateful.

Research for this study has been supported by the Canada Council, the Canada Department of Labour, and the University of Winnipeg. The book has been published with the aid of a grant from the Social Sciences Research Council using funds provided by the Canada Council, and a grant from the Andrew W. Mellon Foundation to the University of Toronto Press.

During the time that Donald Kerr supervised my thesis and then when he helped me turn it into a book, his wisdom and humanity provided me with a standard of academic excellence. Professor Kerr's death in October 1976 saddened me because he was a fine teacher and a good friend.

Without the patience, encouragement, and support of my wife, Carolyn, the book would never have been completed. Not only did she conduct research, criticize interpretations, type manuscripts, and read proof, but she cheerfully assumed family responsibilities which I neglected. To show my deep gratitude for these sacrifices, I have dedicated this book to her.

A.R.M.

R. Parmeter Pettipiece

Fred Dixon

(courtesy Manitoba Archives)

Arthur Puttee

(courtesy Manitoba Archives)

Richard A. (Dick) Rigg

(courtesy Manitoba Archives)

J.W. Hawthornthwaite

(courtesy British Columbia Archives)

William A. (Bill) Pritchard

(courtesy British Columbia Archives)

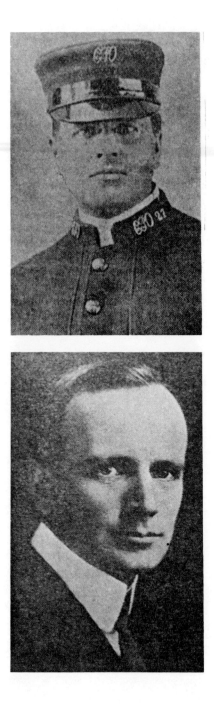

William (Bill) Hoop

Wallis Lefeaux

Charles O'Brien

E.T. Kingsley

Jack Kavanagh

Arthur Wells

Victor Midgley

James McVety

Parker Williams

(courtesy British Columbia Archives)

Ginger Goodwin

REFORMERS, REBELS, AND
REVOLUTIONARIES

Abbreviations

AFL American Federation of Labor
ALU American Labor Union
BCFL British Columbia Federation of Labor
CSL Canadian Socialist League
DLP Dominion Labor Party
FLP Federated Labor Party
ILP Independent Labor Party
IWW Industrial Workers of the World
LRC Labor Representation Committee
OBU One Big Union
PPP Provincial Progressive Party
SDP Social Democratic Party
SLP Socialist Labor Party
SPA Socialist Party of America
SPBC Socialist Party of British Columbia
SPC Socialist Party of Canada
SPM Socialist Party of Manitoba
STLA Socialist Trades and Labor Alliance
TLC Trades and Labor Congress
UBRE United Brotherhood of Railway Employees
UMW United Mine Workers
USLP United Socialist Labor Party
WLP Winnipeg Labor Party
WFM Western Federation of Miners

1

Introduction

The western Canadian radical movement was a product of the economic 'Boom' of the late 1890s - a 'conjuncture of favourable circumstances' which resulted in the great economic expansion of western Canada. Capital - American, British, European, and Canadian - poured into the West to create a boom of unprecedented proportions. Before the outbreak of war in 1914, hundreds of thousands of immigrants had settled in the four western provinces. Many took up farms and pushed the prairie agricultural frontier back to its furthest limits. Others joined in the recently increased exploitation of British Columbia's three great staples, fish, minerals, and timber. Still others built the two new transcontinental railways, which an exuberant and unthinking nation threw across its breadth to carry the wheat of the prairies and the products of the mountain province to the markets of Europe. And many of these immigrants crowded into the sprawling working class quarters of Winnipeg, Calgary, Edmonton, and Vancouver to build the new metropolises, to repair and drive the great trains, to fashion the products of new factories, and to provide the services essential to towns which became cities overnight.

The West's transition to industrial capitalism was astonishingly rapid. Winnipeg was not only a forwarding and distribution point; during the Boom it became Canada's fourth largest manufacturing centre. In 1891 the average manufacturing establishment in the city employed eight workers and was capitalized at $10,000; by 1901 the average had risen to thirty-one workers and a capitalization of $45,000; and a decade later the average number of employees doubled, and capitalization tripled to $147,000. Plants were bigger and more heavily capitalized in Vancouver. In 1891 the average factory employed twelve workers and represented an investment of $40,000; at the turn of the century the average stood at thirty employees and $98,000; and by 1911 the average manufacturing establishment employed seventy workers and was capitalized at $176,000. The capitalization of the average plant in Calgary jumped by nearly 700 per cent between 1901 and 1911. Such unusually accelerated growth characterized the manufacturing sector in all other western cities.[1]

The resource industry was expanding at an equally frenetic rate. While the value of capital equipment in primary fishing operations doubled in Canada as a whole between 1896 and 1914, it tripled in British Columbia. The result was a significant increase in fish production; for example, the halibut catch rose by 700 per cent between 1896 and 1915. British Columbia's forest industry also boomed. Between 1908, the first year for which statistics are available, and 1911, the height of prewar production, lumber output doubled to 1.3 million board feet. This was by far the fastest rate of growth in the country. The most spectacular expansion occurred in the mining industry. BC copper production jumped 1200 per cent to some 50 million pounds per year between 1896 and 1912. In part to fire furnaces in Kootenay smelters, BC coal mines tripled their output in the boom years. During the same period Alberta's coal production increased by an amazing 1800 per cent.[2]

Boom conditions produced a boom mentality. Never were Canadians more confident, more ebullient. The economic promise of Confederation was to be fulfilled, and the twentieth century was to belong to them. Ownership would make them rich. It was a grossly materialistic age. A Vancouver lumberman rhymed,

You can have your golden sunrise and your sunset rich and red,
You can have your summer rose and autumn peace,
But give to us the honey time, the honey time instead
And we'll have every treasure in our reach.

It's fine to watch the apple when it ripens on the bough,
It's fine to see the wheat in the bin,
But there's another season that we're singing for right now,
We want to see THE MONEY COMING IN.[3]

Economic growth was considered an absolute good by many Canadians, and by none more than those in the West. Just as the nation aimed for the achievement of a 'Big Canada' through the National Policy, each province, city, and town strove for its own growth. In the heyday of free enterprise such growth could be promoted only by the entrepreneur, and the captain of industry became the hero of the age. Any obstacle in the way of his schemes was contrary to the public good; equally, though paradoxically, any means to foster those schemes could, only be socially beneficial in the long run.

The growth ethic was not new to western Canada. Boosterism had always been characteristic of Winnipeg. And in BC in the late eighties and early nineties, during 'the Great Potlach,' the government, committed to the rapid development of the province's economy, ceded huge tracts of land to capitalists. The policy resulted in the growth and consolidation of great economic empires.[4] The greatest of these empires was that which the Dunsmuir family held on Vancouver Island. The Dunsmuirs ruled their mines, steamers, and railway in a fashion worthy of any feudal autocrat.

When westerners experienced economic growth, they became even more engaged by the ethic that promoted it. Sir Richard McBride, premier of British Columbia in the decade before the First World War, pledged to make the province 'one which the British and Canadian investor could come to with a surety that his undertaking would not be ... hampered by injurious imposts.'[5] Western cities had similar ambitions. This was natural because the impact of industrial technology was a central part of their historical experience. Vancouver, Calgary, and Edmonton grew up around railways. The businessmen who dominated the life of Winnipeg never suspended their campaign for cheap electric power, population, and industry; the civic government was committed to growth 'at the expense of any and all other considerations.'[6]

Given the boom mentality, the West was not a congenial environment for trade unions. A few workers had been organized since the early 1860s in British Columbia and since the beginning of the 1880s in Winnipeg. But economic growth resulted in the expansion and consolidation of unions. British immigrants, whose skills were essential to industrialization, brought with them a strong tradition of organization; they became the basis of the trade union movement and the dynamic in its growth. In the mid-nineties British craftsmen revitalized Winnipeg's moribund unions by founding a trades council and a number of locals in the building and metal trades. Even some unskilled and female workers organized. In May 1899 *The Voice*, organ of the trades council, observed, 'the past year has been the brightest and most in-spiring in the history of organized labor Winnipeg has ever known.'[7] The Vancouver trades council 'took on a new lease of life' during 1898, and by the end of 1900 there were thirty-four functioning lo-cals in the city, twenty-four of which had been established in the pre-vious two years. Miners were also organizing at this time in the Koot-enays and the Crow's Nest Pass.[8] During the first years of the century, unions of railwaymen and building tradesmen were active in Calgary and Edmonton, both of which cities had trades councils.[9] There were even some stirrings in what was to become the province of Saskatche-wan, though these early unions were short lived.[10]

The trade union movement was confident for the first time. *The Voice* demonstrated the new mood when it predicted, 'the time is in sight when practically all labor will be ranged within organized ranks.'[11] Trades councils discussed the appointment of permanent officers and the acquisition of labour temples. The labour press emerged to speak for a movement now sufficiently strong to support its own organs. To westerners, the decision of the Trades and Labor Congress (TLC) to hold its 1898 convention in Winnipeg indicated that their movement had come of age. But the most significant manifestation of this con-fidence was the belief that, because of an increased demand for labour, unions could gain higher wages and improved working conditions. Dur-ing the early and middle nineties, demands had accumulated, and *The B.C. Workman* of Victoria believed that it was 'natural ... that at such times of inflation the workers should ask for a share of this bounty.'[12] The confidence was misplaced. Western employers beat the unions.

In isolated mining camps on Vancouver Island and in the BC inter-ior, class divisions were stark, and there were few restraints upon rela-tions between workers and companies. Operators fought the unions ruthlessly. The most notorious union-smasher in the West was James Dunsmuir. The Scottish and English miners who dug coal in the Duns-muir mines at Extension, Wellington, and Cumberland were commit-ted trade unionists, but the family never recognized unions during the forty-two years they owned the collieries. James Dunsmuir told a roy-al commission: 'I object to all unions. ... They simply take the man-agement of the mine. ... I want the management of my own works, and if I recognize the union, I cannot have that.' He fought unions with threats, spies, and blacklists. A Scotsman claimed, 'a man could not say union, or if he said union, ... he would not hold his job long.' When Dunsmuir could not break a strike with scabs, he was sufficiently influential to have the provincial government call out the militia.[13] Their unions broken, the miners bitterly resented the low wages and dangerous conditions which the company imposed upon them. They were also incensed by the arbitrary rule which Dunsmuir exercised over their lives. Miners indignantly complained when the coal baron imperiously ordered workers to relocate their homes at a new pit. Life in 'Dunsmuria,' a Methodist minister reported, was 'pregnant with all that ... an Englishman dislikes.'[14]

The new businessmen of the prairies also fought unions. In Winnipeg, Regina, Calgary, and Edmonton, the economies of which were based mainly on forwarding, retailing, and service functions, employers demonstrated the merchant's concern for immediate profit and rapid growth. Frequently inexperienced in the management of large numbers of workers and with only a limited interest in long-term stable industrial relations, employers strenuously opposed the formation of unions.[15] Winnipeg's business community was founded upon mercantile principles and composed largely of self-made men. T.R. Deacon, for example, began his working life as a labourer in logging camps; he became president of Manitoba Bridge and Iron Works and mayor of Winnipeg.[16] Because of their own experience, such men believed implicitly in the free enterprise system. Only entrepreneurs could supply the dynamic in the economy. Unions, by seeking power, interfered with development. While some Winnipeg businessmen treated their workers in a paternalistic manner, they refused to permit a union to dictate rules and wages in companies they had built. As a result Winnipeg was the scene of bitter industrial strife characterized by injunctions, strike-breakers, and on one occasion riots and the use of troops.[17] A British trade unionist described the western city as a place 'where the scramble for dollars and the lack of any restraints of custom have tended to abnormally develop the wolfish instinct and to eliminate conscientious dealing with the man whose very necessities drive him into the market to sell all he possesses.'[18] Long accustomed to the security afforded by organization and to orderly collective bargaining, the British workers who constituted the bulk of the trade union movement bitterly resented the employers' dogmatic and ruthless opposition to unions.

The labour movement's anger increased when provincial governments were reluctant to provide legislative protection for the workers. Fearful that safety and sanitary regulations, age minima, and other labour standards would discourage investment, politicians were slow to enact them. Businessmen reinforced this attitude by claiming that such legislation would irreparably damage their competitive position in the market-place. For example, an industrialist told a royal commission that a minimum wage 'would kill British Columbia.' In addition, labour standards were considered a violation of laissez faire principles. A Winnipeg corporation lawyer warned that 'supervision over and interference in struggles between capital and labor ... would be an attempt to interfere with and control the great natural laws of supply and demand which apply to labor as to any other commodity.'[19] Consequently, despite constant pressure and annual petitions from organized labour, the western provinces generally lagged behind the East in the passage of labour legislation. In 1900 the Manitoba government passed an adequate factory act, but in 1904 Premier Rodmond Roblin, under pressure from Winnipeg's business community, took the extraordinary step of actually reducing the age minima for child labour and increasing the maximum hours of work for women and children. When British Columbia finally passed a factory act in 1908, Prince Edward Island and Saskatchewan were the only other provinces that did not have similar legislation on the books.[20]

Even when provincial governments passed labour standards legislation, they seldom enforced it adequately. Labour bureaus were understaffed and underfinanced, a condition which encouraged employers to ignore factory acts. For example, as late as 1912 one inspector was responsible for the entire province of British Columbia. A Vancouver carpenter, who worked in a sash and door factory, described the results of his employer's refusal to ventilate the works as required by law: 'I have seen machines covered with dust from the fact that no blowers were supplied. ... It effects the lungs. Asthma is very common. I have known men ... who have had to leave the mills altogether on account of the dust.'[21] Such conditions made trade unionists claim that the factory acts were 'practically worthless.' The organ of the Winnipeg trades council stormed 'to hell with trade, business and profit; life and limb must be protected.'[22]

In British Columbia and Alberta, mine owners regularly disregarded safety and sanitary regulations and provincial inspectors were slow to bring them to book.[23] For example, in 1913 none of the mines at Cumberland had gas committees, but the companies were not prosecuted.[24] This state of affairs produced deadly conditions. Mine disasters occurred with terrifying frequency in the coal fields of the two provinces. The mines of Alberta and British Columbia had the reputation of being among the most dangerous in the world. A US Department of Labor study confirmed the validity of this fearsome reputation. Between 1889 and 1908, twenty-three men were killed in the production of every million tons of BC coal; in North America as a whole, which had the highest fatality rate of any continent, six men died to produce each million tons. In 1917 a University of Alberta research team made similar findings.[25] Such conditions outraged miners. An officer of the union in the Crow's Nest Pass dismissed Alberta's Coal Mines Regulation Act as 'a big farce.' And a BC miner charged that operators 'don't care a damn if they kill ten or fifteen men every day. I was here three months, and they got three men killed in No. 2.'[26]

Western workers were the most resentful of federal economic development policies. Central Canadian trade unionists recognized that tariff protection and large-scale immigration to the prairies, by promoting eastern industries and creating a market in the West, would ensure a demand for their skills; thus they recognized a community of interest with employers. Westerners, however, objected to the National Policy. Federal immigration programs were designed to serve the demands of a capitalist labour market. To industrialize the country Canadian employers needed a large pool of workers which could supply varying labour requirements. When the economy was buoyant, men were available for hire; when economic conditions made their employment unprofitable, they could be fired.[27] In addition employers favoured immigration to reduce ethnic homogeneity among workers and thus to impair trade union effectiveness. For example, a BC mine manager explained that 'it is necessary to have a mixture of races. ... They are the strength of the employer, and the weakness of the union. How to head off a strike of muckers or laborers for higher wages without the aid of Italian labor ... I do not know.'[28] Already philosophically disposed to an open-door policy and subject to pressure from corporations, the Laurier government encouraged skilled and unskilled workers to immigrate.

With the beginning of large-scale immigration from eastern and southern Europe, prairie trade unionists recognized that the newcomers constituted a threat to organized workers. Each March when the immigrant trains began to deliver their human cargoes, labour leaders were faced with the difficult task of organizing them in an overstocked job market, and, as a result, each year the bargaining power of the unions was at least temporarily reduced. In 1899 a leader of the Lethbridge miners' union warned that Clifford Sifton, minister of the interior, would destroy trade unions by introducing 'hordes of half-civilized people who can live on ... a crust and an onion.' Soon after the Winnipeg trades council, alarmed by the increased number of eastern Europeans in the city, formally protested to Laurier that the immigrants, who were 'accustomed to a mode of life which enables them to work cheaply,' represented 'unfair and dangerous competition ... [for] the Canadian workman.'[29] In Alberta coal fields, where eastern and southern Europeans were frequently used as strikebreakers, the United Mine Workers organized the Italians and Slavs.[30] Such an effort was unusual, however, and most Europeans remained outside union ranks. This condition was partly the result of the inability of the English-speaking labour movement to communicate with them, and partly the result of the bigotry of union members. In any case, the unorganized Europeans worked for lower wages and, thus, represented a continuing threat to union standards.

Asiatics were an even greater threat to the workers of British Columbia, and resentment of their presence was intensified by racism. The Asiatics, accustomed to an extremely low standard of living, were prepared to work for meagre wages. They were even more attractive to employers because they remained unassimilated and, therefore, impossible to organize. Opposition to Asiatic importation – BC workers never considered it immigration – had been one of the fundamental drives of the province's labour movement from the beginning. In the Island coal fields Chinese coolies were used extensively, and their presence made the maintenance of a union virtually impossible. Japanese workers broke the strike of Fraser River salmon fishermen in 1900, and union effectiveness in the industry was substantially reduced by racial tensions. Hindoos threatened white workers in the third of the province's great staple industries, forestry.[31] Asiatics were not confined, however, to primary industries; by the turn of the century they were working in the building trades and secondary manufacturing. For example, the number of journeymen tailors in Victoria fell from 120 to 40 after Chinese were employed in the city's clothing shops.[32] BC workers never suspended their campaign against Asiatics. The secretary of the Victoria trades council warned Laurier that 'civilization in this country is and will be threatened every day and as long as a system of immigration exists that invites or admits unrestricted numbers of any Oriental nation.'[33] Violence frequently flared against Asiatics; the Vancouver race riot of September 1907 was only the most spectacular example.

Western trade unionists did not object only to Asiatic and southern and eastern European immigration. They also opposed the unregulated flow of people from the United Kingdom into urban labour markets. In the first place, not all British trade unionists comported themselves in the best traditions of the movement. For example, Yorkshire iron workers, scabbing on Winnipeg machinists during a bitter 1906 strike, established a branch of the Amalgamated Society of Engineers and then audaciously marched in the Labour Day parade.[34] In addition, only a small fraction of the British working class was organized and that organization was concentrated in a few industries. Pauper immigrants, those aided by the Salvation Army for example, had virtually no trade union experience and, therefore, few compunctions against taking work at low pay. British pauper immigration was a constant concern, and Kier Hardie, a British Labour MP, reported that in western trade union circles no Englishman was as unpopular as the Cockney.[35]

The other fundamental of the National Policy, the tariff, intensified the workers' anger. From the turn of the century western trades councils and their organs persistently condemned Laurier's failure to make any significant tariff reductions. In part this censure grew out of the British trade unionists' belief in free trade. More important were the workers' perceptions of economic realities. They believed that the tariff forced them to pay artificially high prices for the necessities of life. Western trade unionists, unlike those in the East, were convinced that they derived no benefit whatever from protection. The prospect of its elimination held no fears for them. 'What is the meaning of the tariff ranging from twenty per cent up to fifty or a hundred per cent on nearly everything that the working man has to consume,' demanded the Winnipeg trades council indignantly.[36] But the workers' condemnation of the tariff was caused primarily by a basic sense of grievance at the inequitable nature of federal economic policies. There was free trade only in labour. A Vancouver carpenter complained: 'capital is fenced around with all sorts of safeguards. ... On the other hand labour ... has not only to face world competition without any restrictions, but the Government spend the people's money lavishly to bring competitors into the country so that wages can be held down.'[37]

Western workers did not participate in the prosperity of the Boom. They apparently experienced no increase in their standard of living. While more sophisticated analytical techniques may produce different findings, economists now generally agree that between 1900 and 1920 real wages in Canada declined. This trend was produced mainly by the nature and dimensions of immigration. Workers in extractive industries were in a substantially less favourable wage position in 1910 than they had been in 1900. A specialized study of several occupational groups in Winnipeg concluded that 'a dismal movement in real wages' was characteristic of the city before 1920.[38] There can be no doubt about how western workers perceived the problem; they were convinced that their wages were not keeping pace with prices. In 1903 *Calgary's Bond of Brotherhood* observed, 'everyone knows that the cost of living has gone up by leaps and bounds, and it is with extreme difficulty that working men make ends meet.' In 1907 *The Voice* complained, 'the increase in the cost of commodities has not been offset by an equal increase in wages.' In 1912, after considering the 'phenomenal and persistent rise in the cost of living,' the organ of the British Columbia Federation of Labor concluded that the resulting decline in real wages was 'probably the most annoying fact' of workers' lives.[39]

The conditions under which men and women lived and worked in boom-time western Canada were often appalling. Life for railway construction workers was primitive and brutal. Men frequently worked twelve long and gruelling hours seven days a week.[40] Because construction workers were obliged to pay fees to employment agents, high board charges, and extortionate prices in company stores, they complained that they were working only for 'overalls and tobacco.'[41] Bunkhouses were often poorly ventilated, dirty, and verminous; one worker complained, 'most of the bunkhouses aren't fit, as far as I can see, for animals to live in.' Frequently sanitation was primitive and unsafe. Under such conditions water supplies became contaminated, and typhoid fever was endemic in the camps.[42] Because the power of the contractors was virtually exclusive on the grade, they could resort to the most primitive means to discipline their workers. Foremen who drove their men with fists were not uncommon, and in some cases workers were actually kept under armed guards. A journalist charged that the Grand Trunk Pacific Railway was being built through British Columbia under 'a system that is close to peonage.'[43]

Conditions in the Crow's Nest Pass were equally oppressive. The mining camps displayed all the worst features of company towns. Operators owned everything. Workers were obliged to trade at company stores where, miners charged, prices were outrageously high.[44] The men and their families lived in company houses. Few of the cabins had sanitary facilities, because companies refused to permit municipal incorporation. A Hillcrest miner reported that the house which he rented was 'filthy with bugs; no lights, no water system; ... lots of horses and mules in some places have a better place to live in.'[45] Living conditions were usually even worse for Slavic and Italian miners. At Hosmer, Russian miners lived in a collection of shacks and hovels known as New York. The CPR, owner of the mines, collected the settlement's garbage three times a year. As a result, New York's water supply became contaminated; but there was no alternate source.[46]

Workers who lived in western cities were the victims of rapid urbanization. Edmonton, Calgary, Regina, and Saskatoon mushroomed. The populations of Winnipeg and Vancouver exploded by 500 per cent.[47] The cities grew up too quickly. Because they were unplanned, western cities could not provide adequate accommodation and services for the masses of immigrants. Across the West many workers crowded into houses and tenements which lacked space, ventilation, and plumbing. Such slums were disfigured by industrial pollution and unrelieved by parks and recreational facilities.

The West's most infamous working class district was Winnipeg's north end. To ensure easy access to the CPR, industries located there, and factories made the district dirty, noisy, and smelly. But, to be close to their jobs, large numbers of workers began moving into the north end in the late nineties. Developers built row upon monotonous row of frame cottages and terraces, but these were inadequate to meet the housing needs of the rapidly expanding population. Space was at a premium and rents exorbitant. City inspectors regularly reported three and four families living in tiny houses. In 1912 an official discovered 'one family ... sleeping in a stable and cooking their meals in the cellars of an unfinished house ... [and] another family ... living in a shed intended for a garage.' Less than half of the houses in the north end were connected to the city's water system. Outdoor privies were common. Winnipeg's Medical Health Office reported that 'the filth [and] squalor ... among the foreign elements is beyond our powers of description.' Such conditions produced epidemics of typhoid. They also resulted in an extremely high infant mortality rate; in 1912 one out of every five babies born in Winnipeg died within a year. The deaths occurred mainly in the north end.[48]

Workers considered the West a brutally exploitive environment. Many lived and worked under wretched conditions, yet they knew the country was prosperous. The Edwardian era was a time of conspicuous consumption. Workers saw ample evidence of affluence around them – galas, automobiles, stately houses. Employers' attitudes and government policies seemed to indicate that prosperity was to be achieved at the expense of the workers. 'In no place in the world are the responsibilities of modern industrial growth and development being thrust upon the masses as in Western Canada,' charged a Vancouver union leader.[49] Such a set of priorities violated the workers' most basic expectations. By their very presence in the West, immigrant workers demonstrated a sense of hope. They had emigrated to what they commonly called 'a new country' to achieve upward social mobility. A British immigrant living in Calgary explained that his countrymen came to Canada convinced that they could 'enjoy life free from the demoralizing tendencies of modern civilization, [free] from the long hours of labor for very little pay ... [and thus] raise the standard of living so that all that is good for men and women shall be within their reach.' Many quickly concluded, however, that they could not escape the socio-economic realities of industrial capitalism. After three years in Winnipeg a British trade unionist observed, 'the class lines do exist here, even though they are not quite as plainly marked as back home.'[50] A sense of grievance, if not class solidarity, developed among workers. Many were alienated from the basic ethic of the society in which they lived.

The conditions of western Canadian society were conducive to the growth of radicalism. It was a society in the process of transformation. A study of industrialization has concluded that 'rapid economic growth is a major force leading toward revolution and instability.'[51] Industrialization took approximately a century in Britain and some fifty years in the United States. In western Canada the process was compressed into less than two decades. Such a rapid transition to industrial capitalism produced tremendous social dislocation. It also produced conflict. Unopposed by traditional values, capitalists were able to impose the growth ethic on society, and a predatory social order emerged. But, because social institutions were inadequately developed, the workers' reaction to these conditions was less mitigated by customary constraints. The church could do virtually nothing to discipline workers. And the family was frequently disrupted by immigration and the demands of the capitalist labour market. Young and highly mobile, many workers recognized a relatively slight investment in society. Men who had sufficient courage and drive to cross the Atlantic to start a new life more quickly rebelled against oppressive social conditions.

Radicalism was part of the immigrant workers' cultural baggage, and their prior experience informed their response to the new environment. Ukrainians, Finns, and Germans had been exposed to socialist propaganda in Europe. Many Italians had been indoctrinated with syndicalism. And some Jews were anarchists. Revolutionary intellectuals, like Jacob Penner and Myron Stechishin, led radical movements in teeming immigrant ghettos. Unskilled Ukrainian and Italian workers formed an important component of socialist parties and of the Industrial Workers of the World in mining and construction camps. A leader of the Russian Industrial Union, founded in Vancouver in 1907, had been a socialist member of the second Russian council of state, the Duma.[52]

Men and ideas moved easily back and forth across the border between the United States and Canada. This was particularly true of the far West. A Victoria trade unionist remarked, 'if I leave here and go to Frisco and Seattle, I have no trouble; I simply take my travelling card.'[53] The radicalism which American immigrants carried with them and which Canadian workers learned during sojourns in the mountain states and California had a special relevance in British Columbia. The workers' experience was essentially similar on both sides of the border; in some cases they encountered the same two-fisted employers. Americans directed the development of the militant Western Federation of Miners and led the Industrial Workers of the World. The most important US immigrant was E.T. Kingsley, who did more than any other radical to elaborate revolutionary doctrines in the first decade of the century.

Because of the central role British immigrants played in the trade union movement, their attitudes and experience were most important in the development of western Canadian radicalism. The British artisans who emigrated to Canada in the middle of the nineteenth century had grown up in a trade union movement under the influence of Samuel Smiles, but those who emigrated later and went to the West left a movement inspired by Robert Blatchford and the principles of 'new unionism.' Because of their indoctrination in Britain's politicized labour movement, immigrants from the United Kingdom constituted the great majority of members in urban radical parties. Kier Hardie found it a pleasure to address a Winnipeg rally because he was able 'to meet again the men and women who [have] fought for years in the old country the battle of labour's emancipation.'[54] The leaders of the western Canadian radical movement, men such as Arthur Puttee, Ernest Burns, Bill Pritchard, and Bob Russell, were recent British immigrants.

A recurring image in the western radical press depicted an immigrant worker who, having fled from industrialism in the old world only to be exposed to its ravages again in the new, turned united with his comrades to face and fight capitalism. Certainly, modern, technological society was not peculiar in western Canada. And many men and women rebelled against it, against autocratic employers and an oppressive state. But, while radical workers were united by a common opposition to the social realities of the Boom, the movement was far from monolithic. Because of the variety of the immigrants' cultural baggage and because of the diversity of the workers' experience, the radical movement contained three basic tendencies, distinguished by their ideologies, tactics, or constituencies.

The most moderate radicals, the labourites, founded their indictment of capitalism on Christian ethics, Gladstonian radicalism, and Marxism. Although some envisaged the ultimate inauguration of the co-operative commonwealth, labourites were primarily reformers, committed to an immediate amelioration of social conditions under capitalism. Products of Britain's evolutionary and orderly political culture, they depended exclusively on political action – founding parties, registering voters, and running candidates. Indeed, they perceived the state as the basic vehicle for social change. Because labourism was consciously modelled on the policy and programs of the United Kingdom's Labour party, reformers mobilized significant numbers of British trade unionists in prairie cities, principally Winnipeg.

Militant industrial unionists, advocates of the second tendency, were primarily distinguished by their tactics and a relative imprecision in ideology. They were direct actionists, industrial rebels, who believed that big unions could best prosecute the class struggle. In part this conviction stemmed from the theoretical proposition that amalgamation was the necessary and inevitable reaction to the progressive concentration of capital, and Marxists led each industrial union crusade. Experience, however, converted more workers into rebels. The alignment of corporations and the state convinced many men and women that, because there could be no recourse to an unresponsive political system, only powerful unions could effect social change, if necessary by a general strike. The rebels' ideology was clarified as syndicalism became an increasingly important dimension of the tendency. Militant industrial unionism usually attracted low-status workers in isolated construction or mining camps. But during industrial crises, when collusion between employers and the state was blatant and when solidarity was increased by instability and strife, urban workers perceived a need for more effective, militant organizations. They joined rebellions which challenged the hegemony of craft unionism and disrupted the Canadian labour movement.

The socialists, adherents of the most radical tendency, were Marxist revolutionaries who insisted that industrial capitalism was, by its very nature, an exploitative system of production essentially incapable of reformation. Their basic goal was the destruction of the wage system. Because they perceived the state as the principal means by which the working class was kept in subjugation, socialists considered it the vehicle whereby the means of production would be socialized and, thus, the exploitation of the prolitariat ended. They relied on political action to achieve the revolution. Socialist propaganda found its most eager audience among miners in British Columbia and Alberta and among low-status eastern European workers.

Obviously there were points of similarity between the three tendencies. Reformers and revolutionaries employed the same tactics. Revolutionaries and rebels subscribed to one ideology. And from time to time men and women blurred distinctions even further by enlisting with two or more of these tendencies at the same time, however contradictory such behaviour might appear. Indeed a common opposition to industrial capitalism inevitably resulted in some united action, particularly in times of crisis. Before 1919, however, radicalism usually manifested division rather than unity; each of the tendencies proclaimed, more or less vociferously, the legitimacy of its doctrine. But no single organization in the factious movement could mobilize and direct the workers' alienation. At different times and in different places a party or sect won ascendancy over its rivals, but none could establish a western hegemony. Socialists and labourites, social democrats and Wobblies, fought each other for the workers' allegiance.

2

The emergence of
the socialist movement in
British Columbia

Canadian socialism came of age in British Columbia. In the first years
of the twentieth century, fledgling socialist organizations emerged across the country, but BC became the dynamic centre of the movement.
Beginning in the late 1890s, eastern Canadian, British, and American
socialists laid the institutional and doctrinal foundations of the provincial movement. Because various influences were at work, ideological disputes, which would later become chronic, broke out between
socialists. But these tensions were not yet debilitating; rather they
pushed the movement beyond reformism. Because political and social
conditions were especially conducive to the growth of socialism in the
first two or three years of the century, the new doctrine attracted
many converts, and the movement grew. Maturity came with growth;
BC socialism began to evolve a character independent of the American
and British movements. The basis of this character was a revolutionary doctrine which was peculiar to British Columbia.

Political activism was a dimension of the BC labour movement almost
from its inception: trade unionists ran for office as early as 1882. By
the beginning of the nineties, an independent political tradition was
firmly established among the workers of Vancouver and the Island.[1]
When workers took political action, their platforms were reformist in
character; conventional planks were Asiatic exclusion, labour standards legislation, land reform, the single tax, and direct legislation, all
measures which, while they looked to more or less sweeping changes
in society, stopped far short of revolution.

For radical movements in eastern Canada, the United States, and,
to a lesser extent, Britain, the 1890s marked an ideological transition

from the reformism which had typified the 1880s to the socialism which would characterize the new century. Because BC radicalism had direct and important links to each of these movements, its ideology, to the extent that it can be said to have developed one, was changing in these years. The radicals' progress away from their early doctrines was neither direct nor rapid, however, and, as a result, reformism remained the basic tendency in the movement during most of the decade. Still by the second half of the nineties external influences were at work which ensured that the province's radical vanguard would be socialists.

At the beginning of the economic Boom, many BC workers, certainly the vast majority of trade unionists, were recent immigrants from the United Kingdom. There they had been influenced by the socialist doctrines which were becoming increasingly important in the British labour movement, and some had been members of radical parties. The new breed of British labour leaders, such as John Burns, Tom Mann, Kier Hardie, and Robert Blatchford, had many followers in the province.[2] For example, James Pritchard and Samuel Mottishaw, founders of the socialist movement in the Island coal fields, had been members of the Independent Labour party in Lancashire. And Ernest Burns, prominent in the Vancouver party, received his early education in the Social Democratic Federation where he had known Eleanor Marx.[3] The ideas and experience of immigrants such as these were of essential importance in the development of socialism in British Columbia because they provided personnel for the new movement.

A more immediate influence came from the United States. The ease with which men and ideas moved across the border ensured that propaganda from the American West would have a significant impact in British Columbia. Socialism made significant early progress among unions in the Kootenays because of the presence of large numbers of miners from the mountain states.[4] More important, the two prophets of western socialism, J.A. Wayland and Eugene Debs, led many of the province's workers to the new doctrine. Wayland's *Appeal to Reason*, which preached a highly eclectic and moralistic brand of socialism, circulated widely among western radicals, but it was in British Columbia that the paper had its greatest number of Canadian subscribers. In the late nineties the *Appeal*'s correspondence column frequently contained letters from enthusiastic radicals in Vancouver, Victoria, and the Kootenays describing their efforts to propagate the gospel. Such support caused Wayland to conclude that British Columbia was 'fine country' for socialist propaganda.[5] Debs became known in the province as a result of the formation of locals of his American Railway Union in Revelstoke and Vancouver. He lectured in the latter city at the invitation of the trades council in 1896 and 1897; in the summer of 1899 the Vancouver trades council honoured the American socialist by inviting him to dedicate the city's new Labour Temple.[6]

By the late nineties British immigration and American propaganda had set the stage for the emergence of an institutional socialist movement. During the summer of 1898, readers of the *Appeal to Reason* in Vancouver began to discuss the formation of a socialist party.[7] Arthur Spencer, a Brantford member of the Socialist Labor party (SLP), who had determined to undertake a mission for socialism, learned of these discussions and secured a transfer to Vancouver to organize for the revolution.[8] Spencer was appalled by the reformism he encountered on the coast, and he set about to change the direction of the province's radical movement.[9] In December 1898, his efforts brought twenty-two men together to form the province's first permanent local of the SLP.[10]

In both the United States and Canada, the Socialist Labor party was dominated by the brilliant but doctrinaire Marxist theoretician Daniel De Leon, and the Vancouver party rigidly adhered to the master's revolutionary line.[10] The local stood 'firmly on the everpresent fact of the class struggle and for the complete union of the proletarian forces ... and [for] the socialist reconstruction of society.' SLP propagandists told the workers that victory could be achieved only through political action. Yet, ironically, the local was never in a position to afford the proletariat the opportunity to take political action; its meagre resources prevented it from fielding candidates.[12]

In 1895 De Leon had decreed that the SLP must have an economic arm and proceeded to found the Socialist Trades and Labor Alliance (STLA), an organization which made unceasing war on the American Federation of Labor (AFL) and craft unions. In accordance with party policy, Spencer established a local of the STLA in Vancouver in June 1899, because 'the old forms and spirit of labour unions are almost impotent to resist the oppressions of concentrated capital.'[13] Founded as a general labourers' union, the local never had more than a handful of members, and, though it did make an abortive attempt to organize CPR employees, it seems never to have functioned as a conventional union. Essentially an educational club, which required prospective members to take an examination in socialist theory, the STLA's main functions were to support the SLP in its political activities and to attack the business unionism of the TLC.[14] As a result, relations with trade unions could be stormy. When an STLA speaker told a New Westminster audience, in the charged atmosphere of a fishermen's strike, that successful action by unions was impossible, the meeting broke up in a brawl.[15]

Relations were strained not only with the trade unions. De Leon insisted on a complete and unquestioning acceptance of his revolutionary creed and hurled invective at any who deviated from his line. Because they followed their leader in all things, prominent members of the Vancouver local adopted a dogmatic and sectarian approach to radical politics. They denounced all those whom they perceived as enemies of the militant working class, but especially the 'fakirs' of other competing embryonic socialist parties who were leading the proletariat away from the De Leonite path to salvation. For example, when Debs spoke in the city Spencer sneered, he 'talks to the middle-class.'[16]

Despite poor relations with trade unionists and other radicals, the local tripled in size during 1899 and became sufficiently optimistic to make some attempts to organize on Vancouver Island and in the interior. Much of this growth resulted from the efforts of Will McClain, who had had many years experience in the British socialist movement before he jumped ship at Seattle and went to Vancouver.[17] McClain's less doctrinaire socialism and his dynamic appeal encouraged many to join the party. But his British experience made it difficult for him and others, such as Frank Rogers, to co-operate with the ideologues, and by the autumn of 1899 real tensions had developed between the two factions in the local.

Tensions soon erupted into open strife. In 1899 opponents challenged De Leon's dogmatic and autocratic leadership of the American party, and the SLP was disrupted by the exodus of the 'Kangaroos,' who eventually united with other radicals to establish the Socialist Party of America (SPA). Joining the American struggle, the Vancouver ideologues, led by Spencer, hurled violent abuse at the 'Kangaroos' and attempted to place the local solidly in the De Leonite camp.[18] This McClain and his followers would not tolerate, and in the autumn they bolted the SLP to form a socialist club, which became the United Socialist Labor party (USLP) in April 1900.[19]

In reading McClain and his followers out of the party, Spencer perceptively told De Leon that the USLP was composed of 'the same canaille that the SLP has pushed aside recently.'[20] It was no coincidence that the rebellion in Vancouver had occurred after the bolt of the 'Kangaroos' in the United States. The socialists who established the USLP, dissatisfied with De Leonite dogmatism and the policy of war upon trade unions, saw the rebellion in the United States, which resulted from these very causes, and followed the American lead. They were 'Kangaroos.'[21]

After the spring of 1900 the SLP became an inconsequential, though noisy, sect, and the USLP became the socialist party in Vancouver. The new party adopted a different line than that pursued by the De Leonites. From the beginning it attempted to co-operate with the city's unions; the nature of the USLP's leadership allowed it to implement this policy without difficulty. McClain, president of the machinists' local, Frank Rodgers, president of the fishermen's union, and other leading socialists were active in the trades council. In addition, while the party insisted on the maintenance of its independence and the integrity of its propaganda, the USLP did not make war on other radical organizations.[22] Certainly the new direction appeared to be a sound one. Within weeks of its foundation, the party had made impressive organizational gains, built a hall, formed a brass and string band, and enrolled a paper membership of two hundred and fifty.[23]

The USLP also made a respectable run in the provincial election of 1900 when it nominated McClain as British Columbia's first socialist candidate.[24] The nature of McClain's 1900 campaign represented a new departure in the development of BC radicalism. His platform was cluttered with reformist planks, and his campaign focused on the conventional grievances of corporate domination of the province and Asiatic immigration. However, he sounded a revolutionary call when he pledged to fight for 'a true democracy of happy workers, freed from the abuse of greedy corporations.'[25] McClain enjoyed the active support of the trades council.[26] He also had the active opposition of his former comrades in the SLP, who set out to wreck his campaign; one meeting ended in 'a grand rough and tumble on the sidewalk in front of the Hall' involving twenty men.[27] In the end, McClain polled 684 votes, a result which made the socialists feel 'pretty good.'[28]

By 1900 there had also been some socialist developments outside of Vancouver, and these were associated with Christian socialism. Its most interesting manifestation in the province was the communitarian movement. Although it had its roots in the British Protestant reform tradition, the movement was immediately inspired by the last great wave of utopian colonies in the United States. In 1896 a group of BC workers, inspired by the Ruskin Co-operative in Tennessee, began to plan a colony, and two years later they established their own Ruskin, 'for the purpose of spreading the grand truths that were taught by our Lord Jesus Christ.' The community began as a handful of men engaged in cooperative logging operations near Port Moody; later agriculture became the basis of the colony. After a short probationary period, a prospective member was admitted to the fellowship 'simply for his manhood's sake'; upon joining, he contributed to the co-operative all his possessions, which in most cases appear to have been few. At its height Ruskin was the home of eighty people.[29] The colony was plagued by difficulties from the outset, and by the end of 1899 problems of personalities and economics resulted in its collapse.[30] Ruskin was by its very nature utopian, escapist, and short lived, and in the new century a different intellectual force would inform the socialist movement.

When Ruskin collapsed, its members did not give up the fight for socialism; instead many joined the Canadian Socialist League (CSL). The league had emerged in the East during the summer of 1899 and was dominated by George Wrigley, editor of its organ *Citizen and Country*. A long-time radical, Wrigley based his indictment of capitalism upon a moral indignation at poverty and on an evangelical promise of a better world. His Christian socialism pervaded the league, and the organization's propaganda emphasized reformism and public ownership while it rejected the doctrine of the class struggle.[31] Such a program naturally appealed to the former Ruskin colonists, and Port Moody, which had a CSL local by January 1900, became 'the centre of activity in British Columbia.'[32]

The propaganda of the CSL made rapid progress in the province. The league's secretary told a metal miner, 'the labor unions are doing well by us, especially those in British Columbia.' By early 1900 the province accounted for 15 per cent of *Citizen and Country*'s total subscriptions.[33] The tradition of political action in the BC labour movement facilitated the gains made by the league; it was but a short step from the reformism which was a basic part of the tradition to the platform of the CSL. This pattern was demonstrated by the quick conversion of the Revelstoke Reform League into a CSL local.[34] The CSL's socialism clearly distinguished it from the SLP in the minds of the workers. And the league quickly moved to reinforce this distinction. For example, in line with league policy, John M. Cameron, a former member of Ruskin who had become the CSL's organizer in British Columbia, petitioned the provincial government for labour standards legislation. [35]

Socialists were encouraged by developments in the province during 1900. R. Parmeter Pettipiece, an itinerant Ontario printer who had inaugurated the socialist press when he began publishing the *Eagle* in Ferguson, predicted that, 'British Columbia will be the first to feel the chaos.' So it was natural that socialists should respond positively to Wrigley's call to establish a provincial organization. [36] There already had been co-operation between the USLP and the CSL when in October delegates from Vancouver, Nanaimo, Victoria, and several interior points met in the terminal city to hold the province's first socialist convention. The red flag flew defiantly over the hall for the duration of the meetings despite police efforts to have it hauled down. Consistent with the new direction of the movement, the convention urged socialists to 'assist in building up and strengthening the trade union movement' as well as promoting class conscious political action by workers. The delegates agreed to establish a provincial federation within the CSL, with Cameron as organizer. Although the new organization's program was basically reformist, it did go beyond the league's platform in that it made the collectivization of the means of production its basic demand. [37] The momentum generated at the convention was not sustained, however, and the federation never got off the ground. Cameron soon left the province to take up a position as organizer with the Washington state socialist organization. [38]

Cameron's appointment demonstrated the significant and increasing influence of American socialists on the BC movement. Debs and Wayland continued to be highly regarded, but in 1900 an important new force was at work, the socialist party in the state of Washington. Herman Titus, editor of the Seattle *Socialist*, encouraged by what he considered the revolutionary potential of the province, took a great interest in his northern comrades. He opened the columns of his paper to BC socialists and sent Washington organizers into the province. [39] But patrons can be patronizing, and Titus and his associates adopted a decidedly didactic attitude towards the Canadians. British Columbia's socialists were often criticized for being insufficiently revolutionary to satisfy their doctrinaire neighbours. The Seattle editor set out to save them from the CSL. When Wrigley called upon the province's socialists to reject the revolutionary Washington line and build an inclusive labour party in co-operation with trade unions, Titus charged that the Toronto editor 'stood for capitalistic thought, for compromise and for pasturage on both sides of the fence.' [40]

Titus's concern for the doctrinal orthodoxy of BC socialists clearly grew out of his conviction that they were part of the larger American movement. He considered the USLP to be a kangaroo party. During a visit to Vancouver he wrote, 'socialism knows no national boundaries; ... this province is so close to the states and its interests so closely allied to those of the state of Washington, that it will be a natural and easy step for the socialists to organize as locals in the great Socialist movement of America.' Titus predicted that, after the upcoming American unity convention, BC socialists would probably affiliate with the Socialist Party of America. Some BC socialists found this notion attractive; after the SPA was founded at Indianapolis, a Victoria man called upon party members to form 'one gigantic body' with their American comrades.[41]

The impact of the American movement on British Columbia was best demonstrated by the 1901 provincial convention. In the summer of that year Vancouver socialists, led by Ernest Burns, began efforts to breathe new life into the dormant federation.[42] The convention revived the provincial organization, giving it the name Socialist Party of British Columbia (SPBC), and recalled Cameron from Washington to act as organizer. Most significant was the adoption of the revolutionary platform of the Socialist Party of America which had been hammered out at the Indianapolis unity convention only three months earlier.[43]

The adoption of the American platform was achieved after 'some very warm discussions,' and an executive committee headed by Burns, the provincial secretary, was instructed to draft an additional set of immediate demands which would temper the platform.[44] The controversy quickened between the gradualists, who contended that while the coming of the revolution was assured by history it was only practical for socialists to work for the relief of the working class under capitalism, and the so-called impossiblists,[45] who argued that not only was the reform of capitalism impossible but that efforts to achieve reform could only delay the advent of the co-operative commonwealth by diverting the proletariat from the class struggle. The controversy would rack the party for years. What resulted from the deliberations of the executive committee was 'a composite platform which would represent the average ideas of the membership.' It had three parts: the preamble of the SPA platform; a set of 'general demands' which represented all planks of a national character from the CSL platform; and a set of 'provincial demands' - the last two sections were distinctly reformist in character. In the *Eagle*, Pettipiece appealed to socialists to stay in the party, even if their 'pet ideas' did not appear in the platform, and to fight for these at the next convention.[46]

Criticism of the revised platform came from several quarters, but the opposition to the addition of immediate demands was led by Nanaimo socialists. Conditions in the coal fields, which every day seemed to confirm the validity of the doctrine of the class struggle, had already converted some miners into revolutionaries.[47] The watering-down of the platform caused Nanaimo socialists to reassess their position in the SPBC and to begin to consider the formation of a separate party. Before taking this action, however, the miners felt the need for an accomplished propagandist.[48]

The Nanaimo socialists called E.T. Kingsley to the Island. An industrial accident in California had resulted in the amputation of both of Kingsley's legs, and while recuperating in hospital he read Marx. He joined the SLP, became an active propagandist in Oakland, and was several times the party's candidate for Congress.[49] Kingsley, however, did not gain real prominence in the SLP until the rebellion of the 'Kangaroos.' He remained loyal to De Leon, took an active role in the purge of insurgents, and as a reward was named state organizer.[50] At this time De Leon began to move away from his exclusively political orientation and towards the syndicalism which would lead him into the Industrial Workers of the World in 1905. But Kingsley was not prepared to make this shift, and after a bitter 'face to face' confrontation with De Leon, he left the SLP.[51] The socialism, then, that Kingsley brought with him to British Columbia was that of the pre-1900 Socialist Labor party. It consisted, in its essentials, of a denial of the utility of economic action through trade unions, a rejection of reforms as counter-revolutionary, and a reliance on political action as the only viable tactic available to the working class. The Nanaimo socialists originally engaged Kingsley for only a brief propaganda tour, but his impact on the Island was such that they retained him permanently, setting him up first as a fish seller and later as a printer.[52] Kingsley was not responsible for the introduction of impossiblism to British Columbia; this had its roots in the SLP, the British Socialist Democratic Federation, the Washington state organization, and the realities of life in mining camps. But he did provide impossiblism with a coherent rationale and a dynamic leadership and, as a result, had a profound influence on the development of western radicalism.

When the Nanaimo socialists left the SPBC in the spring of 1902 to establish the short-lived Revolutionary Socialist Party of Canada, Kingsley's influence was already apparent. The party's platform, undoubtedly the most revolutionary drafted in Canada up to that time, called simply for the destruction of capitalism and announced, 'the pathway leading to our emancipation from the chains of wage slavery is uncompromising political warfare against the capitalist class, with no quarter and no surrender.'[53]

By the beginning of 1902 BC socialism had passed beyond its formative stage, and with a province-wide if precarious organization, its own newspaper, and an energetic organizer, it was ready for expansion. Conditions in the province during the first years of the century were highly conducive to the expansion of the movement. The prevailing political confusion arising from the transition from personal to party government encouraged workers to pursue political innovations. Many were convinced that social and economic conditions demanded a radical solution. All signs seemed to point to the triumph of capitalism in the province. From June 1900 to November 1902 James Dunsmuir, the very epitome of repressive capitalism, was premier, and, as if to dramatize his position in the province, a large number of miners were killed at his Union collieries in 1901. Whatever Dunsmuir's motives for assuming office, the labour movement was convinced that his intention was an even greater degradation of the workers.[54]

Of even greater significance to the growth of socialism were several large and violent strikes which rocked the province in these years. In two dramatic confrontations, between Fraser River fishermen and the canneries, and between hard-rock miners and Rossland companies, all the coercive powers of a repressive capitalist state seemed to be employed in breaking the resistance of a united working class.[55] These spectacular defeats in which government complicity appeared to be important made an aroused and bitter labour movement listen more readily to appeals from socialists. The BC vice-president of the TLC observed that, because of their employers' ruthless opposition to unions, workers were 'embracing socialism more than [they have] ever done before.'[56]

Certainly this tendency was demonstrated in the Kootenays when Cameron began organizing there at the end of 1901; the miners, 'fed up' with unsuccessful strikes, appeared to be 'ripe for socialism.'[57] The SPBC organizer met with such success in the interior that Pettipiece became convinced that the province had reached 'the beginning of the final stage of capitalism.' By the end of January 1902, the *Eagle* reported officially that the party had fourteen of its eighteen active locals in the hard-rock camps.[58] Some of these locals were clearly mushroom growths, however, and collapsed within a year. This phenomenon points to a serious problem faced by the BC socialist movement. It had a power base among the hard-rock miners, but the uncertain and transient nature of their occupation made them highly unstable supporters.

Greater numbers of Vancouver Island coal miners were also joining the socialists. In the early autumn of 1902, J.W. Hawthornthwaite, the independent labour MLA for Nanaimo who had been flirting with the socialists for some time, joined the Revolutionary Socialist party. Then in November the socialists nominated a miner, Parker Williams, to contest a provincial by-election; though defeated, he polled 40 per cent of the vote.[59] Such developments caused the labour columnist for the Victoria *Colonist*, to observe, 'the growth of socialism in British Columbia during the past year has been phenomenal.' Early in 1903, Burns estimated that 50 per cent of the party's membership had been socialists for less than two years.[60]

The socialists' new strength was dramatically demonstrated by their ability to cripple the first province-wide labour party established in British Columbia. The Western Federation of Miners (WFM) already had considerable experience in labourite politics when the disastrous Rossland strike caused many miners to conclude that united action at the polls was essential. Events in the United States facilitated developments; in May 1901, the international convention of the union passed a resolution advocating independent political action. Late in October 1901, the socialist local at Slocan City informed the miners' union that there was an 'urgent need' for a workingman's political party and suggested that the WFM sponsor a convention of trade unionists and socialists to establish such a party. This proposal was quickly taken up by socialists within the Slocan City union, and late in November they petitioned the district secretary to convene such a meeting.[61] Initially the district executive refused to consider socialist representation, but under pressure of a campaign mounted by the Slocan City local the question was submitted to a referendum of the locals.[62] Then socialists, both outside and inside the union, began a campaign to have the district pass the referendum and thus to push the WFM toward class-conscious political action.[63] The referendum resulted in a small majority in favour of the socialists, and the call for a convention went out.[64]

In April 1902, approximately sixty representatives of socialist, labour, and reform organizations met in convention at Kamloops to establish the Provincial Progressive party (PPP). One-third of the delegates were socialists, and these, after caucusing, made a concerted effort to have the convention adopt a revolutionary platform. But the socialist offensive was beaten back and, in the words of a comrade from the interior, 'the result was that every vital issue to labor was either ignored or straddled and the platform finally adopted was of a weak and indefinite description.'[65] The convention had been a contest between socialists and labourites, and the adoption of a reformist platform represented a defeat for the socialists.[66]

All socialists could agree on the principle that only their party, or at least a labour party committed to the destruction of capitalism, could lead the proletariat to emancipation, and that any other party claiming the allegiance of the workers could only impede progress. Consequently they immediately initiated a campaign to reverse the decision taken at Kamloops. The party press and propagandists denounced the PPP as *bourgeois*; 'it is no more entitled to special consideration at our hands than either the Liberals or Conservatives,' sneered Burns. Because the new party was committed to the reform of capitalism, the SPBC executive declared that it would be unconstitutional for socialist locals to affiliate with the PPP.[67]

The BC socialists' campaign against the labour party was given substantial assistance by their American comrades. One month after the Kamloops meeting, the international convention of the WFM had met at Denver. Under the urging of President Ed Boyce and Eugene Debs, the delegates endorsed the platform of the SPA. To bring the WMF, and the provincial labour movement, into line, Debs carried the new gospel to British Columbia directly from the Denver convention. He condemned the PPP platform as 'a tissue of contradictions ... well calculated to confuse and muddle the situation' and called upon the workers to reject that 'middle class movement.' At the same time, he told his audiences that the SPBC's 'clear-cut and uncompromising' platform made it the 'party of the future.'[68] Charles H. Moyer, the newly elected president of the WFM, also joined the fight. In June, he issued a circular calling upon the miners to take up the class struggle, and the following month he travelled to the province to proselytize for socialism.[69] The campaign won the hard-rock miners who had been, potentially, the backbone of the PPP. The new party collapsed. Fifteen years would elapse before another labour party could challenge the socialist hegemony of working class politics in British Columbia.

The vitality of socialism encouraged the two wings of the movement to hold a unity convention late in 1902. During the summer and early autumn, the gradualists, led by Burns, and the impossiblists, prominent among whom was Kingsley, debated the question of the inclusion of immediate demands in the platform. At the convention delegates replaced the earlier platform with its immediate demands with a document very similar to the starkly revolutionary program of the Nanaimo party. This was clearly a victory for Kingsley and the impossiblists. Indeed, the *Western Socialist* observed that he had become 'a power in the movement' whose work had 'had a clarifying effect' on BC socialism. [70] The convention did not mark, however, the beginning of the ascendancy of Island impossiblism over all lesser doctrines, as party historians would later claim. The delegates reaffirmed their commitment to trade unions and lifted clauses of the re-united party's constitution verbatim from the Washington state platform. [71] More important, tactical controversies continued to plague the party.

The problem of doctrinal orthodoxy always generated heated debate, because upon it turned the question of whether the SPBC was to be an exclusive sect or an inclusive party. Alex Lang of Vancouver, who had succeeded Burns as provincial secretary, began an exchange early in 1903 when he asserted that it had become necessary, with the growth of socialism, to ensure that persons not fully acquainted with Marxism be barred from the party. The 'scientific' nature of the doctrine necessitated the utmost caution: 'let those who do not understand the ethics of the class struggle serve their apprenticeship on the outside of the party.' Only in this way could the revolutionary character of the SPBC be assured. This was too much for Burns. He condemned such 'intolerant Bigotry,' which impeded the growth of the movement and claimed that socialism could only be considered scientific 'when we find the leaders of socialist thought in complete agreement as to principle and tactics, in the same manner as mathematicians are agreed upon the multiplication table.' Gradualists taunted Lang with the charge that he was following the disastrous policies of the SLP, a ploy favoured by critics of the impossiblists; he replied that the SLP's concern with doctrinal orthodoxy was valid and only De Leon's 'bossism' had hurt the party. [73]

An even more explosive issue, because it affected so many workers intimately, concerned the party's relations with trade unions. As members of the SPBC, socialists were committed primarily, if not exclusively, to political action; the corollary to this commitment was a necessary criticism of economic action in order to turn the workers to the ballot box. By their very presence in the party, all socialists accepted this policy, but controversy arose over the question of what form criticism of unions should take. Kingsley was the most prominent anti-union spokesman. By the beginning of 1903, he had become the epitome of impossiblism in the minds of workers; one defined 'a revolutionary' as 'a Kingsley socialist.'[74] Early in the year Kingsley, now the party's organizer on the Island, told a Victoria meeting that unions, while they provided some workers with relief, played no role in the class struggle. Because unions were 'reactionary products of the present competitive system,' the party could not promote them. Weston Wrigley, George Wrigley's son, condemned Kingsley for making such statements in an official capacity because the vast majority of party members disagreed with the impossiblists' position. Joining the controversy, Burns asserted that, though political action represented the only hope of the proletariat, 'trade unions, strikes and boycotts are all incidents in the class struggle ... [and] afford transient and partial relief.' The Revelstoke local of the party made a formal complaint against Kingsley's statements, and the Victoria local demanded he be relieved of his post as organizer.[75]

Despite this persistent controversy, the party continued to enjoy good relations with the unions. Hawthornthwaite gained the gratitude of organized labour by working sedulously in the provincial legislature for improved labour legislation. In Vancouver, through what Pettipiece called a 'policy of permeation,' socialists continued to work in the trades council and succeeded in having the body endorse the *Western Clarion* when it emerged.[76]

During the first half of 1903, a series of pitched battles between affiliates of the radical American Labor Union and large employers helped to provide the continuation of a climate excellent for the expansion of socialism.[77] Consequently, members of the SPBC were in an exhilarated and confident mood when they entered the provincial election campaign, nominating ten candidates in constituencies from the Island to the Crow's Nest Pass. It was an energetic campaign. After witnessing one election rally in Vancouver, Adam Shortt wrote, 'outside of the hysterical revivalist, we have nothing that quite equals it in the east, either for noise, absence of argument, mixture of metaphor or psychological effect.'[78] The socialists received valuable assistance from ALU affiliates which played a prominent role in the contest. In the Kootenays, the WFM was the basis of the socialist campaign; the union mobilized hard-rock miners as never before, even encouraging some Americans at Greenwood to secure Canadian citizenship in order to vote.[79] But the SPBC's greatest effort was made among the coal miners of the Island. Because they recognized that a long, bitter strike against Dunsmuir had put the workers 'in a particularly good mood for digesting ... the principles of modern socialism,' all the party's leading members campaigned in the region.[80]

The election, early in October, demonstrated the gains which the socialists had made in the province. The SPBC's ten candidates received 9 per cent of the poll; in Vancouver the socialists averaged over 1100 votes each; the standard-bearer in Greenwood failed of election by only a narrow margin; and on the Island Nanaimo and Newcastle returned Hawthornthwaite and Parker Williams respectively. Elected as a WFM candidate in Slocan, William Davidson soon joined the party. The *Clarion*, which significantly pointed to 'the remarkable uniformity of the vote throughout the province,' found the results 'deeply encouraging.'[81] The socialists were elated with the results, and the chiliasm inherent in their analysis of society was reinforced and began to emerge as the dominant component of their thought.

The provincial election of 1903 was a landmark in the ideological development of BC socialism. As a result of their impressive showing, the socialists gained an entirely new self-concept. In the years since its formation the party had become strong and confident, but in the minds of its members the development had been more than one to maturity. They were convinced that in recent months their movement had been transformed from a weak client of established socialist parties to the revolutionary vanguard. The most important statement of this new self-concept was an article published by Weston Wrigley in the *International Socialist Review*. He wrote, 'marvelous as has been the growth of the Socialist vote in many of the United States, ... British Columbia, has by its recent election campaign, taken a foremost place in the American class struggle.' Using a complex and dubious set of formulae, he argued that the party's vote represented, in fact, 13 per cent of the total poll, the highest ever gained by socialists in a North American jurisdiction. Now it was the turn of Canadians to be didactic. The gains came, Wrigley lectured, because the SPBC platform was 'the shortest and most uncompromising statement of the principles of revolutionary socialism that has ever been drafted in any country.'[82]

BC socialists now claimed the leadership of the Canadian movement which, in fact, had been theirs for at least a year.[83] In addition, both the British movement and the Second International were officially criticized by the party for being insufficiently revolutionary.[84] Most instructive was the new attitude towards the SPA. The party which had had such an important influence on the development of the movement in British Columbia was now criticized for doctrinal laxity. Comment began immediately after the election, but it was left to Kingsley to fire the major salvo. When the SPA convention of 1904 made only slight revisions in the party's platform, he sneered, 'the clear-cut and uncompromising attitude of the Socialist Party of B.C. stands out in striking contrast to the halting or confused attitude of the Socialist Party in the U.S.' Burns was quick to criticize this new attitude towards the American party.[85] But developments were passing the leading gradualists by; the majority of party members embraced the new self-concept and its full implications.

The new self-concept clearly had ideological implications in that it entailed a new responsibility for BC socialism. Because the highly developed nature of capitalism in the province had produced the continent's most advanced socialist movement, Pettipiece told his comrades that they must guard their doctrinal orthodoxy: 'fate has decreed this position in the world's history to us, and we should prove to the workers of the world that we can rise to the occasion; let us stand firm; keep our organization iron-clad, aye "narrow" and see that we shy clear of the rocks of danger which have wrecked so many well-meaning movements.'[86] Such an attitude, of course, necessarily entailed a shift to the more doctrinaire line of the impossiblists, and, as a result of the election, the party was prepared for this. The electoral gains had come after the adoption of the revolutionary platform in 1902. More important, success had been achieved in the very centre of the revolutionary propaganda, the Island coal fields where socialism meant impossiblism. Consequently, the SPBC embraced impossiblism because the doctrine appeared to have been vindicated by events, and E.T. Kingsley emerged as the party's leading theoretician. Former critics, like Weston Wrigley, became his supporters. The party's 1903 convention adopted one of his basic doctrines when it explicitly rejected immediate demands as 'liable to retard the achievement of our final aims.' And, most important, late in 1903 the provincial executive, which now controlled the *Western Clarion*, named Kingsley as editor.[87]

Immigration by British trade unionists, determined propaganda by American socialists, violent and dramatic confrontations between capital and labour had, in the space of five years, acted on basic social conditions to produce an almost unique revolutionary movement in British Columbia. By the end of 1903, the socialists had achieved a position of extraordinary power in the labour movement. They would never control the province's trade unions, but in the future socialists would always hold positions of real authority in those unions. More important, the destruction of the Provincial Progressive party had been disastrous for labourism, and it would be fifteen years before another viable, province-wide labour party emerged. In the intervening time, socialists became the political leaders of organized labour in the province and, because of their power base in the mining camps, a force in provincial affairs. The ideology of this unusually influential party also gave it a peculiar place in the North American radical movement. By the end of 1903 the impossiblists' power in the SPBC had become virtually exclusive. The purge of the gradualists ensured that schools of socialism which had their basis in ethics or humanitarianism would be ruthlessly suppressed, to be replaced by a stark and uncompromising materialism. A doctrinaire preoccupation with revolution now was the principal characteristic of BC socialism. And that interpretation of Marxism became the ideological base of the Socialist Party of Canada which emerged late in 1904.

3

Militant industrial unionism and the first western rebellion

From the time the labour movement emerged in western Canada, workers there were isolated from the influence of the eastern-dominated Trades and Labor Congress. This condition was only partly a function of distance. Western economic and social realities which presented the labour movement with special and different challenges tended to estrange westerners from easterners. The same circumstances that produced alienation provided a context favourable to the growth of radicalism, which, in turn, caused further alienation. As more and more western labour leaders moved to the left, they perceived themselves as the progressive element in the congress, always restrained and frustrated by complacent and conservative easterners. Distance, physical and mental, ensured that the TLC would never command the confidence nor direct the will of the western labour movement.

These distances were greatest in British Columbia. Because men and ideas flowed across the American border and because the experience of hard-rock miners was essentially the same in the mountain states and British Columbia, the Western Federation of Miners, a vigorous opponent of exclusive and conservative craft unionism, became powerful in the provincial labour movement. In the first years of the century the leaders of the federation launched a proletarian crusade against the American Federation of Labor and capitalism. At the same time BC workers engaged in a series of pitched battles with great corporations. The exhileration of battle and the frustration of defeat provoked some workers to take up new weapons. They embraced a militant industrial unionism which fought employers with solidarity and socialism. As a result, the first western rebellion against the Trades and Labor Congress began.

Probably more than any other union, the Western Federation of Miners was a product of the conflict between the aggressive, and often brutal, capitalism of the American West and the workers of the region.[1] Initially, the WFM was a typical job-conscious organization, but realities of life in hard-rock camps forced it to ever more radical positions. The radicalization of the miners' union grew out of the labour wars of the mountain states which seemed to epitomize Marx's doctrine of the class struggle – no holds barred, no quarter given. The WFM could not fight the operators with conventional trade union tactics, because the companies frequently enjoyed the support of the state judiciary and executive. Led by President Ed Boyce and Secretary Bill Haywood, the WFM adopted radical tactics. When the operators refused to allow conventional mechanisms of industrial relations to function, violence became a bargaining device. In addition the union developed a strong commitment to political action. Initially this took the form of support for Populism, but Boyce, under the influence of Debs, pushed the WFM towards socialism.

The hard-rock camps of British Columbia were part of the larger American mining society. Prospectors from the mountain states discovered the mineral riches of the rugged, forbidding Kootenays and of the hills of the Boundary District. During the 1890s American corporations inaugurated the modern phase of the province's metal mining industry by building large milling and smelting facilities and railways.[2] Even after eastern Canadian and British capital became important at the turn of the century, American influences remained strong. The essential sameness of mining technology on both sides of the border made American managers a prominent part of BC camps. In fact many British-born managers had worked in the mountain states.[3] The same was true of the men who drilled and shovelled the quartz. The hard-rock miners of the West were highly mobile; the card transfer system of the WFM facilitated mobility. They routinely tramped between American and Canadian camps. Despite a vague official desire to reduce the influence of American workers, companies made no effort to hire Canadian or British miners; one manager observed, 'when a man comes to me for work I do not ask him what his religion is or his nationality; I simply wish to know if he is a good miner.' At the turn of the century at least 50 per cent of the miners in the Kootenays were American citizens.[4]

As the WFM's District 6 developed in British Columbia during the late nineties, it encountered the same opposition that the federation faced south of the border. Following the practice of the mountain states, companies in the Kootenays refused to recognize the union. Time and again mine managers, testifying before a royal commission which investigated the industry in 1899, declared that, while they had no objection to unions in principle and would not discriminate against a man because of membership in the WFM, their only responsibility was to the shareholders, and they would not jeopardize the profit position of their mine by giving over any authority to the union. Some went farther; the superintendent of the Lillooet mine declared that he would employ no members of the WFM, because 'there is always trouble wherever I have been where a Miners' Union is.'[5] When the mechanisms of collective bargaining failed to function, unusually severe tensions emerged between miners and managers. These tensions were exacerbated by the nature of the industry, which created a wide gulf between a few managers representing huge corporations and the men. The absence of a large, relatively neutral business or professional class to mediate disputes in the camps only intensified the condition. A strong feeling of group solidarity among the miners grew out of this experience.

Clearly the hard-rock mining industry of British Columbia shared in what Vernon Jensen has called 'the heritage of conflict.' The great labour wars of the mountain states, particularly those fought in the Coeur d'Alenes, produced a deep and persistent animosity between the companies and the defeated miners. Men driven out of Idaho carried accounts of the struggle across the West, and these became part of the folklore of the camps. By 1899 there was 'a considerable number' of refugees from the Coeur d'Alenes in the Kootenays and the Boundary. The presence of these men allowed BC miners to participate vicariously in what were the most violent confrontations between capital and labour ever to take place in North America. This participation increased the sense of outrage at their own less oppressive, but by no means inconsequential, grievances. The WFM's radical Silverton local declared, 'we do not consider ourselves any better than the miners of the Coeur d'Alenes' and threatened violent reprisals against employers unless conditions improved.[6] Such attitudes produced what one investigator described as 'a feeling of insecurity' among many operators, and they demanded police protection and the exclusion of the WFM from Canada.[7]

The Rossland strike of 1901 dramatized the bitter heritage of British Columbia's hard-rock industry. Late in 1899 tough, anti-union managers in the camp set out to smash the federation's largest and most important local in the Kootenays.[8] In addition to revising customs of work and importing surplus labour, the companies waged what one miner called 'secret warfare' against the union, a warfare reminiscent of the Coeur d'Alenes. Indeed, in his report to the 1902 convention, President Ed Boyce equated Rossland with that notorious region.[9] The operators began blacklisting prominent union miners, a practice which a leading member of the federation described as the 'curse of our unions.' Rossland, naturally, suffered the loss of some of its most active members, who were forced to leave the camp because they were unable to find work, and the local also suffered an over-all decline in its numbers.[10] As were federation locals in the United States, those in British Columbia and the international executive were constantly on the watch for labour spies, and with reason. For example, a detective in the employ of the mine owners rose to become financial secretary of the Morrisey local before giving himself away one night while in his cups. The Rossland companies made extensive use of spies. A miner complained, 'our city, our streets, our unions, are today infested by that Judas Iscariot parasite, too lazy to work, too ignorant to realize their own degradation, known as the spotter, imported here from Idaho.' Agents of the operators reported on the union's activities and its prominent members, provoked factional fights, and at one point came close to controlling the local.[11] Rossland companies also began to assemble a special police force. The municipal council recruited, equipped, and paid twenty-five men who were placed under the orders of mine managers. To ensure the proper protection of the properties, the companies armed the specials with both repeating shotguns and rifles.[12]

The Rossland strike began in July 1901. The miners struck to put an end to union-smashing in Rossland and in Northport, Washington, where Rossland companies were trying to break a WFM local of smeltermen.[13] A confrontation between organized capital, bent on destroying the miners' union, and the WFM's largest and most important local was of critical significance to the federation. Ed Boyce told his BC comrades, 'I am in favor of making a fight to the bitter end, and I care not what it takes to win, nor how we win. I am in favor of winning.'[14] The full resources of the federation were thrown into the Rossland struggle. The *Miners' Magazine* and WFM locals throughout the West advertised conditions in British Columbia and instructed miners to stay away. The federation provided the striking local with legal assistance.[15] Most important was the financial support that the international union gave to the strikers. Although the WFM's war chest had been badly depleted by battles in the Coeur d'Alenes, the Rossland miners received approximately $20,000 from the federation.[16]

The union was fighting strong and ruthless opponents. The men had barely left the mines when the companies called upon the federal government to send in troops to protect their properties and strike-breakers. When Laurier refused, the owners imported American thugs who harassed and intimidated strikers.[17] Early in October the companies obtained injunctions so sweeping that they prevented 'a union man from taking a full breath within a radius of twenty miles of a company office.' Under these instruments, union miners were quickly jailed for the harassment of strike-breakers.[18] The operators made even more effective use of the courts; the Gooderham Syndicate sued the union for damages. Union officers were subpoenaed and ordered to produce their records in court; their refusal to comply brought contempt charges and imprisonment.[19] None of these tactics, however, were the principal means of defeating the union. The companies imported large numbers of strike-breakers from the United States in systematic violation of the Alien Labour Law. Significantly, one manager, a veteran of the Idaho labour wars, secured men from Missouri, the main source of scabs for the mine owners in the Coeur d'Alenes. Appeals from the union for federal action to stop this traffic brought the response from Laurier and his justice minister, David Mills, that they had no jurisdiction. Pettipiece sneered, 'the Laurier government is afraid to enforce the provisions of a law placed in the statutes by themselves.' The importation of miners from the United States provided the owners with 'an abundant supply of labour' and resulted in the effective collapse of the strike by November.[20]

A significant aspect of the Rossland strike was the involvement of the deputy minister of labour, William Lyon Mackenzie King, who attempted to settle the dispute in November. Conversations with the owners convinced King that they had an adequate supply of labour to operate the mines and that the cause of the men was 'hopeless.' He, therefore, advised the union leaders to call off the strike. They refused, and the secretary of the local charged that King was 'unknowingly playing the companies' hand.'[21] The young man had gone to Rossland of the opinion that the strikers' cause was just, but he quickly changed his mind. His first encounter with the radical miners left King uneasy. Recognizing that the strike was in large measure a sympathetic one, he condemned it; the miners had been led into a strike 'by subterfuge and a great deal of crooked work on the part of the executive committee, who were working with the officers of the District Association, and in close communication with the headquarters at Denver.' King concluded that 'this is clearly and simply an agitators' fight.' It would be, therefore, 'unrighteous and disastrous,' King told his minister, for the federal government to take any action which might allow the federation 'to profit by its own wrong.' He recommended that no investigation of the violations of the Alien Labour Law be made. Indeed, if the WFM were not beaten, 'it might be a disastrous thing for the mining interests of this province.'[22] King's mission to Rossland was important because on it he formed his first, and lasting, impression of the WFM. This perception of the federation, as a gang of alien radicals who engineered sympathetic strikes, was the basis of the Laurier government's attitude to militant industrial unions and shaped the federal response to those unions in 1903.

The largest and most important federation local in the province had been beaten and broken by illegal means while government looked on. The defeat at Rossland convinced a large number of miners that conventional unionism was not adequate to meet the ruthless attacks of the operators. The old tactics had failed; now the WFM would adopt new ones. As he watched the violation of the Alien Labour Law at Rossland, a Slocan miner wrote, 'we must make the laws and administer them; it is time, full time, for it is evident, painfully evident, that they are not made nor administered in the interest of the masses, and will not be until the masses take over the power so infamously misused by those into whose hands it has been entrusted.'[23]

By 1901 the hard-rock miners had some political experience. In their early political initiatives they, like their comrades south of the border, had backed middle-class progressives, but by the turn of the century many miners were being influenced by socialist doctrines. As early as 1899 the Silverton local defined its objectives as the achievement of 'the co-operative Commonwealth and the establishment of justice and equality among men.'[24] Socialists played an important role in the locals – D.B. O'Neal and J.A. Foley at Slocan City, Andy Shilland at Sandon, and John Riordan at Phoenix. At the district level provincial organizer James Baker took every opportunity to proselytize for socialism as he travelled among the miners of British Columbia. W.J. Walker, another district organizer, told a Ferguson audience in 1901, 'the time is ripe for the people to rise and with the ballot secure that which is but their own, the product of their toil.'[25]

These developments had parallels south of the border. Since 1897 Boyce had been under the influence of Debs, and in 1900 the *Miners' Magazine* endorsed the latter's candidacy for president. From this time on the pronouncements of the federation's leadership became increasingly revolutionary. For example, John O'Neil, editor of the *Miners'Magazine*, was cheered by a Silverton audience in September 1901 when he urged BC miners 'to lift the banner of socialism to float at once and forever over the silenced battlements of incorporated greed.'[26]

The hard-rock miners were ready for united political action when the Rossland strike ended in disaster; so the WFM called the Kamloops convention early in 1902.[27] The result of the convention, the establishment of a reformist labour party, was unacceptable to socialists in the union, however. The federation's 1902 convention made socialism the official ideology of the WFM. To ensure socialist control of the union – and to wreck the Progressive party – the federation's executive launched a propaganda campaign led by Debs. He reported that he had encountered 'some opposition to the progressive policy adopted at the Denver convention, but this was in the main overcome.'[28] The campaign won the rank and file and placed the socialists firmly in control of the district. In January 1903, Pettipiece rhapsodized, 'in the Kootenays a miners' union meeting is converted into a socialist meeting without turning out the lights.'[29] The federation had been radicalized by the same pressures that had been at work in the mountain states. Now the WFM would become the power base for a spectacular, if ephemeral, rebellion against conservative craft unionism.

At the same convention which had declared for socialism, the WFM, again encouraged by Debs, determined to challenge Samuel Gompers's dominance of the American labour movement. The federation founded a national labour centre, the American Labor Union (ALU). The ALU rejected elitist and exclusive craft unionism and launched a campaign to organize semiskilled and unskilled workers into industrial unions. It emphasized the potential of working class solidarity in strikes. And it was committed to socialism.[30] Immediately after the international convention, District No. 6 began to prepare for the fight against craft unionism by cutting its ties with the TLC.[31]

That Gompers's business unionism was essentially reactionary had become an article of faith among socialists, and from the beginning they actively supported the ALU. They perceived the new organization, with its declaration for socialism, as, potentially, a means whereby the labour movement could be radicalized. In addition, socialists favoured the ALU's industrial unionism which, their reading of Marx told them, was 'the next evolutionary step.' Socialists considered industrial unions as a necessary and inevitable response to the growing concentration of capital. 'Industrial unionism,' said George Dales, a prominent member of the SPBC, 'is the highest form of unionism and the most effective yet devised.'[32]

The socialists also encouraged industrial unionism as a means of increasing class-consciousness among the workers. They were not concerned about the incipient syndicalism which was subsumed in the ALU's commitment to proletarian solidarity. One wrote, 'the sympathetic strike is a manifestation of the solidarity of labor and must be noted with pleasure by those in the advanced labor movement.'[33] This attitude conforms to the general pattern of relations between socialists and syndicalists; members of the SPBC were not opposed to a doctrine which was potentially antagonistic to political action.

Socialist support of the ALU in British Columbia resulted in socialist domination. All the ALU's organizers in the province were leading socialists, Cameron and Wrigley in Victoria, Ben Bakes in Vancouver,[34] and Charlie O'Brien in the Kootenays. At times socialists promoted the ALU unofficially. For example, James Pritchard and Samuel Mottishaw led the drive to organize the coal miners of Extension and then encouraged the local to affiliate with the WFM.[35] Energetic socialists clearly spurred the growth of the ALU in British Columbia. But if the ALU initially derived more benefit from the relationship, by mid-1903 the growth of the SPBC was as much dependent upon industrial unionists as the growth of the ALU was dependent upon socialists. They had become parallel and complementary developments. O'Brien, who told workers that 'in order to be good union men, [you] must become class conscious, politically as well as industrially,' was always as ready to establish a socialist as an ALU local.[36] Workers could join a union, no matter how radical, more easily than the socialist party; but once members of an ALU local, they immediately became subject to Marxist indoctrination. In July 1903, Bertha Merrill, the province's first female socialist leader, surveyed the rapid expansion of the party and observed, 'the effect the A.L.U. has had in setting this "wave" in motion can hardly be estimated; union men, who have long "shyed" at the word "Socialism" ... have been taught by the A.L.U. to look the dubious sign-post squarely in the face, only to find it pointed out a shortcut to the very Mecca they wished to gain.'[37]

The ALU was mainly dependent upon the WFM for its strength,

funds, and membership. So the organization's campaign in British Columbia began in the mining camps of the Kootenays. Here there were relatively few craftsmen, and the great majority of unskilled workers pursued occupations which were in some way related to the mines. These men naturally identified their interests with the WFM - many, indeed, were members of the union - and readily turned to an organization which was so closely linked to the federation. The WFM made every effort to promote the growth of the ALU. For example, Moyer told Shilland to 'use your influence in assisting [the Culinary Employees' Protective Union] in their efforts to thoroughly organize the cooks and waiters' in Sandon. [38] By the autumn of 1902 O'Brien was making good progress among cooks, bartenders, general labourers, teamsters, and lumbermen, and he was able to establish several locals. [39]

The growth of the ALU in the Kootenays was due in part to the failure of the AFL or TLC to organize in the region. Yet industrial growth and inflationary pressures had resulted in the emergence of a significant number of local unions not affiliated with the eastern centres. When J.H. Watson, the TLC's organizer in Vancouver, reported on this neglect to the 1902 convention, he cited carpenters' unions 'all over the Kootenays' affiliated with neither the Amalgamated Society nor the United Brotherhood. Such organizations formed the base for federal unions which the ALU chartered in most camps.[40]

Workers in British Columbia considered the WFM to be a fighting organization, and this reputation for strength contributed to the growth of industrial unionism. Time and again Island coal miners who had watched employers such as Dunsmuir smashing local unions for years, told a 1903 royal commission that they had joined the WFM because it was strong. The Nanaimo union, for example, considered the realities of fighting strikes in the coal fields and joined the WFM because it could call out all BC miners. [41] The federation attempted to implement the ALU's doctrine of proletarian solidarity to the fullest. Recognizing that no Island strike could be won unless the pool of Chinese labour was organized, Haywood ordered Baker to bring those workers into the union. [42]

The rebellion broke out among miners in the summer of 1902. The Phoenix trades council, dominated by Riordan and other socialist miners, left the TLC because it was 'an appendage of a capitalistic party [rather] than a body devoted to the advancement of the interests of the working people of Canada' and endorsed the SPBC. [43] The Nanaimo miners dealt craft union prestige an even greater blow by refusing to issue credentials for the congress convention to Ralph Smith, president of the TLC and a Liberal-Labour MP. Socialists in the union denounced Smith as 'the Gompers of Canada' and led the local out of the congress.[44] Militant industrial unionism spread even more rapidly in the new year. The ALU achieved its greatest success in the mountain strongholds of the WFM, but as the industrial crisis of 1903 intensified, the union moved down into the coast cities. There it fired the imagination and inspired the confidence of workers as an organization of the dispossessed can.

The storm centre of the industrial crisis of 1903 was the strike of the United Brotherhood of Railway Employees (UBRE), an ALU affiliate, against the Canadian Pacific Railway. A purely local union called the UBRE was established in Winnipeg in 1899; early in 1902, it affiliated with an American organization of the same name led by George Estes. By the beginning of the following year the union had locals at all the divisional points of the CPR between Winnipeg and Vancouver.[45]

The UBRE was an industrial union which had as its object the organization of all railway employees, skilled and unskilled, into one union, making them, said the Canadian organizer in a slap at the aristocratic running trades, 'not brothers in name only, but brothers indeed.' Only an industrial union, Estes argued, could function effectively under capitalism; the UBRE, he told a Winnipeg audience, 'has been designed to meet the needs of the hour; ... it meets concentration and consolidation on the part of capital, with the same policy for labor and nothing short of this will protect you.' Estes conducted his campaign for industrial unionism in a rough and ready fashion, instructing his Canadian organizer 'to develop a public sentiment for the U.B.R.E. - the Industrial Union plan - the A.L.U. and against the reactionary and capitalistic party now temporarily in control of the A.F. of L.' Gompers informed the TLC that he considered the radical railway union 'inimical to the interests of the working people everywhere.'[46]

Although Estes was not a member of the SPA, he certainly had a socialist's outlook. He told his audiences that 'labor is entitled to the full product of its labor, and will secure this only when the working class controls the government.' The UBRE's Canadian organizer was under instructions to encourage the growth of socialism in all ways.[47] The union contained a significant number of socialists; the SPBC had, for example, 'the avowed support' of the UBRE's Revelstoke local. The union's attitude resulted in a cordial relationship with the socialists, even though some BC academicians had reservations about Estes' doctrinal orthodoxy.[48]

In January 1903, the CPR began efforts to break the UBRE local in its Vancouver freight department. Estes claimed that this offensive grew out of a realization that an industrial union 'would be too powerful for them to control'; in fact the company had earlier recognized a local union of freight handlers. In any case, the CPR instituted what a royal commission called 'a kind of secret warfare' against the UBRE, and the extensive use of intimidation, dismissals, and spys, virtually one in every meeting, soon weakened the local. This campaign forced the union to strike late in February. The men emphasized that they had made no demands whatever upon the company but were fighting 'to perpetuate their union, nothing else.' To help the Vancouver strikers, Estes called out the other CPR lodges at Revelstoke, Nelson, Calgary, and Winnipeg.[49]

Workers across the West took up the fight against one of the region's most hated corporations. In the words of *The Independent*, the struggle quickly 'passed entirely beyond its original scope and the fight is now upon the part of organized labour ... against the greed and oppression of organized capital.'[50] The spectacle of a fight between approximately one thousand unskilled workers and a great corporation, raging over half a continent produced extraordinary solidarity. Workers in Victoria, Vancouver, Calgary, and Winnipeg demonstrated in support of the strikers, and unions in all western centres contributed funds to the UBRE's war chest.

Refusing to handle scab freight, Victoria sailors, Vancouver longshoremen and teamsters, and Calgary teamsters struck in mid-March.[51] As the strike dragged on, the Winnipeg trades council began a campaign to have the CPR declared 'unfair' across the West, and other councils fell in line. The implications of the campaign were demonstrated when the Calgary council, in deciding to make the declaration, stated that the company would be responsible for 'the immense damage' that would result. Had the boycott gone into effect, no union man could have handled any goods that had been carried on the CPR, a state of affairs that would have produced chaos in the western Canadian economy.[52]

Socialists found such solidarity exhilarating, and they did everything possible to promote it. The workers' united defiance of the great railway was full of promise: 'the general strike has been the dream of labor for years here on the C.P.R.'; now it seemed possible.[53]

The CPR fought the union ruthlessly. Even before the men walked out, the company had begun to import strike-breakers from central Canada, and later it acquired scabs in the United States, without interference from immigration officials.[54] More sinister was the CPR's use of spies and special police. So notorious a part of the strike did such practices become that Pettipiece was moved to complain that 'nowhere else in the British Empire would such a condition be possible, and it has seldom been equalled anywhere in the long and painful history of the tragedy of labor.'[55] The most infamous example of espionage was the subversion of the Canadian organizer of the union, Harold Poore, by the Special Service Department of the CPR. After having sold himself to the company, he continued as the union's organizer, while at the same time giving all union secrets to his real employers.[56] Special police shot and killed Frank Rogers, a popular labour and socialist leader, while he was picketing CPR tracks in Vancouver. When the courts acquitted two suspects and exonerated the company, a thrill of bitter indignation swept through the labour movement.[57]

Not all unions opposed the CPR in its fight against the UBRE. The elitist brotherhoods steadfastly refused to heed Estes' appeals for help and kept the trains running. This ensured that while the strike severely hampered CPR operations it could never cripple them totally.[58] Even more important was the role that the TLC played in the dispute. Of the UBRE men who had gone on strike at Revelstoke, some had also been members of the International Association of Machinists and others of the International Union of Boilermakers, both TLC affiliates and both unions with CPR collective agreements. The company rushed the Machinists' Canadian vice-president to Revelstoke where he ordered his members to return to work. Watson, who had already attempted to supply the CPR with strike-breakers, travelled from Vancouver to order the boilermakers back to work and then, with company help, organized a union of scab metal trades helpers to replace striking UBRE men. An outraged Vancouver trades council expelled the TLC organizer and demanded that his commission be revoked, a demand with which the Congress secretary, P.M. Draper, refused to comply.[59] The *American Labor Union Journal* sneered, 'such reprehensible and traitorous conduct is in direct keeping with the scab-herding policy of the A.F. of L.'[60]

By the beginning of June the CPR's ability to fill the strikers' jobs and the assistance of the brotherhoods had resulted in the collapse of the strike. Despite the UBRE's attempt to put the best face on a settlement reached with the company, the outcome was disastrous.[61]

The UBRE strike, sympathetic strikes, WFM strikes on Vancouver Island and in the Crow's Nest Pass – industrial conflict was crippling BC's economy. Consequently the federal government came under pressure from the business community to restore order.[62] Early in April the western strikes were debated in the House of Commons. The member for Burrard told MPs, 'we in British Columbia ... are face to face with many labour troubles which are practically threatening our existence as a province.' Ralph Smith demanded that the government appoint a royal commission to investigate the industrial crisis.[63] The following day the minister responsible for labour affairs, Sir William Mulock, told Laurier that the 'especially grave' situation in British Columbia, caused by 'interference from the United States,' demanded decisive action. Industrial peace in the province could never be achieved until this harmful influence was removed: 'perhaps it would assist to disillusion [the workers] if an intelligent commission ... were to point out the injuries that have come to them because of the interference of the American unions.'[64]

The royal commission which was given this task was composed of Chief Justice Gordon Hunter of British Columbia and the Reverend E.S. Rowe, with Mackenzie King as a very active secretary. Some findings clearly confirmed the deputy minister's perception of militant industrial unions formed two years earlier. The commissioners and King discerned unusual working-class solidarity and became alarmed. After observing that it was 'a singular fact' that all the 1903 strikes involved ALU affiliates, the report went on to posit an elaborate conspiracy against the economy of British Columbia directed by foreign agitators. While the brotherhoods were described as 'legitimate and responsible unions,' the UBRE was accused of having 'latent possibilities of evil,' because its industrial structure and Estes's willingness to employ sympathetic action allowed it to cripple the whole transportation system.[65] Then the report linked the UBRE strike to that of the Island miners: anxious to stop the CPR's supply of coal, the ALU engineered the strikes in Dunsmuir's mines. It was clear to Hunter, Rowe, and King that 'there was an understanding between the American Labor Union and both the United Brotherhood of Railway Employees and the Western Federation of Miners whereby the three were to act in conjunction in the event of either of the latter requiring the aid of the other.'[66] The commissioners condemned as 'reprehensible' the tactics of militant industrial unionism – sympathetic strikes, boycotts, and intimidation of non-union workers. And because they were 'really nothing more than conspiracies against society in general and employers in particular,' the report recommended that the ALU and its affiliates 'be specially declared to be illegal.'[67]

There was no conspiracy. It is clear that low-status CPR employees joined the UBRE in the hope that an industrial union could take on the giant corporation. Island miners enlisted in the federation because they believed it to be a strong fighting machine. The workers' desire to organize and the strikes grew out of economic and social conditions and employers' repressive tactics. It is equally clear, however, that the leadership of the ALU unions, Canadians as well as Americans, were prepared to take advantage of the discontent of the Island miners to apply pressure on the CPR.[68] The radicals of the ALU, committed as they were to proletarian solidarity, had no compunctions whatever against the use of sympathetic action; indeed, they regarded it as wholly salutary.

The report of the royal commission did not retard the growth of the militant industrial unions, as it was intended to do; indeed, it probably produced the opposite effect. The western reaction to the commission's findings was almost universal indignation. The rebellion continued. The ALU remained strongest in the metal mining regions of British Columbia, but the influence of the radical centre was, by the summer of 1903, extensive in the cities of the province, and to some extent beyond its boundaries.

When it began organizing in the cities, the ALU moved into what had been formerly the exclusive preserve of the TLC and thus posed a direct threat to craft unionism. The workers of the coastal cities proved responsive to the ALU's radical gospel. In the three or four years before 1903, there had been a rapid expansion of unions, and many of the new organizations represented semiskilled or unskilled workers, freight handlers, laundrymen, teamsters, building labourers, and longshoremen. The entrance of these occupational groups into the labour movement tended to radicalize it in two ways. First, they diluted the influence of the conservative craft unions. Second, because their memberships lacked the skills served by the traditional methods of market regulation, the new unions were more disposed to consider radical tactics. Early in 1903 an ALU organizer in Vancouver reported to his Denver headquarters that the city's workers were rapidly becoming convinced that 'the American Labor Union is the only organization that holds any hope for the working class.'[69]

The year 1903 was not a good one for international craft unions in Canada. Harassed in the East by a campaign to exclude American unions from the country, they could ill afford to be driven out of the West.[70] Gompers's Canadian lieutenants were obliged to prevent the ALU making important inroads into the country's second most industrialized and unionized province. The TLC leadership realized that if the Congress was to be a truly national organization it must retain British Columbia. In addition, Gompers feared that if the rebellion spread and radicals captured the TLC, they could attack craft unionism in the United States.[71] So during 1903 the congress and Gompers fought the ALU for control of the coast province.

The commitment of the Vancouver trades council to the TLC was, at best, never more than half-hearted. During the early months of 1903 the council, under the leadership of President George Lamerick, an exponent of industrial unionism, moved steadily out of the orbit of the eastern centre. Although the ALU organized some large locals in Vancouver, for example, the civic labourers and factory and wood mill hands, the union's strength on the council was never sufficient, by itself, to produce this development. The radicalization resulted mainly from the enthusiasm for the ALU among delegates from other unions. The anti-TLC trend was first manifested in socialist attacks on Watson as a Liberal politician. Then late in March, about the time the congress organizer was enlisting strike-breakers for the CPR, the council instructed its organizing committee to secure all federal charters from the ALU. The actual break with the TLC came early in April when the council endorsed the principle of industrial unionism and refused to pay its per capita tax to the congress.[72]

Watson, now expelled from the council, denounced the ALU as a scab organization which would not serve the needs of its members because it was primarily concerned with socialism. Because he recognized that socialists were promoting the radical centre, the TLC organizer attacked the ALU by attempting to discredit the SPBC: 'fancy these men running a country without a God, without religion, and where free love reigns.'[73] Watson had some support among conservative craftsmen who were alarmed and offended by the radical orientation of the trades council.[74] Nonetheless, throughout 1903 radicals were in control of the most influential central body in British Columbia. In July, a depressed Draper told a colleague that the Vancouver council was 'doing everything in its power ... to disrupt the A.F. of L., the Trades and Labor Congress of Canada and the International trade union movement.'[75]

An organization campaign by Cameron and Wrigley resulted in a short, sharp fight between old and new unionism in Victoria in mid-1903. In June the two socialists organized locals of hackmen and mill-workers, and these applied to the trades council for affiliation. T.H. Twigg, the AFL organizer in the city, immediately announced that the two unions were barred from affiliation by the council's constitution. Nevertheless, the council overrode the constitution, seating the two ALU affiliates, and then proceeded to elect a full slate of socialist officers.[76] The radicals gloated over the victory. And Twigg fumed. The AFL organizer, who made no distinction between the SPBC and the ALU, warned that 'socialists, under the cloak of what they call industrial unionism, are trying to pull the foundations from beneath the old line trade union movement in hopes of making converts to socialism out of the wreckage.'[77] Like Watson in Vancouver, Twigg was able to muster support among the more conservative crafts in the city. The elitist attitude of some unions was well demonstrated by their reaction to an extraordinary effort by Cameron, his organization of the city's newsboys. The council refused to admit the 'socialist kindergarten.'[78] Pressure from the craft unions forced a review of the decision to seat the ALU affiliates, and when Draper was asked for a judgment on the matter, the TLC secretary, acting on direct orders from Gompers, instructed the Victoria council to require the hackmen and mill-workers to secure AFL charters.[79]

By the autumn of 1903 the workers of British Columbia were, in the words of the province's TLC executive, 'excited and heated' by ALU propaganda. The Victoria council remained rebellious. Vancouver was locked in the radical centre's orbit. And 'in the mountains,' Wrigley boasted, 'the A.L.U. and its affiliated bodies are all-powerful.'[80] Congress President John Flett's call for western workers to end the 'lamentable lack of unity' and resolve all differences at the congress convention was ineffective. In a blistering reply, Ernest Craig, the socialist secretary of the Fernie trades council, declared 'when you quit sending lobbyists to legislative halls, when you are willing to recognize the class struggle, ... when you admit that the conflicting interests of labor and capital can only be harmonized by doing away with the system that creates the two classes, when you declare for Socialism as the only solution to the labor problem and enter the field for a pure democracy, then and only then, will this Crow's Nest Valley Trades and Labor Council, now holding a charter from the great and progressive A.L.U. around whose flag thousands of wage-slaves are rallying for physical and intellectual liberty, talk affiliation with you, or you with their organization.'[81] At the congress convention there were no delegates from west of Winnipeg. In his presidential address, Flett denounced industrial unionism as a cancer in the labour movement. Draper reported that during the year fourteen British Columbia unions had returned TLC charters - most of these were picked up by the ALU - and that the Vancouver trades council was 'now actively opposed to Congress.' Despite opposition from Winnipeg delegates, the convention condemned all ALU affiliates and gave a qualified approval to the report of the Hunter Commission.[82]

In July, Draper had observed regarding the ALU, 'this sort of thing may succeed for a while but any movement that goes up like a rocket is bound to come down like a stick'; by the end of 1903 developments proved his analysis to be valid.[83] The UBRE was completely broken except for a struggling local in Winnipeg which soon faded away.[84] In Victoria the crafts regained control of the trades council and purged the socialists from the executive.[85] But Vancouver's return to the TLC was to be slower; indeed, it only re-affiliated with the congress in 1906 in order to send a large radical delegation to the Victoria convention of that year.

The ALU had never enjoyed an existence truly separate from the WFM, and by the beginning of 1904 the latter organization had entered a period of rapid decline. In Canada the federation had been driven out of the Island coal field and was in the process of losing the miners of the Crow's Nest Pass to the United Mine Workers. Even more important was the labour war which the WFM fought in Colorado in 1903-4; this great strike, which required its full attention and resources, eventually brought the union to its knees. Without the support of the federation, the ALU began to collapse. Large assessments for the fight in Colorado drove away members, and the organization faded even in the Kootenays.[87]

Though it was only short lived, the first western rebellion inaugurated the tendency of militant industrial unionism. The rebellion provided an institutional connection with later similar movements. ALU leaders, including Canadians, would found the Industrial Workers of the World which sought to mobilize the same unskilled men and women whom the ALU had organized. In addition the rebellion left a doctrinal legacy. Although the radicalism of the early rebels had a primarily political orientation, it contained the elements of syndicalism, even if these were only vaguely formulated. The elements were part of the rebellion - the primacy of the union, the determination to organize all workers, even the despised Chinese, and the commitment to solidarity. The Phoenix local of the ALU even believed that a general strike would be 'of valuable assistance' in achieving the revolution.[88] Perhaps most important in the long run, the rebellion furnished an example of industrial unionism in action. The solidarity of two or three thousand workers had crippled British Columbia's economy, and they were only beaten by an open alliance of the state, employers, and conservative craft unionists. Such a fight was not easily forgotten by workers who won few victories.

4

The ascendancy of the
Socialist Party of Canada

Between 1904 and 1910 - the period of ascendancy for the Socialist Party of Canada (SPC) - revolutionaries had real vitality and influence in the western Canadian radical movement. The party, the successor to the SPBC, maintained its position in the BC labour movement and forged an important place in provincial politics. Because it had a national vision, the SPC organized significant numbers of workers in Alberta and Winnipeg. Among those who joined the party were many of the European immigrants who were crowding into the West. The socialism which the SPC taught its new members was impossiblism, the BC doctrine. The revolutionary creed was most acceptable in the class-polarized mining camps of the mountains and Vancouver Island, and in these places the party was powerful. The SPC's importance declined in a ratio inversely proportional to its proximity to that power base. Nonetheless, because of its vitality in British Columbia, the party emerged as the revolutionary vanguard of western radicalism.

From the time that the SPBC emerged at the head of the Canadian movement, socialists across the country hoped that it would take the lead in the formation of a national socialist party. Early in 1903 the Ontario league urged the executive of the SPBC to unite the country's several socialist organizations. Initially the BC party responded coolly, but after the election of 1903 the SPBC concluded that it could not escape its destiny. British Columbia was 'the Cradle of Socialism in Canada,' and therefore, capitalism would be 'fought from West to East.'[1] The SPBC carried on negotiations with socialists in Winnipeg and Ontario cities during 1904. At the party's fourth annual convention in December delegates amended the platform and constitution of the SPBC to give them national application and founded the Socialist Party of Canada.[2]

The SPC prided itself on being a 'scientific' socialist party, teaching the pure Marxist creed, but so did virtually every other socialist party in the world. What made the Canadian party highly unusual in the North American movement was its impossiblism.[3] The doctrine was based on three fundamental propositions: first, that capitalism could not be reformed and attempts at amelioration had no place in the class struggle; second, that trade unions could not benefit all workers in the short run or any workers in the long run; and third, that class-conscious political action was the only means by which the proletariat could destroy the wage system and establish the co-operative commonwealth.

The platform of the SPC contained no immediate demands; it called only for the destruction of the wage system. By refusing to demand reforms in its platform the party became unique in the North American socialist movement. Party theoreticians believed that, because workers were essentially victims of the wage system, the socialists' only responsibility was to strive for the destruction of capitalism. And because capitalism was fundamentally incapable of reformation, tinkering with the system was useless. 'Do not think that a revolutionary socialist is opposed to reform as such,' explained Ed Fulcher of Brandon: 'he would gladly make things better for the working class were it possible; but he knows that nothing short of socialism can benefit the workers.' Reforms were 'powder sprinkled over the festering sores of that organism called human society.' To illustrate this proposition, party members liked to cite the experience of the British working class which remained in degradation despite progressive legislation. Socialists could point to cases closer to home. Bill Pritchard, an important party activist, recalls, 'they had the finest ... coal mine regulation act in this province, [and] it was violated everyday and in every clause.'[4]

Not only were reforms useless to the working class; they were, in the opinion of some party members, 'poison to the revolution.' To reform the present system was to interfere with the onward march of history by promoting 'a return to a played out phase of Capitalism' and was, therefore, 'reactionary.' Alex Paterson of Winnipeg argued that 'to improve conditions under any system is surely to strengthen that system and to strengthen a system surely means to prolong its existence.'[5] The logical extension of this formulation was extreme, but some socialists did not hesitate to make it. Kingsley persistently argued that the progressive degradation of the working class was directly beneficial to the advancement of socialist propaganda, because 'when their miseries become no longer bearable, ... the slaves will take the necessary action to strike the fetters from their limbs.'[6]

Probably the majority of party members, however, simply believed that the reform of capitalism was not the province of revolutionaries. Pritchard claims that the attitude of the SPC was one of 'indifference' rather than antagonism.[7] While they persistently and vehemently rejected any suggestion that the platform be expanded to include immediate demands, most socialists were prepared to accept any reforms available. A popular view in the party was that, by adhering strictly to the SPC's revolutionary creed, socialists could force the ruling class to grant some short-term relief to the workers. 'If you want palliatives don't go after them,' counselled D.G. McKenzie, who in 1908 succeeded Kingsley as editor of the *Clarion*, 'pick up the revolutionary club and go after the earth and the first thing you know you will have palliatives galore from the cowardly capitalist tribe fleeing for their lives from the wrath to come.'[8]

The official policy of the Socialist Party of Canada on trade unions was much the same as that on reforms. Unions were simply products of capitalism directing their efforts against 'effects which are absolutely inevitable,' and for this reason their battles with capitalists did not constitute part of the class struggle. In addition, there was general agreement that conditions in a capitalist labour market - particularly the West's immigrant-glutted market - precluded unions from providing workers with long-term relief; the SPC's *Manifesto* declared, 'in the industrial field defeat is inevitable.'[9] Even union leaders who were party members took this view; for example, Frank Sherman, president of District 18 of the United Mine Workers (UMW), asserted, 'the day of the trade union has passed; a union is now only useful to grapple with the petty tyranny of bosses.'[10]

But though superficially the SPC's policy on unions appeared to be monolithic, the party actually contained a rather broad range of opinion on the subject. What should be the socialists' attitude towards unions in the short run? All agreed that the party must be kept absolutely separate from unions, but beyond this common ground, two basic schools of thought developed. Some socialists considered unions at best useless and potentially detrimental to the party's propaganda; others insisted that unions were the workers' only defence under capitalism. The SPC never adopted the policy that its members could not become officers of unions. George Dales might say that 'only a recruit in the devotee stage' would actually disparage unions, but many influential socialists, who were hardly neophytes, regularly did.[11]

The two most prominent critics of unions in the party were Kingsley and McKenzie. Kingsley persistently told trade unionists that their efforts to increase real wages, however heroic, were utterly futile. Vexed at their obstinate refusal to accept his advice, he complained, 'this union superstition seems as firmly fixed upon its followers, as was the religious superstition of the middle ages upon its devotees.'[12] If these 'traders' organizations' refused to see the light, those who had seen it could easily ignore their unseemly wrangling in the market place. McKenzie sniffed, 'we have no concern with the traffic in labor any more than we have with the trade in turnips.'[13] Yet despite the disdain which some socialists regularly affected, their attitude towards unions clearly went beyond indifference.

At times disdain gave way to antagonism. Some party members denounced unions as being reactionary because they eroded class solidarity by making short-term gains for their few select members at the expanse of the great majority of unorganized workers. Any improvement in the lot of workers, even a small number, tended to prolong capitalism. The purpose of the SPC would best be served by the destruction of unions, thereby removing any hope of relief for the working class under the present system. Kingsley asserted 'in the labour unions of today are the statesmen of tomorrow. To "smash the unions" is to transform craftsmen into statesmen, and, if need be, into Soldiers.'[14]

The experience of the party appeared to substantiate the anti-union attitude. SPC candidates were regularly returned from constituencies in the Island coal fields where the miners' union had been broken. The party also won elections in the Kootenays and the Crow's Nest Pass where industrial relations were chaotic and the unions constantly under seige. Socialists could easily conclude that the operation of strong and effective unions was actually detrimental to their propaganda.

Nevertheless there were socialists who considered unions capable of affording some short-term relief to workers and organizations potentially useful to the SPC. A significant proportion of party members were trade unionists – estimates ranged from 60 to 90 per cent. Trade union leaders were prominent among socialists who adopted the pro-union attitude. Pettipiece, the leading pro-unionist, was a respected member of the Vancouver local, the very seat of impossiblism. Though he acknowledged that unions were products of the wage system, Pettipiece insisted that they were 'the correct plan for defence under the present plan of industry.' Because members of unions were part of the working class, history ensured that they would become a part of the revolutionary movement; it was, therefore, essential for the SPC to carry on an active propaganda among unionists. And in response to opponents' sneers, Pettipiece asked, 'what other "trader's organization" has ever helped to finance the Socialist Party.'[15] Leading party activists whose revolutionary credentials were impeccable also adopted this attitude. For example, J.H. Burrough, who became editor of the *Clarion* in 1913, believed that 'unions are absolutely necessary as long as the labor-power of the worker is a commodity that has to be sold in the competitive market. ... Without the union the position and standard of living of the worker would be absolutely at the mercy of the capitalist.'[16]

In large measure the socialists' attitude towards unions was based on the conviction that only through class-conscious political action could the emancipation of the proletariat be achieved. Party members believed that only the 'stupendous assininity' of workers prevented them from making the proper analysis of society and then setting out to destroy capitalism. This obstinacy was, in part, a product of trade unionism which encouraged workers to believe that social conditions under capitalism could be improved. Every socialist, including those who believed that unions were useful in the short run, told workers to take up the fight on the political field. 'For the love of liberty,' pleaded Pettipiece, 'join the rest of your class [at the ballot box] in an endeavour to put an end to the whole thieving swindle perpetrated upon them by the conscienceless rule of capital.'[17]

In the economic field the workers' numbers were a weakness because a strike's effectiveness could always be destroyed by the unorganized unemployed resuming the interrupted work, but in the political field those same numbers were a source of strength. An SPC pamphlet on unionism advised that 'only by themselves conquering political power for the purpose of abolishing capitalist ownership of the means of production can the workers ever obtain any easement.' To abolish the wage system the proletariat must gain control of the state, the citadel of capitalism. The party's *Manifesto* made this plain: 'by means of the state the workers have been held in subjection, and by means of the state they shall be emancipated. The state it is that guarantees to the master class, ownership in the means of production. ... The state is the sword of the master class. It lives by the sword and by this sword it shall perish.'[18]

Like other socialist parties, the SPC took the position that in states with a liberal franchise, the ballot was the revolutionary's best weapon. John Siemon, a prominent member of the Winnipeg local, called it the 'nearest and quickest' means by which the co-operative commonwealth could be achieved.[19] Consequently socialist MLAs worked assiduously to protect and extend the franchise.[20] Party propagandists never ceased to call upon the proletariat to take the ultimate revolutionary action, striking at the ballot box. The act of casting a socialist ballot was not sufficient in itself, however; the voter needed to understand the implications of the act. O'Brien observed, 'a political movement on the part of the working men takes on the form of a class struggle only ... when the aim of such a movement has [revolution] in view.'[21] The education of the proletariat was, therefore, the ultimate political function, and party leaders claimed that they ran candidates primarily to promote propaganda.[22] Given this purpose, some SPC campaigns took on an other-worldly quality. Without immediate demands in the platform, candidates could only present the party's analysis of capitalism, and, as a result, socialist election meetings at times resembled a lecture on Marxist economics rather than a campaign rally.

The revolution for which party members prepared dramatized the SPC's special place in the socialist movement. Theirs was an apocalyptic vision of the revolution. This grew out of the SPC's fundamental rejection of the principle of the rule of law. Under the laws of the state, enacted to protect capitalist ownership of the means of production, the working class had no rights. Indeed, because they held power, capitalists were totally justified in using the laws against the workers or flouting those laws.[23] Given this attitude, socialists did not believe that capitalists would voluntarily relinquish power through the democratic process. History taught that every advance by the working class had been ruthlessly resisted by the ruling class. Nothing else could be expected in the final battle. Some party activists, such as J.W. Bennett and Bill Pritchard, believed that violence could be reduced, perhaps eliminated, if a sufficiently large proportion of the workers were committed to socialism so as to persuade the bourgeoisie that opposition would be useless. But other prominent socialists were convinced that the proletariat would have to drive the capitalists out of power by force of arms. A party primer even warned workers not to expect a peaceful revolution. Kingsley described the final battle: 'the earth will tremble from the shock as slaves and masters meet in the death grapple in that supreme hour; ... there will be a smell of blood in the air and the torch will light the heavens with the glare of destruction.'[24]

Workers who sought both solace and hope in visions of a co-operative commonwealth frequently urged SPC propagandists to discuss post-revolutionary society. Only a few party members would, and even their vague descriptions reflected little systematic consideration. Most socialists simply refused to speculate on the post-revolutionary future. In part their reticence was caused by the failure of Marx and Engels to leave a detailed prospectus. But this lacuna did not prevent other socialist parties from providing their followers with sources for hope. Impossiblism precluded members of the SPC from developing such propaganda. The concept of distributive justice, usually basic to visions of the co-operative commonwealth, was incompatible with their stark ideology. To a party that had ruthlessly subordinated humanitarianism to materialism, such fantasies appeared vulgar and superficial, the utopianism of pre-Marxian idealists. In any case speculation was 'not susceptible of scientific verification.' History would be the only arbiter. Consequently party members urged workers to destroy capitalism but did not inspire them with a vision of the new order. Impossiblists would only assert that, after 'a short spell of working class autocracy,' the means of production would be collectivized and the state would become 'purely an administration of industry by the working class for the working class.'[25]

That the revolution was inevitable was never doubted. There was a degree of chiliasm in all socialist parties, but in the SPC, which took pride in its Marxist orthodoxy, this tendency was more pronounced. Marx had taught that the onward development of capitalism would result in its collapse, and the master's principles were 'as absolute in their operation as the laws of gravitation or the laws which govern the growth of trees or icebergs.' Secure in the knowledge that their aim was in tune with the forces of history, party members could ignore setbacks which might discourage or dissuade the uninitiated. A coal miner said simply, 'we are invincible.'[26]

But if the chiliasm of the SPC found expression in dogmatism and, at times, an insufferable intellectual arrogance, it never found expression in inaction. Party members were never guilty of waiting for the millennium to arrive of its own accord, as critics charged. Marx had also taught that, within certain limits set for them by the conditions of their times, men made their own history and that it was necessary to work for the revolution. The Socialist Party of Canada was imbued with a sense of mission. The historical role of the revolutionary, explained Percy Chew of Winnipeg, was 'to rouse the workers of the world from apathy and indifference ... to implant a hope of better things in every heart, to lead and [to] point the way to social salvation.'[27]

The impossiblism of the SPC bore a striking resemblance to the doctrines of the pre-1900 Socialist Labor party and the Social Democratic Federation. Observers frequently commented on the similarities. For example, Kier Hardie, a perceptive student of radicalism, believed that the SPC was 'imbued with the De Leon spirit.'[28] The party's interpretation of Marx was the work of a few theoreticians who dominated the Vancouver local and the Dominion Executive Committee which sat in the city. The group included Wallis Lefeaux, a lawyer, John Harrington, a party organizer, and Hawthornthwaite, the MLA for Nanaimo. More important were D.G. McKenzie and J.G. Morgan. Born in India, McKenzie had developed his hatred of capitalism working as a miner in the mountain states and British Columbia. He was a quiet and intelligent man whose editorials in the *Western Clarion* demonstrated wide reading in revolutionary literature.[29] Geordie Morgan, who named his son Karl to honour the master, had been a member of the Social Democratic Federation in Britain. For a time he was party secretary, but he did his most important work directing the Vancouver local's study clubs and conducting classes in Marxist theory.[30] At the centre of the group was E.T. Kingsley, the link between the SLP and the SPC.

It became an article of faith among party members that the 'inspiration and life force' of the SPC sprang from Nanaimo. This conviction indicated the socio-economic basis of impossiblism, but it also emphasized the major intellectual influence on the SPC. 'Thanks to that old war horse Kingsley,' wrote Lefeaux, 'the platform of the Socialist Party of Canada is the most clear cut and revolutionary of any Socialist Party of any country of the world.' Harrington remembered that Kingsley was 'the real founder' of the party.[31] In the years of the SPC's ascendancy, Kingsley, in the words of Alex Paterson, 'pretty well ran the *Western Clarion* and the Party.' Until 1908 he edited the party organ; even after his resignation he financed the paper and only discontinued the support, which put him deeply in debt, in 1912. An extraordinarily effective propagandist, Kingsley was the SPC's most popular speaker; he inspired and delighted audiences across the West. To the members of the party, Kingsley was the 'Old Man,' a title which said much about his status.[32] Opponents as well as supporters testified to Kingsley's pre-eminence. Labourites, De Leonites, Wobblies, social democrats, and later Communists, all decried his ruinous influence on western Canadian socialism.[33] In 1910, W.H. Stebbings of Winnipeg reviewed the history of the party and made an assessment of Kingsley's importance which was largely valid: 'the movement today in Canada is the result of one man's interpretation of Marx.'[34]

In the years before 1910 the Socialist Party of Canada was a vital and expanding organization. It won the confidence and support of many workers. Some elected socialists to lead their unions. Even John Mortimer, a prominent critic of trade unions, played an important role in the tailors' locals in both Winnipeg and Vancouver. Perhaps more significant, miners elected socialists to represent them in provincial legislatures, and the party emerged as a force in the working class politics of British Columbia and Alberta. After a tour of Canada in 1907, Kier Hardie, in an essay on the western labour movement, observed, 'beyond Winnipeg only Socialists need apply; Winnipeg itself has a fair proportion of both phases of thought.'[35]

The SPC was never an important political force in Winnipeg, but its members were, nonetheless, influential in the city's trade union movement. If the workers were not prepared to vote for socialists, they were prepared to elect them to office in their unions. As representatives of a number of organizations, party members worked actively, though in most cases unsuccessfully, to promote the interests of the SPC in the Winnipeg trades council. The most prominent of these were George Armstrong, a carpenter, Bill Hoop, a letter carrier who served as president of the council, and Dick Rigg, a bookbinder, who became the council's first permanent business agent.[36]

Party members had some influence in the Calgary and Edmonton trades councils.[37] But the SPC's power base in Alberta was among the coal miners of the Crow's Nest Pass. Prominent executive officers of the UMW's District 18, like Frank Sherman and Clem Stubbs, were members of the SPC. Socialists, first J.W. Bennett and then H.P. Nerwich, edited the official *District Ledger*. There was no outcry when they told the miners that political action was always more effective than economic action. Bennett could observe, 'a strike is a game of matching the pennies of the strikers against the dollars of the capitalists and when the last cent of the strikers is gone, the capitalists have lots of dollars left.' Some UMW organizers also carried credentials from the party and promoted its doctrines at every opportunity.[38] Clearly such sympathies were not limited to a few leading union members, however. There was a close association between the UMW and the party at the level of locals in the camps. The SPC frequently held economic classes and lectures in miners' halls. In 1909 the UMW's district convention endorsed the party's platform.[39] A special relationship developed between the party and the radical coal miners in the Crow's Nest Pass. Even though the socialists insisted that the union could afford no long-term relief under capitalism, party members did what they could to support the UMW in its fight against the coal companies.[40]

The relationship paid political dividends for the SPC in Alberta. In December 1907, the provincial TLC executive held a convention to found a labour party. Led by Pettipiece, the delegates, many of whom were miners, endorsed the SPC's platform by a two-to-one majority. Socialists using TLC funds then proceeded to found a number of party locals before the congress could end the escapade.[41] Early in 1909, the SPC nominated Charlie O'Brien in Rocky Mountain, a miners' constituency. O'Brien conducted a tough campaign in which he focused on the hardships of the miners' lives; with the active support of the UMW, he won a solid victory.[42]

With only some extravagance Pettipiece could boast, 'British Columbia belongs to the Socialists.'[43] The Vancouver trade union movement, the most important in British Columbia, never elected an SPC candidate to the Legislature, but it was, nonetheless, favourably inclined towards socialism, and, to an important extent, led by socialists. In certain unions, the most important of which were the machinists and the longshoremen, support for the SPC was quite strong.[44] Even more significant was the continuing influence party members had on the Vancouver trades council. Led by James McVety, a machinist who served several times as president, and Pettipiece, also a sometime president and the council's first permanent secretary, socialists did everything possible to protect and promote the party's interests. The council newspapers, *The Trade Unionist* and *The Western Wage-earner*, edited by Pettipiece and McVety respectively, were a remarkable blend of trade unionism and SPC propaganda. Most striking were the editors' frequent critiques of trade unions. McVety, in particular, was capable of writing tortuously doctrinaire editorials. One such, written in June 1910, resulted in a motion of censure being brought against him in the trades council, but it was voted down by a two-to-one margin.[45]

The hard-rock miners of the Kootenays continued to support the socialist party, despite the Western Federation's brief connection with the Industrial Workers of the World. William Davidson, elected as a miners' candidate in the provincial election of 1903, emphasized the connection between party and union when he joined the socialist caucus. The miners continued to elect socialists to lead their union; Davidson later became district president. In the hard-rock camps, WFM locals had very close relations with the SPC. The party was able to rely on the union for financial help; eventually the district amended its constitution to require support of the SPC by affiliates.[46] After John McInnis, an SPC candidate, was elected from the Kootenays in the provincial election of 1907, a hard-rock miner boasted, 'Phoenix has the distinction of casting a greater number of Socialist votes than any town of its size in America.'[47] The miners maintained their commitment to the SPC in the face of stiff opposition from employers. Companies frequently attempted to disrupt socialist campaigns by laying off men, and thus driving them out of camp, immediately before election day.[48]

The SPC enjoyed its most solid support among the coal miners of Vancouver Island. Hawthornthwaite and Parker Williams had been elected to the legislature from Nanaimo and Newcastle respectively in 1903. In the provincial election of 1907 the miners returned them again. And when they went back to Victoria after the election of 1909, which marked the height of the SPC's electoral success, Hawthornthwaite and Williams became the effective opposition to the overwhelming Conservative majority.[49] Because of this record, party members believed that the coal miners' votes were 'ours till the revolution.'[50]

In their campaigns Hawthornthwaite and Williams promoted revolution, but they also worked at being elected. Clearly in constituencies where the prospects of victory were good, SPC candidates accommodated their impossiblism to political realities. This process was demonstrated in the campaign of 1907. Both socialists sought to educate and mobilize the proletariat by elaborating the doctrines of the SPC. But they also promised the workers relief from such conventional abuses as corporate domination of the province and oriental immigration. They even campaigned on their records in the House. Williams, for example, told a Nanaimo meeting, 'if you can put your finger on one solitary thing from 1903 to the close of the last session that ... has been detrimental to the working class we would be glad to hear of it.'[51]

To an important extent, the vitality of the SPC reflected the fact that the party's practical policy on current issues was not always consistent with its impossiblism. As the SPC became an increasingly important force in the labour movement, especially in British Columbia, internal and external pressures developed which made it more difficult for the party to remain completely doctrinaire. Consequently a reluctant pragmatism developed within the party. This ambivalence was probably best demonstrated by the record of socialist MLAs.

The socialist members of the BC Legislature refused to conform to the standards of parliamentary decorum. For example, at the opening of the 1907 session Hawthornthwaite and McInnis remained seated while Lieutenant Governor James Dunsmuir entered the chamber.[52] The socialists also used the House as a forum for party propaganda. But Hawthornthwaite believed that it was necessary to 'take advantage of every opportunity of introducing any reform whatsoever that may be of even temporary benefit to the working man.'[53] The best opportunity presented itself when the socialists held the balance of power after the election of 1903. Even though Hawthornthwaite recognized that co-operation entailed compromise, he supported the Conservative government and was able to wring a number of concessions from Premier Richard McBride.[54] The workers were grateful.[55] In fact the socialists' record of achievement was impressive. Concentrating on safety and labour standards reform, they were able to effect important improvements in the mining industry, including an eight-hour day in coal mines and in smelters.[56]

Charlie O'Brien, Alberta's socialist MLA, conformed to this pattern. Always affecting a red necktie in the House, he was the most flamboyant of the party's legislators. His most spectacular defiance of the fitness-of-things occurred during the 1910 session. When a resolution of sympathy for Edward VII's widow was introduced, O'Brien moved an amendment extending condolences to the wives of miners killed in a recent disaster. His refusal to withdraw the amendment reduced the House to chaos.[57] But O'Brien did not consider himself only a propagandist. He worked tirelessly to improve the lot of his constituents; for example, at the beginning of the 1912 session he had twenty-four questions relating to mining on the order paper. As a result of his efforts, O'Brien was regarded as the UMW's representative in the Alberta Legislature.[58]

This reluctant pragmatism produced a dilemma for party theoreticians. On the one hand, Kingsley and his associates recognized that the work of the socialist MLAs resulted in increased support for the party. The theoreticians regarded election results as an indication of the level of socialist awareness, and they were encouraged by results in British Columbia and Alberta. Consequently party propagandists attributed the passage of virtually every piece of legislation, in any manner beneficial to workers, to the efforts of the socialist members. Even Kingsley praised the British Columbia members as 'a little band of Ishmaelites,' working for 'the benefit and advancement of the proletariat.'[59] But, on the other hand, were the activities of the legislators reformist? The platform's 'rule of conduct' for SPC parliamentary representatives, which made the welfare of the working class the ultimate test for legislation, would seem to have answered this question, but some party members were not satisfied. They were embarrassed, particularly under prodding from labourites, by the apparent contradiction of representatives of their party working to improve conditions under capitalism. This embarrassment produced an interesting rationale. MLAs were, the theoreticians asserted, engaged in an aspect of the commodity struggle in which all workers must participate. If their efforts, like the activities of unions, could be kept separate from the class struggle, the revolution would not be impeded.[60]

An important dimension of the SPC's vitality during these years was the organization of European immigrants in the West. The ethnic heterogeneity of the western Canadian labour force tended to militate against working class solidarity. And it took some time for immigrant workers to be incorporated into the English-speaking trade union movement. Even the SPC was slow to begin organizing non-Anglo-Saxon workers. Despite the fact that it contained a significant number of Finns and Germans from the time of its formation, the party did not translate any of its literature until 1908. Initially it was only in Winnipeg's north end that a local proselytized among non-English-speaking immigrants. Socialists in the city attempted to have the party's platform translated into German and held classes in the English language and Canadian history.[61]

The interest of the Winnipeg local, and that of the party as a whole, increased when the Russian internal crisis, beginning in 1904, resulted in the immigration of revolutionary intellectuals who provided the emerging eastern European socialist movement with a leadership which promised to make it a force in the immigrant community. Herman Saltzman, a Jewish socialist, Jacob Penner, a prominent Winnipeg Marxist, and Peter Ternenko, editor of the first Ukrainian socialist paper in Canada, were Russian exiles.[62] Like all socialist parties, the SPC was very sympathetic to the Russian revolutionary movement, and when in 1906 and 1907 men who had been active in that struggle became a prominent part of immigrant socialist groups, party members recognized 'a common source of inspiration' linking them to the eastern Europeans.[63]

The most important result of this new attitude was the contact between the SPC and the Ukrainian Socialist Labor Committee. Founded in 1907, the committee was a loose federation, with headquarters in Winnipeg, linking a handful of socialist groups across the West. In November 1907, Myron Stechishin, the leading member of the committee, proposed to the dominion executive of the SPC that his organization become an autonomous national unit within the party. The Ukrainian socialist believed that such an arrangement would serve 'our special purposes'; he claimed that the SPA had established national units to promote propaganda in foreign languages.[64] Although the Vancouver leadership was highly encouraged at the prospects of making such an important gain among the eastern Europeans, it was, at the same time, reluctant to jeopardize its commanding position in the party by sanctioning the erection of a potentially parallel power.[65] Apparently the solution to the problem, worked out late in 1907, provided for the chartering of autonomous language locals and financial support for Ukrainian propaganda.

In 1908 the party initiated a major propaganda campaign among non-English immigrants. The SPC's platform was translated into Ukrainian, Finnish, and Italian. The party designated *Chervony Prapor* a Ukrainian paper, and *Tyokansa*, a Finnish journal, as official organs.[66] Early in the year the SPC commissioned Thomas Tomashavsky as its organizer in Alberta, and he spent most of the year working among the Ukrainians in the province. He was aided by O'Brien who was often forced to adopt the awkward expedient of delivering lectures through an interpreter. Also important in the drive was Mike Susnar, the UMW's eastern European organizer. Some gains were made among the immigrant farmers of the province. But a more important response came from the Slavic, Italian, and German miners, many of whom were socialist 'veterans.' For example, Frank Poch, one of the founders of the Frank local, had been a member of the German Social Democratic party for twenty years.[67] When O'Brien was elected from this region a few months later, the *Coleman Miner* grumbled, 'illiterate Slavs and Dagoes' were responsible for the victory.[68]

The party also appointed Herman Sliptchenko as Ukrainian organizer in Manitoba. He attempted to organize his countrymen who farmed in the southeastern section of the province but met with no significant success. The power base for the immigrant socialist movement in the province was, and would remain, Winnipeg's north end. Even if the British and Canadian socialists would, for a time, retain control of the party, the importance of the north end ensured that the Winnipeg movement's numerical strength, and to a large extent its character, would be eastern European. An English-speaking comrade remarked on the city's 1908 May Day demonstration: 'it certainly was not Canadian in character, the great bulk of the feeling and sentiment exhibited there had not been born [in], nor was it the outcome of, Canadian life and conditions.'[69]

During the years of its ascendancy, the SPC was a small exclusive party led by British immigrants. Initially such men and women constituted the great majority of the membership. In 1903 it was estimated that 'nine out of ten' of the Clarion's readers had recently arrived from the United Kingdom. [70] Even when eastern European immigrants began to join the party in important numbers, British domination was never threatened. Only men with Anglo-Saxon names were prominent in BC locals. The composition of the Dominion Executive Committee remained almost exclusively British. Eastern European representation on the Alberta provincial executive did not reflect the numerical importance of that group to the party in the province. Only in Winnipeg, where they constituted the bulk of the party's numbers, did non-English-speaking immigrants play a significant role.

Relations between British and eastern European party members demonstrated that the SPC was never ethnically integrated. In Vancouver Pritchard recalls that the Finnish and Lettish language locals tended 'to step into clans,' and, therefore, relations with the English local were 'cordial' but not warm. [71] Much the same was true of Alberta. After a tour of the province in 1908, O'Brien reported that the British and eastern European socialists were 'strangers to each other,' largely because the latter tended to 'huddle together in groups, speak the languages and retain the ideals of the place from whence they came.' [72] In Winnipeg, where the non-Anglo-Saxon immigrants were influential, relations between them and members of the English local were neither cordial nor correct. Indeed, tension was so great between the two groups that at times 'it almost came to blows.' [73]

The size of the SPC is difficult to determine. Except for a few reports from the Manitoba executive committee published in 1908 and 1909, the *Clarion* contained virtually no membership data which could be used systematically. The Vancouver English local was the party's largest, with a membership of approximately one hundred and twenty-five. Next in numbers was a group of three locals, Nanaimo, Cumberland, and Winnipeg (English); these had a membership of approximately fifty each. Then followed the locals in Calgary, Edmonton and Victoria, each with approximately thirty members. The remaining locals in other smaller centres and mining camps probably had no more than a couple of dozen members each; Pritchard recalls that the 'average' local numbered twenty.[74] Similarly, no conclusive evidence is available on the total membership of the SPC, but it probably was, at the party's height and including eastern locals, approximately 3000.[75] But this small group of dedicated and able men and women exercised a much greater influence in the radical movement than their numbers would suggest.

The size of the party was to an important extent a function of its sectarian nature. The impossiblists' triumph in the SPBC ensured that the SPC would be an exclusive rather than an inclusive party. This orientation, manifested in an insistence on doctrinal orthodoxy and, hence, an intolerance of 'unscientific' socialism, was embraced by the faithful across the West. W.H. Stebbings of Winnipeg defended the party's sectarianism, because 'it not only prevents fusion but gives you a platform which is in no danger of collapsing.'[76] Because they believed that socialists' basic function was to educate the proletariat, the SPC's leadership insisted that party members be well-schooled in Marxist theory. The revolution would not be achieved by 'a wave of enthusiasm stirred up by glib-tongued orators and facile pen pushers appealing to the sentiment, the passion, the prejudice of the mob' but by a thorough understanding of the wage system.[77] To ensure the doctrinal orthodoxy of applicants, most locals required them to sit for an oral examination in socialist theory. Pritchard justifies this practice by arguing that 'it's from these people you expect to produce your writers and speakers, and if they don't know what they're saying, they [are] going to be easy pidgeons ... for the opposition.'[78] Watchfulness did not cease with initiation. In the locals, members continually tested comrades on doctrinal points. Pritchard recalls, 'we were highly critical one of the other, seeking only "truth"; there was no quarter asked and none given in our verbal fights.' No member of the party, no matter how senior, was free from criticism. If the *Clarion*'s editor were to make 'a slip even in terminology,' he would 'hear from some local with a blast.'[79] In this continuing process of self-criticism, if a comrade's orthodoxy or his commitment to the party appeared dubious, he was given short shrift. A miner boasted that a 'reformer' could not survive in the SPC, because 'he is so quickly "sat on" that he promptly "transforms" himself to the tall timers.' Similarly, any socialist guilty of co-operation with other parties was quickly expelled; even a man as important to the SPC as Frank Sherman could be purged for this reason.[80]

One manifestation of the SPC's sectarianism was an attitude similar to what Daniel Bell has nicely called 'the cult of proletarian chauvinism.'[81] Impossiblists believed that a revolutionary party must be representative of and controlled by the working class. The party spurned middle class intellectuals and reformers as reactionary elitists who involved themselves in the cause of the workers only to retard the progress of the revolution. Members of the party regularly complained that the bourgeoisie, because they had not shared in the suffering of the workers, failed to understand the mortal nature of the class struggle.[82] Only the worker who suffered under capitalism was a 'natural revolutionist'; only the worker, driven by this lash, would be properly motivated to persevere against all opposition and destroy the wage system. Morgan told a Vancouver audience, 'the proletarian revolution must be the work of the working class alone.'[83]

Working class credentials became, therefore, a mark of distinction in the SPC, and the party took great pride in the proletarian origins of its lecturers and representatives. After allowing that Parker Williams was 'not an orator,' Kingsley observed, 'more effective and lasting propaganda can be done by the plain, common and unpretentious working man who has acquired his knowledge of Labor's needs in the bitter school of experience than by the polished and windy jawsmiths.'[84] The party's most prominent politician, Hawthornthwaite, a university graduate and former mining promoter, hardly fitted the proletarian definition, however. 'Intellectuals' were anathema in the SPC, and one of the customary charges brought against members who broke party discipline was that they had compromised with 'high-brows.' Ed Fulcher boasted that the Brandon local had 'no bourgeois notions,' because 'we have no "intellectuals" – our membership is composed wholly of plugs, dirty faces and all.'[85] However, the SPC's high opinion of the sons of toil never became a romantic fetish as it did with Wobblies; indeed, the party regularly said some very harsh things about workers.

Directly related to SPC's exclusiveness was its self-concept. The concept that had evolved in the SPBC during 1903 was reinforced by the Socialist Party of Canada's expansion in the West during the years before 1910. Of the SPC's electoral record, Pettipiece boasted, 'this is a showing that at least cannot be duplicated upon this western continent, if it can anywhere else in the world.'[86] Consequently, the belief developed and persisted in the SPC that the support the party was able to command in British Columbia, and to a lesser extent in Alberta, demonstrated the primacy in the revolutionary movement of what was sometimes called the 'British Columbia school' of socialism. The Winnipeg local considered Kingsley 'the best exponent of scientific Socialism on the American continent.' Only half-humorously, McKenzie observed that 'since Marx died nobody was capable of throwing light on [economic] matters except the editor of the *Clarion*, whoever we may happen to be.'[87] Because of this perceived pre-eminence, the SPC believed it could properly stand aloof from virtually all other socialist parties.

The SPC's leadership dismissed the British Labour party with its trade union and Liberal connections without hesitation. But the impossiblists were no more sympathetic to the Independent Labour party though its doctrines were Marxist.[88] The SPC demonstrated tremendous antagonism to ILP leaders who came to Canada to instruct the colonials in the ways of working class politics. When Kier Hardie toured the country in 1908 urging Canadian workers to form an inclusive labour party and denouncing the SPC's doctrines as a 'dogmatic, arid, blighting creed of withering materialism,' party members were enraged. Mortimer told Hardie that 'Canadian Socialism is much too "modern" for you or any other British labor leader to catch up with.'[89]

The SPC had no higher opinion of the Socialist Party of America. Because it was dominated by 'intellectuals and opportunists,' the party was moving 'in the direction of ever greater confusion.'[90] The SPA's right wing was simply dismissed as a group of charlatans. But the SPC felt some affinity with the left wing. From time to time the *Clarion* reprinted pieces by Jack London, and Debs continued to enjoy the high regard of the Canadian revolutionaries.[91] The only development in the American socialist movement which had a noticeable impact upon the SPC was the publication of Upton Sinclair's *The Jungle*. The book became a standard propaganda item for the party, and Hawthornthwaite took up the fight for wholesome meat in the BC Legislature.[92] Despite the Canadian party's aloofness, members of the SPA's left wing had a high regard for the impossiblists. Debs described the *Clarion* as 'a rattling good paper,' and A.M. Simons, a leading left winger, respected Kingsley's work, though he believed the BC leader to be 'best suited to the Pacific Coast.'[93]

The members of the Socialist Party of Canada considered themselves part of the international socialist movement. Their attitude was probably best demonstrated by the ritual observance each year of the anniversary of the Paris Commune, the glories of which constituted one of the principal myths of international socialism. Though the SPC did not regard the Commune as a truly revolutionary event, its memory remained, nonetheless, 'sacred.'[94] In 1904 Kingsley had been able to block the party's affiliation with the Second International, but the SPC continued to have informal contacts with the organization. In a report to the 1907 congress at Stuttgart, Morgan assured the International that 'Le Canada est en communauté d'ideés avec le mouvement universel et il n'entend pas faire défaut dans la lutte internationale contre le capitalisme.'[95] The party, however, never affiliated. Initially it claimed that precarious finances prevented it from doing so. But as pressure for affiliation from the newly organized eastern Europeans mounted, SPC leaders frankly explained their reluctance. The International was a 'reformist' organization which contained 'certain non-Socialist bodies, particularly the British [Independent] Labour Party,' and, therefore, the SPC could not consider affiliation.[96] After 1910 calls for affiliation ceased, and the Socialist Party of Canada remained in splendid isolation.

At the beginning of 1909 socialists were gratified by the SPC's recent progress, but in the very expansion which they found satisfying were the beginnings of the party's disruption. After 1905, party locals were established in Ontario, Quebec, and the Maritimes. From the outset western ideologues had reservations about the doctrinal orthodoxy of their eastern comrades. The easterners, for their part, were prepared to accept the impossiblist gospel, the truth of which had been made manifest at the polls in British Columbia. But when socialist candidates were wiped out in the provincial election of 1908, Ontario locals began to question the party's doctrines. By mid-1909 these locals were in full-scale rebellion. The Ontario socialists demanded the inclusion of immediate demands in the platform, a less antagonistic policy towards trade unions, and a national convention to end the autocratic control of the Vancouver leadership.[97] The crisis reached its climax late in 1909 when favourable returns from the British Columbia provincial election were coming in. The Dominion Executive Committee regarded these returns as additional confirmation of the validity of impossiblism and refused to consider the easterners' demands.[98] The SPC disintegrated in the East.

While the Vancouver leadership and their English-speaking comrades across the West were reading the easterners out of the SPC, the language locals remained ominously silent. It was already apparent that they were becoming increasingly reluctant to accept party discipline. In Winnipeg the language locals were discouraged by the indifferent progress the SPC was making among the workers of the north end.[99] The basic reason, however, for their growing dissatisfaction with the SPC was the fact that they formed part of the social democratic tradition of eastern Europe. There Marxist parties tended to be much more pragmatic than the SPC, combining revolutionary doctrines with reformist politics. These parties were also much more inclusive than the Canadian one. They regarded trade unions as natural and necessary allies, having in some cases actually taken the lead in forming unions. In addition, the eastern European movement, particularly in Germany, had been affected by the theories of the 'revisionists,' led by Edward Bernstein, who rejected Marx's analysis of capitalism and argued that society must be transformed by gradualist, rather than revolutionary, tactics. Although the SPC regarded 'revisionism' as anathema, Bernstein was highly regarded by party members in Winnipeg.[100]

As eastern-European socialists 'became more mature politically,' they recognized that there were significant differences between their social democracy and the doctrines of the SPC.[101] The criticism that the language locals made of the party line grew directly out of their European experience. They considered the SPC's attitude towards unions as unsound; an eastern European veteran wrote, 'social-democracy represents the working man. The trades union movement and the political movement are the two arms; we cannot work with one arm.'[102] In addition, eastern Europeans demanded the inclusion of immediate demands in the party's platform. Not only would these afford the proletariat some relief under capitalism, they would help 'in rousing the slumbering energies of the working class.' By expanding its platform, the SPC would abandon its dogmatic insistence that the party's sole function was education and become part of the mainstream of the labour movement. A less rigid platform would end the sectarianism of the SPC which the eastern Europeans found highly offensive.[103] Because they equated the Canadian party's doctrines with the teachings of the young Marx, the European socialists condemned the SPC as 'reactionary.'[104] It was, therefore, imperative that the SPC affiliate with the International so that it could profit by the experience of the European parties and thus join the 'modern' socialist movement. When the Dominion Executive Committee rejected the language locals' demands for affiliation, they were further alienated by what they regarded as autocracy.[105]

There was a new and important element in the developing rebellion of eastern European socialists. That was, paradoxically, nationalism. In a strange land, immigrants, who had no knowledge of English and few, if any, family connections, naturally tended to congregate in national groups. Socialists were no different than other immigrants, and the revolutionary organizations of Winnipeg's north end, for example, had an important social, as well as political, purpose. Indeed, the immigrant socialist movement grew out of various education and cultural organizations.[106] The practice of socialists to proselytize compatriots tended to increase the feeling of group consciousness. Fred Tipping, a prominent social democrat, admits that nationalism had 'a strong pull' on north end socialists.[107] The tendency was most pronounced among the Ukrainians, the largest language group in the SPC. As a result, they became dissatisfied in the British-dominated party. By 1909 relations between Ukrainian locals and their English-speaking comrades had become openly acrimonious, and the compromise fashioned at the end of 1907 to curb the nationalistic aspiration of Stechishin and his compatriots was in ruins. The Ukrainian leader complained bitterly that 'the humiliating alliance' with the SPC was 'strangling' the Ukrainian locals.[108]

Nowhere was the SPC's failure to integrate the non-English-speaking immigrants into the party better demonstrated than in the burning dissatisfaction of the Ukrainians. Late in 1909 representatives of Ukrainian locals from across the West met in Winnipeg and decided to establish a separate language federation which would have 'complete autonomy in matters of organization, propaganda and publications' and the right to deal with the socialist parties of other countries. In demanding that the SPC's constitution be amended to provide for this arrangement, Stechishin claimed that such a federation was necessary because 'the Ukrainian Locals are only nominally in the Party; ninety-five per cent of the membership of our Locals do not read English at all.' The Dominion Executive Committee refused to afford the Ukrainians the degree of autonomy they demanded.[109]

By early 1910 the language locals on the prairies were in full revolt. In February Stechishin and his compatriots founded the Ukrainian Social Democratic Federation. Though the organization professed to be a part of the SPC, it was virtually autonomous and declared *Robochy Narod*, a Ukrainian socialist paper, its official organ.[110] In Winnipeg, where impossiblists had already been purged from the provincial executive, the north end locals fought to exclude their English-speaking comrades from the movement in the city's immigrant quarter. In July the crisis was precipitated by a dispute over local politics, and the north end socialists left the SPC to begin laying the foundations for the Social Democratic party (SDP), the party which would unite the eastern European and moderate British socialists.[111] One month later a convention of the Ukrainian federation met at Edmonton and decided to affiliate with the SDP, 'the only representative of the true spirit of international socialism.'[112]

Once it began, the revolt even spread into party strongholds in British Columbia and Alberta. BC Finns, who had resented the Dominion Executive Committee's refusal to accommodate their special language requirements, followed the Ukrainians into the more tolerant SDP.[113] Convinced that the SPC's weakened condition ensured that it could not mobilize the working class, leading trade union socialists, such as McVety and Pettipiece, left the party.[114] A doctrinal dispute disrupted the Nanaimo local.[115] And the SDP replaced the SPC among eastern European miners in the Crow's Nest Pass.[116]

By 1912 the SDP could claim the status of a national party. After exhausting all possibilities of compromise with the Vancouver leadership, the expelled eastern locals of the SPC established the Canadian Socialist Federation in April 1911. Immediately the organization established contact with the Winnipeg social democrats and, at a unity convention held at Port Arthur in December, the eastern and western groups amalgamated to form a national Social Democratic party.[117]

The revolt did irreparable damage to the SPC. The exodus of the eastern locals and most non-English-speaking socialists shattered the party's organization outside of British Columbia, and even there the party was severely weakened. The split also slashed revenues which, in turn, disrupted propaganda. Beginning in the autumn of 1911 the *Western Clarion* staggered through an irregular publishing schedule and then in 1912 failed to appear for a number of months. The emergence of the SDP confronted impossiblists with a viable Marxist competitor, and for a time their response was ineffective. The party reached its nadir in 1912. Early in the year Kingsley surveyed the wreckage and made the unprecedented admission that 'the Locals ... are either semi-defunct or in a state of philosophic dry rot.'[118]

Impossiblism was directly relevant to the experience of BC coal and hard-rock miners and, given this power base, had a general relevance in a largely proletarian province experiencing a rapid transition to industrial capitalism. But these conditions were peculiar. Not confronted with the same ruthless capitalism which BC miners faced, workers in places such as Calgary, Edmonton, and Winnipeg did not develop a similar degree of class consciousness. As a result, impossiblism had considerably less relevance for men and women outside British Columbia. The failure of the revolutionary doctrine to mobilize significant numbers of workers east of the Crow's Nest Pass cannot, however, be explained entirely by social conditions. SPC propaganda was unsuccessful in prairie cities because it was inappropriate to political realities in those places. Supreme rationalists, socialists were convinced that workers needed only to learn Marx's analysis of capitalism and they would become revolutionaries. The tactic was too cerebral. It sought only to explain the workers' exploitation and posited an inevitable, though ill-defined, new order. Impossiblism could not win the workers' hearts or, in the short run at any rate, fill their stomachs. Eastern European immigrants had been indoctrinated in a humane socialism. British trade unionists on the prairies were engaged by such mundane issues as higher pay, shorter hours, and improved municipal services. Perhaps paradoxically, while party members accommodated propaganda to political realities in their mining-camp strongholds, impossiblists became even more sectarian and doctrinaire when workers, in places such as Winnipeg, refused to vote for the SPC. Similarly the party's strict internal discipline and ethnocentricity were incompatible with the eastern European immigrants' cultural baggage. Because the party could not accommodate these ideological and ethnic tensions, it disintegrated. The Socialist Party of Canada became a prisoner, and then a victim, of its experience in British Columbia.

The lesson was not lost on the impossiblists. They insisted that the revolt of the social democrats made them even more determined to preserve their doctrinal orthodoxy, and in fact party doctrine demonstrated a good deal of continuity over time. Thus the SPC remained the revolutionary vanguard in the West. As with other aspects of the Socialist Party of Canada, however, the matter of doctrinal continuity needs to be qualified. Because it had been disrupted by the split, and because a new group of young activists became influential, the party made significant revisions in tactics and doctrine after 1912. These changes allowed the SPC to gain a crucially important place in the radical movement at the end of the Great War.

5

A case study in labourism:
Winnipeg 1899–1915

In the years before the general strike, political activism was a significant and persistent dimension of Winnipeg's labour movement. This
radicalism, however, was not the impossiblism of British Columbia.
Winnipeg workers were not threatened by incoming waves of Asiatics.
Nor were they influenced by a revolutionary power base, the miners,
as workers in Vancouver and Victoria were. And geography ensured
that western American socialism would not be important in the city.
Winnipeg's dominant radical tendency was the less militant doctrine
which was part of the British trade unionists' cultural baggage – labourism. Because it was British in origin, labourism was one of the basic tendencies of western political radicalism. In the first two decades
of the century, labour parties were formed in several prairie cities –
Regina, Edmonton, Calgary, Lethbridge. But Winnipeg was the centre
of the phenomenon. The city was also the centre of the social democratic movement based principally on eastern European immigrants.
Because the social democrats were Marxists, their ideology distinguished them from the labourites. The two parties were, however,
similar in tone and tactics; consequently, before the Great War, social
democrats joined labourites in moralistic campaigns for stronger trade
unions and improved social conditions. Their propaganda was the basis of Winnipeg's radical tradition.

As they were in British Columbia, British trade unionists who settled
in Winnipeg were inspired by the radicalism which was becoming increasingly influential in the United Kingdom's labour movement. Winnipeg workers were delighted by the progress of the militant 'new unionism' and the consequent shift to the left by the Trades Union Con-

gress.[1] The new breed of British labour leaders – John Burns, Tom Mann, and Kier Hardie – had a large following in the city. The British radical who stood out above all his comrades was Robert Blatchford. His moderate and moralistic socialism, expressed first in the weekly *Clarion* and then in *Merrie England*, was tremendously popular among British workers and was important in the foundation of the Independent Labour party.[2] *The Voice*, organ of the Winnipeg trades council, described him as 'the leading English Socialist of the English school,' and contributors aped his style and adopted his pseudonym, Nunquam. After 1895 *The Voice* regularly offered for sale, and sometimes presented free with subscriptions, *Merrie England*, 'the best book on socialism ever written.' By the turn of the century the paper announced, however, that it was no longer necessary to stock the book on a regular basis, because 'all our friends and readers' owned it.[3] The paper also regularly reprinted material from the *Clarion* and in February 1898 began to publish the full series of letters which was later published as Blatchford's second book, *Britain for the British*.

Like their comrades in the United Kingdom, early Winnipeg radicals were inspired, in part, by a crusading zeal learned in Nonconformist Sunday schools and chapels. From the outset many contributors to *The Voice* based their critique of capitalism on Christian ethics. In 1894 one regular correspondent wrote, 'the more the people know about Christ the more they feel the injustice of their position.' The basic tenet of this critique was that the development of capitalist society had taken it away from the teachings of Christ; it was essential to reconstitute society by 'bringing into active operation the golden rule.'[4] Although Winnipeg workers were alienated from the church, some clergymen were active in their movement. For example, the Reverend Hugh Pedley, a Methodist who had read Marx, was a regular speaker at radical meetings; he told an audience in 1896 that socialism was the force which 'will drive us back to Christ.'[5]

A group of British trade unionists laid the institutional foundations of Winnipeg's radical movement in the summer of 1894. Encouraged by labour gains in the British general election of 1892 and the formation of the Independent Labour party the following year, they set out to establish their own labour party, so that Winnipeg workers could participate in the 'social revolution' which had begun in the homeland.[6] Before this could be achieved, however, it was necessary to convince many trade unionists that the introduction of politics into the labour movement would not result in fatal disunity. By the beginning of 1895 the trades council was able to take the lead in forming an organization which by no coincidence was called the Independent Labor party.[7] Almost immediately, however, this organization collapsed, and it was not until March 1896 that the party was revived. The Winnipeg Labor party (WLP), as it was now called, was a reformist organization, which had as its primary objective the political education of workers.

The radical movement which emerged in Winnipeg was class oriented. From the outset the advocacy of independent political action was based on the assumption that only a worker could represent workers. Labour's interests could not be effectively promoted by middle class politicians, because 'they do not shovel mud nor carry bricks nor a thousand other things that we do for a living; they never walk miles and months on a hopeless search for work, nor go hungry to bed, nor tell their children fairy tales to try and make them forget their hunger.'[8] But if the movement was class oriented, it was never doctrinaire or sectarian. The radicalism of the British trade unionists who led the movement was the moderate political labourism of the United Kingdom. Rather than revolution, labourites sought certain basic reforms which would reduce the inequities in society and improve the quality of the workers' lives. This objective could best be achieved by an inclusive labour party which could unite all workers and thus utilize their commanding strength at the polls. The model was the British Independent Labour party. Like the leaders of that party, those in Winnipeg refused to include the word 'socialist' in the party's name for fear that it would alienate potential support among conservative trade unionists. Nevertheless, socialists were members of the party and came to play an increasingly important role in its counsels. But, because of its inclusive nature, the WLP was also able to gain some middle class support. It became a meeting place and forum for progressives and intellectuals in the labour movement and the community at large.[9] Indeed, this first party came closest to the inclusive organization for which the city's labour politicians would work in future years.

When Winnipeg's member of Parliament died in February 1899, Arthur Puttee called for the nomination of a labourite candidate. His was a voice of some authority. British-born and much-travelled, Puttee was a printer who had settled in Winnipeg in 1891 and had taken a leading role in the founding of the trades council, the labour party, and *The Voice*; by 1899, he was the editor of the paper. Early in March the party and the trades council began to make preparations to contest the vacant seat. Much to the satisfaction of the labourites, the unions responded 'generously' to appeals for support. It is in this context that the labourites' desire for an inclusive party can be fully appreciated; the unions were essential to the establishment of a viable organization. In June a joint meeting of the labour party and the trades council nominated Puttee to contest the Winnipeg seat.[10]

Puttee was not entering a normal race. The Winnipeg Liberal party was badly split as a result of a rebellion against Clifford Sifton's leadership, and only the rebels nominated a candidate, E.D. Martin.[11] In addition, the 'kickers,' as the rebels were called, had the active support of the Conservatives who chose not to run a candidate in the hope of prolonging the insurgency and discrediting Sifton.[12] Consequently the by-election became a straight contest between Puttee and Martin.

When the campaign became active in January 1900, Puttee ran on a conventional reformist platform which advocated direct legislation, a land tax, and public ownership of 'all natural monopolies.'[13] Despite their essential moderation, Puttee's platform and speeches provided the ammunition with which he was attacked. As a result, the basic issue in the campaign emerged as the question of labour's right to have independent representation. Both he and Martin, who fancied himself a sort of Canadian populist, admitted that they agreed on general principles, but Martin claimed that he was running as the candidate of all the people whereas Puttee could only represent the workers to whom he made his primary appeal.

The charge obviously caused Puttee concern. He had carefully avoided being identified as simply a class candidate. The accusations levelled against him could alienate not only potential middle class supporters but also conservative trade unionists. In reply, *The Voice* insisted that the reforms which Puttee advocated would benefit all classes. But, despite these claims, his campaign was dependent on the support of the workers. To make an effective appeal to this constituency, Puttee and the labourites were obliged to emphasize the legitimacy of the movement for independent labour representation. On one occasion, William Scott, president of the WLP, went so far as to trace its origin to 'an upper room in Jerusalem.'[14]

Puttee carried the by-election held in January 1900 by ten votes and thus became the first labour member elected to the Canadian House of Commons. The victory came as a result of the prevailing political abnormality in Winnipeg. Party allegiance broke down, and both the Liberal and the Conservative vote split between Puttee and Martin.

An examination of the returns in the three sections of the city demonstrates that party allegiance was replaced by class allegiance. In the affluent south end Martin received 69 per cent of the vote. In the north end, the city's working class quarter, the response was almost as decisive for Puttee. Only in the centre of the city was the contest relatively close, reflecting the mixed socio-economic composition of the area.[15]

The split in Liberal ranks continued during 1900, and the party's weakened condition caused the Siftonites to conclude that only by supporting Puttee in the forthcoming general election could they retain some measure of political control in Winnipeg. It is impossible to state categorically that Puttee made specific commitments to the Liberals. However, it seems likely that he did, and, certainly, it became obvious that the labourite MP was willing to accept their help in his campaign. Ironically, had it not been for this help Puttee would probably have carried the seat by acclamation. But the Conservatives and the 'kickers' refused to allow Sifton's candidate, as they perceived Puttee, to take Winnipeg unopposed and so, at the end of October, they nominated Martin.[16]

Nevertheless, Liberal backing spelled the difference in the second campaign. Puttee received a majority of 1200 votes; he even got 50 per cent of the poll in the south end. The *Free Press* called it a 'splendid victory,' and Puttee attributed his success 'to the fact that the labor people had won the confidence of the citizens generally.'[17]

Winnipeg radicals had been united in Puttee's second campaign of 1900, but this unity did not continue. The need to assume a position separate from, and to the left of, reformist labour parties was an essential dimension of the growth of the socialist movement. But this process was impeded in Winnipeg by the presence of the labourites. In the minds of many Winnipeg workers, labourism was vindicated by the British example and, more directly and dramatically, by Puttee's election to the House of Commons. The slow and difficult birth of the city's first socialist party demonstrated the importance of this constant in Winnipeg and to some extent anticipated the bitter struggle which would develop between labourites and socialists in later years.

Socialists had been active in the city's labour movement since the mid-nineties. German workers had established an SLP local in the city, but it had never amounted to much.[18] More important were the British socialists who formed an influential faction within the labour party. They were an odd group. Geordie Morgan, later an important impossiblist theoretician, was one of their leaders; the other was James

Stott. For a number of years secretary of the Bradford Labour Church, he numbered Kier Hardie, Robert Blatchford, and Ramsay MacDonald among his friends. Stott was really a British 'gas and water' socialist, who should have been satisfied to remain in the labour party, but he felt obliged to push the movement farther down the road to utopia.[19] In 1900 encouraged by socialist growth in British Columbia, this group demanded that the labour party affiliate with the Canadian Socialist League.[20]

The league took a direct part in the controversy when its organizer John Cameron arrived in Winnipeg in March 1902. At the end of the month, the socialists bolted the labour party, and Cameron organized a 'small' CSL local.[21] Inaugurating what was to become a radical institution in Winnipeg, the socialists began holding propaganda meetings on the Market Square, which on warm summer evenings would draw crowds up to five hundred people. During the summer of 1902 socialist propaganda made good progress, and this resulted in the formation of the Socialist Party of Manitoba (SPM) in November. The party's platform had as its essential object the collective ownership of the means of production, but, at a time when BC socialists had already decided that they could be satisfied with nothing but the destruction of the wage system, the manifesto also advocated a number of reforms.[22]

When the socialists left the labour party, it collapsed. Puttee who had emerged as the leading labourite found the growing disunity disturbing. His early commitment to a broadly based party had been reinforced by a visit to England in 1902. There he met, and came under the influence of, Kier Hardie and Ramsay MacDonald. After his return Puttee began to promote the British Labour party as the ideal working man's political organization; he would do this throughout his career. In Puttee's view, the main obstacle preventing the formation of such a party in Canada was the 'irreconcilable' socialists, of whom he had always been suspicious. He told his readers that European socialists, who were 'well versed in Marxian economics,' had long since rejected the impossiblism which was becoming a disruptive force in the western Canadian radical movement.[23] Socialists naturally resented such criticism, but, at this point, their opinions on Puttee were divided.[24] When he was in Parliament, no open breach occurred between Puttee and the Marxists. The editor had too much tolerance in his make-up and was too committed to working class unity to make all-out war on the socialists. For their part, Winnipeg's socialists, in these early years, were more tolerant and less sectarian than their BC comrades.

Factionalism hurt Puttee in his campaign in the 1904 general election but not so much as the loss of Liberal support. The growing importance of socialists in the labour movement and the trades council's endorsement of militant industrial unionism precluded the broad support Puttee had enjoyed in earlier elections. But more important, the Liberals no longer needed Puttee; political normality had been restored by the Siftonites, who had suppressed the rebellion of the 'kickers.'[25]

The united Liberals nominated a candidate and began an energetic campaign, an important aspect of which was a drive to undermine Puttee's power base in the north end. Perceptively, they recognized that the emerging eastern European vote would be an important factor in the election and made plans to capture it.[26] The main vehicle of this campaign was a newspaper printed in Ukrainian and edited by the dominion immigration commissioner in Winnipeg.[27] So thorough were their efforts that the Liberals organized the foremen of the Winnipeg Public Works Department, a traditional place of employment for eastern Europeans.[28] The campaign to draw the trade union vote away from Puttee was no less painstaking. The Liberal candidate judiciously distributed patronage among leading trade unionists, but probably the most effective aspect of the campaign was a labour column in the *Free Press* conducted by a local Liberal wheelhorse, John Appleton. Capitalizing on the division in the city's radical movement, Appleton charged that the trades council was dominated by 'socialistic parasites' and urged responsible trade unionists to support Laurier, the working man's champion.[29]

From the beginning Puttee was on the defensive, and as a result, his campaign took on a new aggressive tone. Although he ran on essentially the same platform that he had used in 1900, Puttee emphasized the independence and legitimacy of labourism as never before. But this became a class line, and thus a tactical principle which had been observed since the inception of the movement in Winnipeg was violated. In previous contests Puttee had campaigned as a representative of all classes; but in 1904 he was the candidate of 'Mr Workingman.' Appleton skilfully took advantage of the campaign's new tone; he told his readers, many of whom had always been suspicious of the radicals, that Puttee and his associates were 'revolutionists' and 'assassins.'[30]

In the election Puttee ran a poor third and lost his deposit. The vote in the north end explained Puttee's humiliation and demonstrated the two fundamental obstacles faced by radical politicians in the city.

In the general election of 1900, he received 71 per cent of the vote in that area; in 1904 his proportion fell to 21 per cent. In part the dismal showing indicated the return of British workers to the old-line parties when political normality was restored. Puttee admitted most workers were not class-conscious when he complained in an election post-mortem that 'the labor vote is still as unstable as water and will remain so until experience and right thinking bring [the workers] to a clear perception of the real issues in human society.'[31] In addition the collapse in the north end dramatized the emergence of the eastern European vote which was controlled mainly by the Liberals and Conservatives. The labourites – British in personnel, preconceptions, and prejudices – could not mobilize these immigrants. Because of the labourites' strong trade unionism, they despised the 'hunkies' as scabs. For their part, the eastern Europeans were not attracted to an alien movement without patronage to distribute. A straight labourite candidate would not appeal to these immigrants again for nearly twenty years.

After his defeat, Puttee began to elaborate and enunciate his political philosophy – an amalgam of Marxism and Christianity, populism and liberalism. His indictment of society, which could be severe, was more rational than emotional. Puttee considered industrial capitalism unjust and inefficient, a system of production which 'starved little children' and 'burned unsold boots.' His basic political objective was a classless society. Each component of his thought made him an optimist, persuaded that the inauguration of the co-operative commonwealth was inevitable. Puttee also believed, however, that the process of change would be gradual. And, although capitalism was evolving as a result of technological change, democratic pressure, and ethical improvement, development would be facilitated and accelerated by ever-increasing state intervention and municipal enterprise. Indeed the cumulative effect of amelioration would be decisive. Because he abhorred the spectre of violent revolution, Puttee consecrated his political career to the achievement of peaceful and orderly change. He was more reticent about his vision of the new order than any other prominent western radical; in fact, he never discussed it. Puttee avoided speculation on the future because his political philosophy planted him firmly in the present.

Puttee's immediate objective was the amelioration of social condition. He believed that, in addition to educating the workers, radicals were obliged to agitate for reform. He lectured, 'we have to bring changes about ... not sit by and hope to see them evolve into perfection.' And Puttee was prepared to accept whatever reforms capitalists made: 'it would be stupid to refuse the half loaf because the whole one cannot be acquired from the enemy.'[32] Labour standards legislation, public health regulations, a workmen's compensation law, these and many other schemes were promoted in *The Voice*. To cite the most characteristic manifestation of his British philosophy, Puttee was a tireless advocate of 'gas and water socialism.' When the city of Winnipeg began supplying its citizens with low-cost electrical power, he observed 'public ownership as an antidote to corporate monopoly has something of the sweetness of liberty itself in it.'[33] He was convinced that such state intervention not only improved the quality of workers' lives in the short run but contributed to the evolution of a co-operative society.

Puttee was no ideologue; he eschewed systems. Although he considered himself a socialist who was obliged to promote a cause, he never lost sight of political realities, particularly the need to found an inclusive party. It was apparent to him that circumstances could develop in which principle would necessarily be subordinated to expedience. Puttee tolerated compromise. He was a pragmatist who believed that labourite politicians must 'be ready to face all kinds of readjustments and positions.'[34]

In the columns of *The Voice*, Puttee campaigned for an inclusive labour party 'bigger than unionism, wider than the Socialists.'[35] The unity which he perceived in the British movement inspired him to hold the Labour party up to Winnipeg workers as the example they were to emulate. *The Voice* was never without detailed reports of the party and the activities of its members at Westminster. Hardie was described as 'the head of British democracy and the most conspicuous personality of the whole English-speaking labour movement.' Puttee campaigned for a party on the British model, because he believed that the emergence of Labour had marked 'the breaking of a new day for the toiler, the aged and the industrially oppressed of the land.'[36]

Puttee's ideas and objectives brought him into direct conflict with the sectarian SPC. The impossiblists were convinced that only a revolutionary party, theirs, could serve the working class. Indeed, reformist parties were actually counter-revolutionary because, by holding out false hope to the workers, they kept them from taking up the struggle to overthrow the wage system. Consequently, the SPC persistently refused to compromise or to co-operate with labour parties. Initially, the SPC considered Puttee an opportunist lacking sufficient moral courage to declare for socialism and treated him with contempt. But when he persisted and his efforts contributed to the failure of their party in the city, the impossiblists came to regard Puttee as an enemy of the proletariat in league with the capitalist parties, and their denunciation of him became bitter. For example, a member of the Winnipeg local demonstrated the SPC's special talent for invective: 'there is nothing too mean or dirty for him where his masters' interest are at stake; talk about prostitution, the most degraded woman that ever prostituted her sex is was white as snow in comparison with this cur.'[37]

Puttee, who was sympathetic to most varieties of socialism, refused to consider the impossiblists as socialists but rather perceived them as political aberrants spawned in distant and different British Columbia. Like his friend Hardie, Puttee scorned the SPC's rejection of immediate demands: 'if they would study human nature they will find that the more comforts a man gets through organization the more he demands and by giving a helping hand to immediate demands, [they] will soon lead the great mass on towards Socialistic thought and once started from the bottom no power on earth will ever stop the flow towards Socialism.' His bitter experience with the intransigent SPC caused the long-suffering Puttee to lament, ' "Workers of the World Unite!"; when we attempt it, the Socialists say "No." '[38]

Developments during 1906 provided Puttee and the labourites with an opportunity to put their ideas into practice. Winnipeg workers were aroused in the spring by a dramatic and violent street-car strike, which was climaxed by the use of the militia, and then strikes in the building and metal trades.[39] Equally important in promoting labourism were the great gains made by the British Labour party in the general election of 1906. To many British immigrants who had been active in working class politics in the United Kingdom, these gains represented 'our' victory, and they were encouraged to take up the fight in the new land. Puttee wrote, 'hundreds of men, and women too, are here now who have been trained in the SDF and ILP of the old land and something should be done to bring us all together.'[40]

During the summer a group of 'old-time I.L.P. men' began a campaign to establish another labour party.[41] Then the TLC's 1906 convention instructed the congress's provincial executives to establish labour parties with reformist programs.[42] Ramsay MacDonald visited Winnipeg in the autumn and urged the workers to follow the example of their comrades in the United Kingdom. In October the trades council established the Independent Labor party (ILP) and named Puttee chairman. According to *The Voice* the party, which adopted a reform-ist platform, was 'the British expression of the socialist aim of other countries.'[43]

The new party could easily have been established in a factory town in Lancashire or Yorkshire. One of its objects was to provide members with 'reasonable [and] rational recreation,' and the ILP became an or-ganization which sponsored both social clubs and lectures.[44] Similarly the Nonconformist sentiment, important in the British radical move-ment, was a dimension of the Winnipeg party, which was sometimes called the 'Industrial Church.' Unlike the stringent materialism of the SPC, Christianity always informed the beliefs of labourites. They em-ployed the forms of the church - Sunday meetings, hymns, sermons, socials. And they continued to base their critique of capitalism, in part, on Christian ethics, though this justification was much less evi-dent after 1900 than before. Still some labourites employed Christian-ity, the scriptures, and the historic and divine person of Jesus Christ to justify their crusade against capitalism. A speaker told a meeting of the labour party in 1907 that 'the genuine religious impulse is the heart and soul and only hope of the struggle for social justice.'[45]

Since the emergence of radicalism in the city, there had been an im-portant link between the movement and progressive men in the church. Leading radicals like Fred Tipping and Dick Rigg had taken up the workers' fight after theological experience. And Puttee, whom Richard Allen regards as the 'most notable' advocate of the social gospel in the Unitarian Church, regularly opened the columns of his paper to radi-cal theologians.[46] Methodists were the most important influence upon the movement. While labourites across the West were affected by the social gospel, nowhere was the impact so great as in Winnipeg, because nowhere was there collected such a group of brilliant and energetic radical churchmen. Wesley College became the dynamic centre of the social gospel in Canada when Salem Bland went there in 1903. Because of his sympathy for the workers and his commitment to reform, Bland was respected by all radicals and was influential among the labourites.[47] In 1907 J.S. Woodsworth began his mission in the north end; and, al-though he was not political in his early years at All People's, his work among the immigrants won him the respect of the labourites.[48] The regard that most radicals had for the Methodists was demonstrated when Tipping persuaded the trades council to allow the Ministerial Association to affiliate so that Woodsworth, Bland, and his students could sit in the labour body.[49]

The political baptism of the Independent Labour party came in the municipal campaign of December 1906. Because local politics, concerned with franchises, contracts, and transportation, affected the workers directly, labourites took an active interest in them, and labour party candidates regularly ran, and lost, in civic contests. Following this practice, the ILP nominated W.H. Popham and Ed McCann to contest two north end wards. Running on platforms which emphasized the 'gas and water' socialism so dear to the hearts of British workers, they suffered the usual fate of labour candidates. In addition to the workers' ordinary reluctance to cast a class ballot, municipal candidates were hampered by the franchise which, based on property ownership, excluded a significant proportion of workers from the vote.[50]

The SPC treated the campaign with studied contempt. Popham had complained about the street railway's ban on smoking, and so a member of the party sneered, 'the bold demand for the "right" to smoke on street cars ... is a reform ... too far in advance of its times. ... We suggest that a start be made by working for the right to chew tobacco on street cars on condition that those who do this shall expectorate in their pockets or in their sleeves – or on one another – but not on the car floor.'[51] Such ridicule demonstrated the SPC's attitude towards municipal politics. W.H. Stebbings, a leading Winnipeg impossiblist, explained that civic government was solely concerned with property matters, and because the proletariat owned no property the issues were purely bourgeois. In addition, impossiblists believed that no real power was vested in local administrations, and, therefore, they were compelled to concentrate their efforts in provincial and federal politics.[52] This attitude helped to isolate the SPC from many workers who were vitally concerned with those local issues which the socialists contemptuously dismissed.

To contest the provincial election in the spring of 1907, the labour party nominated Kempton McKim, president of the trades council, in the constituency of West Winnipeg, which contained a substantial number of skilled tradesmen who worked at the CPR shops. McKim's campaign emphasized labour standards legislation, which was badly needed in Manitoba, and public ownership of utilities. Much to Puttee's chagrin, the Liberals nominated Tom Johnson, a popular reformer, against McKim. This exasperation demonstrated the labourites' belief, stemming from their British experience, that an informal connection existed between them and the more advanced members of the Liberal party. As it would until the progressive breakthrough of 1914, the labour vote went Liberal, and Johnson was returned. *The Voice* lamely described the contest as 'a fine educative campaign,' but in the pragmatic British tradition actual gains were more important than the education of the working class.[53] The defeat in the provincial election, and that earlier in the municipal campaign, dealt a severe blow to the labour party.

Another persistent problem for labour parties also contributed to the decline of the ILP. Their inclusive nature ensured that memberships would be relatively substantial. Because of doctrinal tolerance, and low initiation fees, each of the Winnipeg parties appears to have contained approximately three hundred men and women drawn from trade unions, the professions, the church, and white-collar occupations. Such memberships meant that these organizations, while they lasted, were larger than other urban radical locals. But almost every type of dissident joined labour parties, and this tendency substantially increased the potential for factionalism. As long as the vague goal of the workers' betterment was kept before the membership by the hurly-burly of active campaigning, unity could be maintained. But when the party came to discuss the actual means by which the condition of the workers could be improved, the number of solutions which were pressed produced division.

Puttee might fondly believe that the Winnipeg party was 'largely composed of men of socialistic tendencies,' but it also contained a significant number of non-ideological trade unionists and middle class reformers.[54] Early in 1908 the fragile unity of these groups was destroyed when pressure began to build for the party to define its philosophic position. Some socialists urged the Winnipeg party to endorse socialism in the light of the gains made by the Socialist Party of Canada in Alberta and British Columbia. But more important was Kier Hardie's call, made when he visited Winnipeg in the autumn of 1907, for the ILP to declare itself a socialist party. Then the British Labour party's 1908 convention announced that the collective ownership of the means of production was its ultimate aim.[55] As a result, some former members of the British ILP, led by W.J. Bartlett and W.C. Turnock, began demanding that the party make a similar declaration.[56] The campaign immediately ran into bitter opposition from middle class reformers led by Fred Dixon, a single-taxer. Dixon argued that if it were to declare the collective ownership of the means of production its ultimate aim, the party would have declared for socialism, and that was repugnant to the liberalism of his single-tax creed. When in June it came out for collective ownership, the party split and ceased to be an effective organization.[57]

The year 1910 saw the beginning of a new political ferment in Winnipeg. By then, because of the long Conservative ascendancy, middle class reformism, which would be an important force in Manitoba politics for a decade, was in full swing. The labourites were associated with this movement in its early years and, to capitalize on the ferment, they began to work for the formation of yet another labour party. Another new factor encouraging them was the propaganda of the People's Forum established by Woodsworth, who was now taking a direct role in the city's radical movement. Labourites and socialists spoke at the Sunday afternoon meetings of the Forum, and at one of these Bland called for a new workers' party.[58] In addition, the continuing strength of the British Labour party in the first general election of 1910 once again provided encouragement for the labourites' efforts.[59]

By early spring what had become the conventional labourite campaign was under way. In *The Voice* Puttee denounced the SPC as an isolated and useless sect, and in the trades council Bartlett and Turnock pressed for a political convention. In anticipation of a provincial election, the labourites formed the short-lived Manitoba Labor party early in May. The platform of this organization, which again contained moderate socialists, trade unionists, and middle class reformers, was made even broader than that of earlier parties in an attempt to avoid divisions. The founding convention declared 'the ultimate object of attainment shall be to preserve to the worker the full product of his toil' instead of a more radical declaration in favour of the collective ownership of the means of production. In addition the platform contained a number of reforms very similar to those advocated by the Liberal party.[60]

The platform did not find favour with the English local of the SPC, which professed to see a sinister influence in the party's formation: 'the Manitoba Labour, Liberal, Single Tax, any old crank party, must be another case of the immaculate conception – Puttee, political pimp and spineless animal though he is, could not have gathered such an aggregation.'[61] The usual sectarianism of the impossiblists had come to verge on paranoia because of the growing recalcitrance of the eastern European socialists. Isolated in a movement dominated by the non-English-speaking immigrants, the British comrades had become alarmed when the other locals began a campaign to exclude them from north end politics. Early in the year friction developed over the question of the party's candidate in the provincial constituency of North Winnipeg, the eastern Europeans pressing for 'an opportunist, step-at-a-time guy.'[62] With the approach of the election, the SPC held a convention. Neither the choice of the impossiblists, George Armstrong, nor of the language locals, Herman Saltzman, was nominated, but a compromise candidate, Ed Fulcher of Brandon, was chosen for North Winnipeg. Armstrong ran in West Winnipeg.[63]

To avoid a fight with the SPC, the Manitoba Labor party chose to nominate only in Centre Winnipeg, a constituency which, because it contained many boarding houses, had in it a substantial number of workers. The party's candidate was Dixon, who despite the earlier doctrinal dispute, accepted the nomination, because, he said 'it will give me scope to work for several much-needed reforms.' Although he made it clear that 'this is not a Single Tax fight,' Dixon also ignored the basic principles of the labour party and campaigned as one of the progressives who could rid the province of the corrupt and incompetent Roblin administration. Puttee was confident that his party's candidate could carry Centre Winnipeg and thus inaugurate the process of change.[64]

If Dixon's prospects appeared relatively good, they seemed to be immeasurably improved when the Liberal party gave him its support. His deep involvement in the progressive movement, his commitment to free trade, and his essential liberalism made Dixon feel a real sympathy for the Liberal party. Recognizing this, T.C. Norris and his associates accepted him as one of their own.[65] But this support, rather than assuring an easy victory, resulted in his defeat. Because they viewed his acceptance of Liberal help as a betrayal of the working class, the impossiblists' were determined to defeat Dixon, and they nominated a spoiling candidate, W.S. Cummings. The members of the Socialist Party of Canada believed that by fighting such Lib-Labs they could turn the workers away from the shibboleth of Liberalism. Dixon lost the election by eighty-three votes; Cummings polled ninety-nine.

Bitterly disappointed, Puttee told the trades council that the SPC's nomination in Centre Winnipeg was 'the most despicable piece of political work which has been done in the labor movement in Canada' and charged that the socialist campaign against Dixon had been financed by the Conservatives. Although they denied the charge that Conservative money had actually been used, the impossiblists were delighted by the election's results, because 'we dealt Puttee a good blow.' They called upon all socialists to unite to 'destroy the Labor paper and the Labor Party.'[66]

In fact it was the SPC which soon faced destruction. The party's spoiling tactics resulted in a strong and bitter reaction against it in labour movement. More important, the incident precipitated the long-expected exodus of language locals, by far the largest component of the party in Winnipeg. A delighted Puttee found this development 'full of encouragement for the real Socialist cause in the country.' In reply Stebbings claimed, 'what the S.P. of C. lost in numbers she gained in prestige,' but he was whistling in the dark. After the split, the SPC 'sunk very low' in the city; indeed, for a time, it ceased to exist.[67]

Three months after the disintegration of the SPC, the Social Democratic party published its platform, which had been drafted by Dick Rigg, Jacob Penner, and Herman Saltzman. The document was firmly based on Marxist principles, but it also contained a list of reforms which would facilitate 'active practical work.'[68] The platform's blend of the revolutionary and the pragmatic epitomized the philosophy of the SDP which firmly believed that some relief could be afforded workers under capitalism. The party, therefore, pledged itself 'to work unceasingly' for reforms and was 'determined to wrest from the ruling class every concession for the improvement of the life of the workers within the present system.' The social democrats' commitment to immediate reforms was tactical as well as practical; they believed that by effecting some improvement in the workers' lot, or at least holding out the hope of some relief in the not-too-distant future, they could mobilize the workers and make them a part of the proletarian army. The reforms for which the SDP pressed were many, ten in all, and varied, ranging from the eight-hour day to the abolition of the Senate.[69] Social democrats had a similar attitude towards trade unions. They regarded unions as 'the only means of preventing the working class from sinking into a condition of depravity more absolute than the mind can conceive'; therefore, the party pledged 'its sympathy and active co-operation' in every strike. Indeed, because unions contained 'the germ life' of the revolutionary movement, social democrats gave strikes an official place in the class struggle.[70] The party persistently emphasized, however, that reforms and unions could only 'minimize the present effects of capitalism.'[71]

The SDP's pragmatism should not, therefore, be misconstrued as indicative of an absence of revolutionary zeal. Social democrats were not reformers who affected revolutionary rhetoric. They were Marxists. Their propaganda emphasized that capitalism was destructive and that the workers were obliged to take up the class struggle as a matter of 'self-preservation.' The social democrats, like the impossiblists, conceived of themselves as a revolutionary vanguard whose historical destiny it was to educate the proletariat. This task had but one end, 'the overthrow of capitalism and the establishment of the co-operative commonwealth.'[72]

Indeed, the essential difference between the Social Democratic party and the Socialist Party of Canada was one of tone and tactics rather than principles. Social democrats eschewed the academic formalism which distinguished the SPC. Instead, their propaganda, even though they believed it to be 'scientific,' was decidedly moralistic. David Orlikow has called it 'almost a religion, golden rulish.' Similarly, the social democrats shunned the jargon which often cluttered the SPC pronouncements. Fred Tipping, one of the founders of the SDP, recalls, 'the doctrinal body is liable to use terminology that is peculiar to itself, [but] the language of the social democrat tended to be more the language of the street.'[73] By rejecting the SPC's dogmatism and sectarianism, the SDP became a more inclusive party which contained a rather broad range of socialism. Social democrats were much more tolerant of other varieties of radical opinion than were the impossiblists.[74] This difference in tone and tactics was by no means insignificant, however. The SPC alarmed and alienated the great majority of Winnipeg's workers, but the SDP was able to develop a significant measure of support.

The Social Democratic party was far stronger in Winnipeg than in any other centre in western Canada. Nearly 20 per cent of the SDP's national membership of 3500 lived in the city.[75] The party's strength was based on the support it enjoyed in the north end. The membership of the SDP was drawn almost entirely from eastern European immigrants organized in language locals. As the SPC had found earlier, the north end's various national and cultural organizations provided valuable recruiting places. Indeed, Tipping believes that the SDP was 'really a reaction from life in Europe.' But the importance of the various non-Anglo-Saxon groups to the party meant that their particularism would also be a part of the SDP. As a reaction to what was regarded as the autocracy of the Socialist Party of Canada, the Social Democratic party emerged as a loose federation of national units. Although relations between the various locals were good, they were not particularly close. The periodic conventions, which Tipping remembers were 'long' because each speech had to be translated into four or five different languages, were the best co-ordinating mechanism which the party possessed. Despite the party's multinational character and the relative numerical insignificance of the English local, the British-born were significant in the SDP, 'simply because they were the men who could express themselves on behalf of the party.'[76]

The English-speaking face of the SDP probably contributed to the prominent role the party immediately began to play in the city's labour movement. More important was the social democrats' attitude towards trade unions. They believed that the SPC's official policy on unions had been 'a fatal pedagogical mistake' and therefore actively supported unions. For example, during the summer of 1911, social democrats led a campaign to organize immigrant carpenters in the north end.[77] Such activities made for friendly relations between the SDP and the unions and allowed party members such as Rigg, Tipping, Ed McGrath, and A.A. Heaps to be elected to offices on the trades council. The unions' sympathy for the party was given formal expression in 1914 when the SDP was invited to affiliate with the trades council.[87]

The Social Democratic party's strength in the north end and its good relations with the unions made it a much more significant political force in the city than the SPC had ever been. In addition, the party's inclusive nature allowed it to co-operate with the labourites; this co-operation became as aspect of Winnipeg radicalism from the time the SDP was formed. The new spirit in the movement encouraged labourites to begin building yet another party, and late in 1912 they succeeded in establishing the Labor Representation Committee (LRC), modelled, once again, on a British organization. The LRC's platform contained conventional reform planks, such as the eight-hour day and municipalization of utilities, but it declared the organization's ultimate aim to be the collective ownership of the means of production.[79] Despite the radical tone of the platform, the SDP's reaction to the new organization was cautious. The social democrats believed that, like earlier labour parties, the new organization lacked sufficient revolutionary zeal and for this reason they refused to affiliate.[80]

The caution of the SDP did not, however, preclude co-operation with the Labour Representation Committee, and the two organizations worked together in the municipal campaign of 1913. This joint action and a solid immigrant vote resulted in Rigg's easy election to an aldermanic seat from a north end ward.[81] The victory was a landmark in Winnipeg radical politics; from this time onward there would be labour representation on city council.

Rigg's election and the labour unrest caused by the prewar depression encouraged radicals to launch their most ambitious political effort to that time in the provincial election of 1914. Both socialist parties and the LRC nominated candidates in ridings with high concentrations of working class voters. As usual the campaign was damaged by radical disunity. But in the north end the Social Democrats' campaign, which was directed almost exclusively at the immigrant community, encountered an additional serious problem. In a period of severe unemployment, which was almost daily being aggravated by the arrival of new immigrants, British-born trade union leaders, including Rigg, the SDP's most prominent member, had been demanding that the traffic be immediately stopped. Such demands, were, of course, highly unpopular in the north end, and the social democrats were hard pressed to reconcile their claims to be the champions of the trade unionists and the immigrants.[82] None of the radical candidates was returned. This failure gave rise to the usual bitter complaints from leading labourites about the workers' failure to recognize their class interests.[83]

The most significant fight of the campaign was that in Centre Winnipeg. There Dixon, unlike other labour candidates, chose to retain his connection with the middle-class progressives and ran as an Independent, instead of an LRC candidate. His platform was virtually the same as that of the Liberals, and he was completely identified with their cause.[84] Puttee participated to a limited extent in Dixon's campaign, but, because of Liberal connections, the editor refused to regard him as a true labour candidate.[85] The impossiblists were even less inclined to support Dixon, whom they despised, and they pledged to do everything possible to defeat the 'fake.' Wherever Dixon spoke he was followed and harassed by George Armstrong and Bill Hoop, the SPC's spoiling candidate in Centre Winnipeg.[86] These tactics again gave rise to charges from the labourites that the impossiblists had become the 'tools' of the Conservatives. The SPC officially denied these charges, but the help that one Tory labour boss gave the socialists lends some credence to the allegations.[87]

Despite socialist harassment, Dixon was able to win a convincing victory and thus begin a political career which would span the years until his premature death in 1928. Liberal support, the progressive upsurge, and the discontent caused by the depression all contributed to Dixon's election in 1914, but something more played a part in his victory and his continuing popularity. The additional, and most important, factor was Dixon's essential moderation. He might make violent and emotional attacks on the inequities of society and the privileged few who ruled and robbed, but the remedies he proposed threatened no fundamental change in society. He was a safe man. In addition, he had about him an air of respectability, derived from his middle class associations and his acceptance by the Liberals, which the labourites and certainly the socialists lacked. This characteristic the British-born workers who formed his constituency found reassuring.[88]

During the legislative session which followed the election, Dixon was a staunch defender of labour's rights and won the approval of Winnipeg trade unionists. But he also maintained a cordial relationship with the Liberal party, and this drew criticism from leading labourites such as Puttee.[89]

In the election of 1915 called by Norris after Roblin's resignation, Dixon again enjoyed the support of the Liberal party. Again the SPC nominated a spoiler, even though they now regarded Dixon as unbeatable. Certainly the results indicated that Dixon had great strength in the riding; he carried all but two of Centre Winnipeg's sixty-one polls.[90]

In North Winnipeg the SDP nominated Arthur Beech and Rigg, both of whom were officially endorsed by the LRC.[91] The social democrats refused to trade on the popular corruption issue but instead conducted a vigorous campaign which, though it stressed reforms, was firmly based on the class struggle.[92] Despite this tactic the impossiblists, who regarded the social democrats as a 'conglomeration of Labor Fakirs, Justice seekers, sentimentalists and Christ lovers,' continually harassed Beech and Rigg. Relations between the two parties were so inflamed that impossiblists were physically ejected from SDP election rallies.[93] Nevertheless, Rigg won what Tipping called 'a glorious victory.' High unemployment and the general political ferment of the times contributed to his election. Probably most important was the unity of the various ethnic groups. Rigg was a popular radical politician who had proven his sympathy for eastern European immigrants by fighting their battles for a number of years. Not identified with any single ethnic group, he was able to unite the north end politically.

Political initiatives that Winnipeg workers made before the war demonstrated the many impediments faced by radicals. Labourites, socialists, and social democrats were plagued by factionalism both within and among their parties. Tension precluded the emergence of a broadly based radical organization which could appeal to all workers. For their part the workers were divided into mutually suspicious and antagonistic ethnic groups. Diversity did not prevent the establishment of radical organizations; indeed it usually promoted their proliferation. Ethnic heterogeneity compounded the effects of perceived upward social mobility to retard even more the development of class consciousness among workers. But to concentrate exclusively on failures would result in a fallacious assessment of the Winnipeg radical movement.

Labourites developed an appeal which became increasingly more viable in an urban context. Their British inspiration allowed them to establish a model for an inclusive labour party which could accommodate radical philosophies ranging from Methodism to Marxism. Similarly, like their British mentors, Puttee and his associates were pragmatists who placed primary importance on political considerations. Their theoretical objective seldom interfered with practical programs of reform. As a result labourites addressed issues which concerned workers immediately, such as unsafe factories, long hours, and extortionate municipal franchises. The labourites' tactics were relatively successful. As the experience of the SPC demonstrated, radical parties could not restrict their appeal if they were to achieve broad political viability. Before the Great War, Winnipeg labourism was the only tendency to develop substantial support in a large city, the most significant potential constituency for radical doctrines. Labourites elected Canada's first labour MP. Then, along with British social democrats, who eventually migrated to the labour party, Puttee and his associates established a tradition of working class political action. By the beginning of the war they had achieved secure municipal and provincial representation. This radical tradition was the foundation upon which J.S. Woodsworth built after the Winnipeg General Strike.

6

The Industrial Workers of the World and militant industrial unionism

The development of the Industrial Workers of the World (IWW) in western Canada demonstrated the ease with which men and ideas moved back and forth across the forty-ninth parallel in the years before 1914. The same revolutionary industrial unionism which inspired thousands of wretched unskilled workers in the United States was carried to the western provinces by such Wobbly luminaries as Bill Haywood, Elizabeth Gurley Flynn, Frank Little, and Joe Hill.[1] But more important propaganda was conducted by faceless Wobblies who agitated while they worked beside hard-rock miners, loggers, construction workers, and harvesters and then tramped to take up the fight on another job. The IWW was able to inspire the western Canadian workers whom it organized in the same manner it did American workers because the men's experience on either side of the border was essentially similar. If there was nothing peculiarly Canadian about Wobbly doctrines or appeal, the IWW became, nonetheless, part of a western radical tradition. By 1905 the experience of workers in British Columbia had already produced a manifestation of militant industrial unionism. Indeed the IWW grew directly out of the first western rebellion against 'pure and simpledom.' And Wobblies played a role in the second campaign, weak and abortive though it was. Part of the tendency which culminated in the One Big Union, the IWW conformed to the pattern of militant industrial unionism in western Canada. Its doctrine was Marxist; its syndicalism was pragmatic; and it flourished during industrial crisis.

Like the Western Federation of Miners and the American Labor Union throughout the mountain states, BC locals were in a severely weakened condition when, in the summer of 1904, the leaders of the miners' union began a drive to found a new organization better able to fight aggressive western capitalism. In January 1905, after a meeting in Chicago, a call was issued to reorganize the American labour movement on the basis of industrial unionism.[2] John Riordan, a miner from Phoenix, British Columbia, who was international secretary of the ALU, was invited to Chicago to help direct the propaganda campaign for the new cause; in fact he even loaned his personal savings to finance the movement.[3] In the Kootenays the WFM's district vice-president, James Baker, assiduously promoted industrial unionism because 'it will become the most beneficial factor to the toiling masses the world has ever known.' BC members of the WFM and the ALU responded enthusiastically to the campaign because, like their American leaders, they believed that a stronger and more effective organization was necessary. Canadian delegates to the federation's 1905 convention voted overwhelmingly in favour of their union taking part in the upcoming Chicago convention.[4]

The Continental Congress of the Working Class, which convened in Chicago at the end of June 1905, brought together representatives from a number of radical organizations and sects. They founded the Industrial Workers of the World, the basic purpose of which was, in Bill Haywood's words, 'the emancipation of the working class from the slave bondage of capitalism.' This objective was to be achieved through the organization of the wretched of the world into great industrial unions.[5] Apart from reminding the convention of the need to emphasize the international character of the new organization, the BC delegates, Baker and Riordan, played no important role in the proceedings. But Riordan was elected to the Executive Committee and was named assistant secretary-treasury of the IWW.[6]

Before 1909 the Kootenays were the IWW's power base, and the WFM, as it had been for the ALU, was the dynamic in the union's growth. Within six months of the Chicago convention a miner from Phoenix reported that 'the principles enunciated by the IWW have found a firm, abiding place in our midst.'[7] Led by Fred Heslewood, officers of the federation organized unskilled workers, such as civic employees, teamsters, and building labourers. In some camps the WFM men were only reviving moribund ALU locals. By the autumn of 1907, the IWW had five functioning locals in the Kootenays, and even after the WFM left the organization the Wobblies enjoyed support in the region.[8]

On the coast the IWW made only modest gains before 1909. In Victoria and Vancouver the IWW built on the foundations laid by the ALU, organizing workers who had formerly belonged to that union.[9] But in the latter city members of the tiny Socialist Labor party, who followed Daniel De Leon into the IWW, were initially more important to the local.[10] Characteristically the DeLeonites subordinated organization to propaganda, and it was not until 1907 when Joe Ettor and John H. Walsh began agitating among longshoremen, lumber handlers, teamsters, and general labourers that the IWW demonstrated any vitality in Vancouver.[11]

Before 1909 the IWW's ideology might best be described as incipient syndicalism. Industrial unionism was the means whereby the proletariat would be emancipated. All members of the IWW, whether they were veterans of the WFM, the ALU, or the SLP, could agree that the new unionism could be created only by destroying Gomperism and all its forms. For example, a BC miner condemned time contracts as 'a snare and a delusion ... [by which] the workman's only weapon is taken away from him and he is left on the dung hill of impotence.'[12] IWW propagandists urged workers to subordinate political action to 'revolutionary unionism.' Heslewood believed that 'the ballot is the reflex of the union,' and therefore members of the IWW were obliged to 'concentrate our efforts to building up a great industrial organization.'[13]

Neither Heslewood nor any of his fellow workers totally rejected political action, however. This ambivalence was most obvious in the Vancouver local where the DeLeonites were influential, but in the Kootenays members of the IWW maintained their ties with the socialists. They gave active support to SPC candidates in the provincial election of 1907. Such attitudes and activities were a function of the miners' experience. They had elected members to the provincial legislature and those members, working with other miners' representatives, had achieved beneficial legislation. One miner argued that if the IWW were to abandon political action completely it would degenerate into 'a Hobo's Protective Association.'[14]

In the sectarian conflicts that racked the IWW between 1906 and 1908, BC locals were aligned with the syndicalists. At the 1906 convention Heslewood and Riordan helped drive the 'reactionaries,' who were committed to political action, out of the organization because BC members of the IWW perceived themselves as 'revolutionists.'[15] But this alignment placed BC miners on the wrong side of a power struggle within the WFM which resulted in the federation's departure from the IWW. The split crippled revolutionary industrial unionism of the Kootenays.[16] The alignment also contributed to the exodus of the De-Leonites, though this did not represent a great loss.[17]

In the years between 1908 and the outbreak of the Great War, the IWW organized the same constituency in western Canada as that of western American Wobblies: unskilled, itinerant workers - loggers, harvesters, longshoremen, construction workers. They called themselves blanket-stiffs, because they packed their blanket beds as they tramped about in search of work. The unskilled labour market of western Canada was both regional and continental in scope. Within what one BC Wobbly called the 'migratory work-shop,' a stiff might spike ties above Lake Superior in the summer, harvest the Saskatchewan wheat crop in the autumn, and saw trees in British Columbia during the winter.[18] Wobblies perceived these unorganized, exploited, and wretched men as 'the leaven of the revolutionary industrial union movement in the West.'[19] The IWW's commitment to the itinerants was based on a perceptive analysis of their lives. The very nature of the stiffs' existence ensured that they would have little commitment to industrial capitalism. The native born were alienated from society; the immigrants had never been part of it. Wobbly propaganda flattered these workers. The stiffs were told that they were the basis of the economy and the hope of mankind.

Wobblies organized cooks and waiters in the Kootenays, laundrymen in Prince Rupert, 'newsies' in Saskatoon, workers on the CPR irrigation projects south of Calgary, teamsters in Victoria, and street excavators in half a dozen cities.[20] The IWW's campaign to organize the BC lumber industry began in 1907 when loggers informed Wobbly leaders that the province's bush camps and saw mills would be fertile ground for revolutionary industrial unionism. Many loggers were IWW sympathizers or carried the red card of membership, and for a time Vancouver's Lumberworkers' local was the largest in Canada.[21] Wobblies made their most impressive gains among the workers who built the Canadian Northern Railway (CN) and the Grand Trunk Pacific Railway (GTP); the peak of IWW strength coincided with the railway construction boom. In 1912 the union had some 5000 members, the largest following attained by a revolutionary organization before the war; the twelve Wobblie locals stretched from Winnipeg to Victoria. While this membership constituted only an insignificant proportion of the industrial labour force in western Canada, nearly 40 per cent of

workers engaged in railway construction in the region belonged to the
IWW. [22]

An important characteristic of the unskilled labour force was its
ethnic heterogeneity. Unlike craft unions, the IWW did not ignore low-
status immigrant workers but rather attempted to overcome the diversity that made them attractive to employers and to organize them into effective unions. A Prince Rupert Wobbly exhorted, 'when the factory whistle blows it does not call us to work as Irishmen, Germans,
Americans, Russians, Greeks, Poles, Negroes or Mexicans. It calls us
to work as wage-workers, regardless of the country in which we were
born or color of our skins. Why not get together, then ... as wage-
workers, just as we are compelled to do in the shop.' The IWW even
advocated the organization of Asiatics in British Columbia. This attitude reflected pragmatism as much as it did the Wobblies commitment
to the proletarian solidarity of the working class. Because 'wops' and
'bohunks' constituted the major component of unskilled occupations,
Wobblies considered it impossible to organize this sector of the western economy if the immigrants were excluded from the union.[23] Consequently the IWW circulated propaganda in at least ten different languages in western Canada, and when agitators with language skills were
not available, speakers frequently had their remarks translated for immigrant audiences. There was an Italian local in Vancouver, a Swedish
local in Edmonton, and a Ukrainian and Polish local in Winnipeg. [24]
The first IWW local to conduct a strike in western Canada was a remarkable organization; a Vancouver union of longshoremen and lumber handlers, it was composed of eighteen different nationalities. [25]

Although employers perceived European immigrants as docile, an
attitude which was a function of Anglo-Saxon xenophobia, these
workers demonstrated a marked capacity for spontaneous rebellion. [26]
Wobblies recognized their revolutionary potential and enrolled them
in the one big union. Immigrants from societies which had traditions
of peasant violence, Italians for example, were probably attracted to
the IWW partly by its doctrine of direct action and partly by the heroic and romantic image cultivated by Wobblies.

The tactics and structure of the IWW were intended to overcome
the difficulties inherent in the organization of itinerants. As Wobblies
worked their way back and forth across the West, they preached their
revolutionary doctrine, and stiffs were exposed to IWW propaganda on
the job. This tactic was formalized in the camp-delegate system by
which any Wobbly could act as a full-time organizer while he tramped. [13]

The IWW charged low initiation fees and dues and allowed universal transfer of membership cards. These practices were designed to make it easy to join the union; 'all we ask of one in becoming a member of the IWW is to swear allegiance to the working class,' declared a member of the Vancouver local.[28]

The IWW provided services of real importance to its membership. Wobbly halls functioned as mail drops and dormitories for itinerants. Most locals provided job information, and Prince Rupert's hall even functioned as an employment agency for unskilled workers. The Vancouver local appears to have furnished some medical services for stiffs passing through the city.[29] Camaraderie was an important dimension of the IWW's appeal, and Wobbly halls were one of the few social centres, apart from bars and brothels, that were part of the itinerants' experience. At the Vancouver hall workers could swap tales about life on the road in the club rooms, read Marxist classics or copies of 'nearly every Socialist and revolutionary paper of the world' in the library, or listen to regular lectures on revolutionary industrial unionism.[30]

If the IWW was fighting ultimately for revolution, it never lost sight of the need to secure immediate improvements in the working conditions of its members. The organization's official demands for itinerants in British Columbia focused on many of the hardships endured by these workers: exploitation by employment agents, long hours, low pay, unsanitary camps, inadequate medical services, and so on. By pressing these demands, Wobblies made an appeal itinerants could easily appreciate: 'the I.W.W. will take the blankets off your back, Mr. Blanket-stiff. It will make the boss furnish the blankets. And, further not only the blankets, but springs and mattresses; yes and as we grow stronger sheets and pillows. Just imagine yourself in camp snoozing away, tucked up between nice clean sheets, with your head resting on a feather pillow and a good mattress and springs under you.'[31] Wobblies believed that workers would join a union which promised them immediate benefits; once members, the itinerants could be indoctrinated with revolutionary propaganda. In addition it was valuable to fight for immediate improvements because each strike trained the workers for the general strike; Bob Gosden, a prominent Prince Rupert Wobbly, called strikes 'miniature revolutions.'[32]

The propaganda that Wobblies directed at unskilled workers was the peculiar American syndicalism of the IWW, based upon a conviction in the primacy of economic action in the class struggle and a belief in the industrial organization of the new order.[33] While this doctrine was not classical syndicalism, it did nonetheless display certain similarities with the French system.[34] Wobblies told workers that they must fight their oppressors on the job, because the job was the basis of capitalism and was dependent upon their labour power. Joe Biscay, an itinerant intellectual who led the drive to organize BC construction workers, declared, 'everything is founded upon the job; everything ... comes from conditions on the job which is the environment and life of the toiling slaves. The job is the source of civilization.'[35] To control their jobs, the workers had to be organized by industry. To Wobblies, who sought above all the solidarity of the proletariat, craft unionism was ridiculous and perfidious. The 'American Separation of Labour' divided the labour movement into scores of exclusive and rival organizations, instead of uniting the workers against their common enemy. IWW agitators persistently argued that craft unionism was 'behind the times.' Workers were obliged to model their unions on the organization of modern industry. The industrial union, a Wobbly from the Kootenays asserted, 'is the logical evolution of working class organization and tactics in the same way that the trust is the logical evolution of capitalist class organization and methods.' Only unions that organized all the workers in an industry could defeat concentrated capital. 'We must all come into the ONE BIG UNION,' a BC logger told his fellow workers, 'and whenever a fight comes on, all the battalions have got to fight. ... If we all go into the battle the parasites won't last long.'[36]

The final battle would come in the general strike that would destroy capitalism. Wobblies never provided a precise definition of the general strike, but those who agitated in western Canada appear to have anticipated some general refusal to work which would 'paralyze' capitalism. A Wobbly on the CN grade told a Toronto journalist how the proletariat's final fight would end: 'the working men ... might begin expropriation by taking possession of the warehouses and means of production, without the sanction of the dictators. ... The farm workers might imitate the workers of the city and seize the possessions of the great land owners.' There would then evolve what a cook in a camp near Penticton called 'industrial socialism.'[37] Once again the structure of utopia was ill-defined, but generally Wobblies envisioned a society organized on the basis of industrial unions and directed by the workers.

This syndicalist commitment to the union and the general strike necessarily resulted in a denigration of working class political action.

Wobbly agitators persistently sneered at the proposition that by stuffing pieces of paper into a box workers could destroy capitalism. 'On the coast the sentiment [in the IWW] is strongly anti-political,' declared Biscay; 'to me the "ballot" ... is NOT a debatable question. No more so than industrial unionism. If the latter is right, the former is entirely unnecessary.' Under Biscay's leadership the Vancouver local burned copies of Haywood's pamphlet *The General Strike* because they considered it to be 'soft' on political action. [38]

Such an excess, for which the local was condemned by the General Executive Board, does not, however, indicate any significant departure from the western American norm. Like their fellow workers south of the border whose attitudes have been described by Dubofsky and Conlin, the Wobblies in western Canada were essentially non-political rather than anti-political. Their syndicalism was pragmatic. The IWW disdained political action because the great majority of its constituency was, what Wobblies called, constitutionally 'dead.' Either because they had not been naturalized or because they could not meet residence requirements, most itinerant workers were without the franchise. After addressing three thousand strikers on the Canadian Northern, a member of the SPC inquired how many of the men would vote against capitalism; only a handful could vote. [39] In addition the workers to whom the IWW directed its propaganda were deeply suspicious of government. Immigrant workers who had feared the state in Europe had their anxieties confirmed when Canadian police broke up strikes or drove them from the streets. Long and bitter experience caused itinerants to reject the efficacy of legislation passed by governments allied with capital. BC loggers and construction workers considered sanitary regulations for camps worthless because of inadequate enforcement. [40] To unskilled itinerant workers, excluded from the political process and suspicious of the state, the IWW's doctrine of direct action made good sense.

Wobblies discovered that one of the most effective means of organizing itinerant workers was through street meetings. While the IWW did attempt to agitate on the job, organizers always had to contend with hostility of employers and the mobility of workers. But on urban skid rows, to which the itinerants periodically returned for rest and recreation, Wobblies could preach the gospel of revolutionary industrial unionism and induct workers into the faith. Henry Frenette, who organized loggers on Vancouver Island, reported, 'nearly all the men I have spoken to have heard of the I.W.W. from the speakers on the streets.'[41] In addition to preserving a basic civil liberty – a liberty upon which Wobblies in Canada placed a peculiarly American construction – maintenance of the right to agitate in the streets was essential for the union's growth. Wobblies were obliged to resist any attempts by civic authorities to restrict or prohibit their open-air meetings. As a result the IWW fought to preserve its right to speak on the streets in Victoria, Nelson, Edmonton, and Calgary.

The most spectacular free speech fight began in Vancouver early in 1912. Winter unemployment was a normal part of the unskilled workers' experience. Because Vancouver's moderate weather attracted itinerants from across the West, the city ordinarily had a labour surplus in the three or four months after November. But late in 1911 a slowdown in the city's construction industry ensured that the usual surplus would become an unemployment crisis.[42] In December Wobblies began organizing the jobless, holding marches and street meetings to protest against the workers' plight.[43] Alarmed by the union's recent American fights, the city's administration determined that the IWW would not humiliate and intimidate Vancouver. In January the mayor banned street meetings and prepared for trouble.[44] It came on January 28 when unemployed workers taking part in a demonstration refused to obey a police order to disperse. With the grounds surrounded by troops in mufti, almost one hundred police, mounted and afoot, charged the crowd, injuring a number of people. As demonstrators fled, they were pursued by police and beaten. Twenty-five demonstrators were arrested.[45]

Other radical organizations took up the fight for free speech in the city, but none like the IWW. A Wobbly declared, 'if they want to down free speech in Vancouver, they will have to bury us with it.' Vincent St John condemned the civic administration and called upon Wobblies all over the continent to go to Vancouver and fight for free speech.[46] In the same way that they went to Spokane, Missoula, San Diego, and Aberdeen, Wobblies now marched on Vancouver. Alarmed at the prospects of this 'horde of ruffians' causing disturbances, immigration officials closed the border to members of the IWW; at least one hundred and fifty Wobblies were turned back from BC ports of entry. Others, using mountain trails, avoided border guards and made their way to Vancouver.[47] There, in the face of police harassment, the IWW fought for free speech with courage and audacity. On one occasion, agitators, always introduced as 'John Brown,' addressed crowds from boats moored off Stanley Park beaches; another time they used a megaphone ten feet long and eight feet in diameter to harangue the unemployed.[48] A number of Wobblies were arrested and jailed on vagrancy charges; deportation proceedings were immediately instituted against them. The mayor, who refused to negotiate with the IWW, announced his 'cast iron determination' to rid the city of 'alien undesirables' who were 'preaching sedition' and attempting to 'ruin' Vancouver.[49] Despite this attitude, the radicals' campaign forced the administration to rescind the law, and by early spring the Wobblies were able to hold their street meetings without harassment.[50]

A few weeks after the Vancouver free speech campaign ended, the IWW led the construction workers on the Canadian Northern out on strike. From the time work began along the Fraser River, camp delegates, led by Joe Biscay, had tramped along the grade organizing the stiffs. To the CN and its contractors the Wobblies were 'the biggest curse to railroad construction in this western country.' The contractors disrupted IWW meetings, encouraged provincial police officers to harass organizers, and placed Pinkerton agents in the union.[51] The contractors' opposition reached a violent climax when Biscay was beaten by police in a Savona bunkhouse and jailed for carrying a concealed weapon. Despite efforts by the companies to have him sentenced to a long prison term, Biscay was exonerated at the assizes.[52] Instead of driving the IWW off the grade, the contractors' campaign of intimidation only encouraged more Wobblies to migrate to the CN camps during the winter.

The strike that began late in March effectively stopped work on the CN grade from Kamloops to Hope, a distance of 300 miles. The men struck primarily to protest conditions in the camps; 'they treated us like swine,' charged a Swede. The strikers, approximately 7000 strong, were 'nearly all foreigners,' representing sixteen nationalities. Floyde Hyde, one of the strike leaders, claimed the men realized that 'there are only two nationalities, and ... these nations are divided by class and not by geographical lines.'[53] To keep the men in the strike zone and thus maintain solidarity, the IWW established camps at several towns along the line. One of the more important strike camps was located at Yale. Here an IWW committee, led by Charles Nelson, a young Swede, provided food and crude accommodation for more than five hundred men. When the strikers were not on picket duty, they spent their time listening to lectures, debating industrial unionism, and singing revolutionary songs. The songs, such as 'Where the Fraser River

Flows,' were composed by Wobbly bard Joe Hill who arrived in Yale shortly after the strike began. The organization of the Yale camp prompted a reporter to describe it as 'a miniature republic run on Socialist lines.'[54]

To win, the IWW recognized it must ensure that the strike was non-violent. Despite alarmist and xenophobic newspaper accounts, the strike was non-violent, as far as the men were concerned. BC Provincial Police reports demonstrate this condition. Strike leaders had received explicit orders from Chicago headquarters to take no provocative action; they assured the senior provincial constable in the strike zone that 'all the I.W.W. have been instructed ... not to give the police any trouble.'[55] The strike committees maintained strict discipline; for example, they requested that all saloons on the grade be closed and appointed their own police to control the men.[56] It was difficult, however, for the IWW to prevent provocative acts. The federal government relaxed its immigration regulations to allow contractors to procure strike-breakers, and the provincial government encouraged the companies to employ large numbers of private detectives to guard the scabs.[57] Most of the strike-breakers were Italian, and a circular in a crude southern dialect warned 'we are coming with a large force to ... drive any scab off the work.' Strikers adopted the tactic of using massed pickets to intimidate the strike-breakers.[58]

From the beginning of the strike the Canadian Northern and its contractors sought the aid of the BC government in their fight against the IWW. At a meeting early in April contractors told Sir Richard McBride, the premier, and William Bowser, the attorney general, that Wobblies had duped simple-minded immigrant workers into striking as part of the IWW's 'stupendous scheme for tying up the leading industries of the Pacific Coast.'[59] In addition to the companies' campaign, the government came under popular pressure to break the strike. Citizens of Yale demanded the IWW camp be removed from the town because they feared for their property and because the strikers were 'foreigners who do not practise the laws of sanitation or even common decency.'[60] In Vancouver *The Sun* carried out a violent editorial campaign against the IWW; on April 8 the paper declared, 'the whole movement represents an invasion of the most despicable scum of humanity. ... The government must show its strength and drive these people out of the country even if the use of force is required to do so.' In the circumstances it was not difficult for the BC government to go to the aid of its political railway.

On April 16 the attorney general informed the superintendent of police that 'the time has now arrived to prosecute and imprison [the IWW] on every possible occasion.'[61] Bowser told the officer to use the Public Health Act in the campaign. Health inspectors now began attempting to close IWW strike camps which, in fact, conformed better to sanitary regulations than did the contractors'establishments.[62] Then in the third week of April police raids began; these followed a general pattern all along the grade. The strikers were ordered to return to work; when they refused, the police tore down the camps, closed the IWW halls and forcibly ejected the men as vagrants. Police detachments then drove the strikers along the line to ensure that they left the strike zone.[63] A number of men were arrested, and local magistrates joined in the campaign against the IWW. A New Westminster judge warned Wobblies against preaching their doctrines because Canadians 'are a free and law-abiding people, and above all will not tolerate the red flag of anarchy.' Strikers were sentenced to terms ranging from three to twelve months on such charges as vagrancy, unlawful assembly, intimidation, and conspiracy. By June 250 Wobblies were in BC jails.[64] Simultaneously the provincial government sought the deportation of Wobblies because Bowser was 'anxious' to rid British Columbia of 'these undesirables.'[65] The police campaign broke the strike and destroyed the IWW organization on the CN grade.

Another defeat on the Grand Trunk Pacific followed the CN strike, and in subsequent months employers and government intensified their campaign against the IWW. Under this attack Wobblies began to promote and employ a tactic of the defensive and defeated – sabotage. What they advocated was that form of resistance which their fellow workers south of the border urged, essentially harrassment on the job, which forced employers to make concessions.[66] BC Wobblies had explicitly advocated sabotage for some time.[67] The tactic had great appeal for eastern and southern European immigrants, pre-modern workers, who had traditions of machine-breaking and direct action against oppressive employers.[68] Indeed during the CN strike Wobblies warned that they were prepared to resort to sabotage, and in one case Russians and Ukrainians who were forced back to work destroyed their tools.[69] It was not until after the defeats of 1912, however, that sabotage became a significant dimension of IWW propaganda. In an article published by the *Industrial Worker* in 1913, Bob Gosden argued that, given the capitalists' offensive, Wobblies could no longer employ conventional tactics: 'the only way is for every member of the I.W.W. to sabotage at every conceivable opportunity.'[70] As the construction season on the GTP and CN opened in 1913, Wobblies told workers that the 'walk-out strike ... [was] old fashioned;' they must strike on the job. IWW agitators believed the men 'understood' the concept of sabotage and enthusiastically reported incidents in which workers wearing 'wooden shoes' disrupted construction operations. Jim Rowan, an organizer on the GTP, announced that sabotage had passed the acid test; scowmen on the Fraser, who had wrecked their boats, won increased wages. [71]

The Wobblies' last major fight for the itinerants of western Canada occurred in the unemployment crisis of 1913 and 1914. The prewar depression and the completion of railway construction threw thousands of the unskilled out of work. [72] The resentment of men who trudged the streets in search of a job or stood self-consciously in breadlines burned hot, and they naturally responded to a familiar revolutionary gospel. In every major western city the IWW organized the unemployed.

The IWW was most active among the jobless in Edmonton. A large proportion of the unemployed in the city were workers from the railway construction camps where they had heard IWW propaganda. Now Wobblies told the stiffs that they were unemployed because 'you have produced too much and have allowed it to fall into the hands of a bunch of parasites who do no work.' Led by Jim Rowan, the IWW organized an Unemployed League late in December. The league demanded work for wages, 'regardless of race, color or nationality,' and backed up its demands with marches and street demonstrations. [73] 'To avoid outbreaks of lawlessness,' the civic administration expanded its relief program, instituted public works, and established a camp for the unemployed. But when the Wobblies attempted to organize the camp, the city fathers became alarmed and closed the facility. [74] The IWW now urged the jobless to use 'a little direct action.' Members of the Unemployed League occupied one of Edmonton's most fashionable Methodist churches until they were given food and accommodation. Others ate large meals in restaurants and then refused to pay the bill. [75]

Edmonton's elite was outraged by the IWW campaign as it intensified during the late winter and spring of 1914. The city's newspapers denounced the 'inflamatory' nature of the Wobblies' speeches and emphasized that the unemployed were mainly 'foreigners.' Citizens discussed forming vigilante groups to rid the city of the IWW. And a divided civic administration came under pressure to call out the militia. [76]

In February city police and health officers raided the IWW hall and evicted two hundred jobless men who had been living there. During the spring a number of league members were jailed for vagrancy; then at the beginning of July Rowan was arrested for murder. Although he was eventually released, he remained in prison six months; Wobblies charged that he was kept in jail 'for being true to [his] class.'[77] There appears to be a good deal of substance to the allegation.[78]

By the very nature of its tactics and doctrine, the IWW was isolated from workers organized by the AFL and the TLC. This condition was substantially reinforced by the nature of the Wobblies' constituency. Unskilled, unorganized, and un-British, the itinerants never constituted a part of the trade union movement. The Winnipeg trades council, for example, was simply unaware of a north end IWW local composed of approximately four hundred Ukrainians and Poles.[79] In some cases ignorance gave way to animosity. From 1906 onward Gompers was troubled by the possibility of the IWW making gains in western Canada, and AFL and TLC organizers fought what they perceived as the 'dual union' heresy. C.O. Young, the AFL's organizer in British Columbia, considered the Wobblies 'lawless brigands,' and he did whatever he could to retard their propaganda.[80] At times the crafts' fight against industrial unionism was spontaneous and local. 'A.F. of L. slaves' conducted a strenuous campaign to prevent the IWW from organizing loggers at Port Alberni.[81]

In its campaign to promote industrial unionism, the IWW compounded the isolation and antagonism by levelling strident and hostile criticism at the AFL and the TLC. Wobblies never tired of asserting that because craft unions divided the workers, the AFL and the TLC were allies of the bosses. The 'bushwah' leadership had betrayed the workers. Wobblies asserted that Samuel Gompers could not lead the working class because he was no longer of that class; a member of the Prince Rupert local charged that the AFL president lived in luxury and had a personal fortune of $5 million. When Gompers visited Vancouver in 1911 Wobblies disrupted his meeting and denounced him in what Gompers called 'the vilest language I have ever heard.'[82] In some cases Wobblies took their fight against craft unionism directly to the rank and file. For example Paddy Daly believed that it was 'our duty' to prevent the formation of a local of the United Brotherhood of Carpenters in Prince Rupert, and in the northern city relations between the IWW and the craft unions were stormy.[83] However, because of their commitment to the solidarity of the proletariat, Wobblies found it difficult to make general war on the rank and file of AFL and TLC affiliates. Consequently, in normal times, the relationship between craft unionists and Wobblies in western cities was one of peaceful but distant co-existence.

The IWW's relationship with socialists was more significant. In the United States the Wobblies' precarious position in the radical movement was, to an important extent, dependent upon its unstable alliance with the left wing of the Socialist Party of America. In Canada no such alliance existed. Because the IWW's syndicalism rejected political action for industrial action, the SPC made all-out war on the heresy. To a party dominated by the conviction that the revolution could be achieved only through political action, the IWW's advocacy of the general strike seemed to demonstrate total ignorance of the class struggle. Although they admired the courage of the Wobblies' crusade to organize the wretched, the socialists were convinced that the IWW's activities were essentially futile because its doctrines were unsound. After travelling with Haywood and coming to know him during the IWW leader's western Canadian tour of 1909, Charlie O'Brien observed, 'he confuses the struggle between the buyers and sellers of commodities with the class struggle.' Much worse, because the Wobblies were attempting to lead the working class down the wrong road, they were enemies of the proletariat and 'should be classed with the thugs, detectives, specials and other pimps of capitalism.'[84]

The IWW repaid the SPC in kind. Members of the IWW derided the party for its insistence that only political action could free the workers. Bill Craig of Nelson denounced the socialists' refusal to consider other tactics as a 'fatalism' which would ensure the continuation of wage slavery.[85] Even more offensive was the SPC's persistent denial of the essential utility of economic action through unions. One of the socialists' more extravagant attacks on unions caused a Vancouver Wobbly to explode, 'if poor old Karl Marx could return he would braid his whiskers into a cat-o-nine tails and scourge these super-scientific spittoon philosophers until every drop of milk and water ran out of their veins.'[86] Despite such invective, and the doctrinal antagonism which produced it, there was a recognition by some Wobblies, particularly those in the Kootenays, that 'internecine warfare is absorbing the best of our energies.' There appears to have been some co-operation between the rank and file of the SPC and the IWW in several western cities.[87]

Given the IWW's isolation it would be easy to conclude that the organization was only tangentially significant in the development of militant industrial unionism in the Canadian West. In fact historians have reached this conclusion.[88] But in the two years before 1914, the IWW's courageous leadership of the construction workers and the unemployed substantially raised its stock with the labour movement, especially in British Columbia. Both socialists and craft unionists joined the fight against government repression of the Wobblies.[89] Because of this altered relationship, the IWW became an influence, though not the most significant one, in the second western rebellion against craft unionism.

The most explicit, though least important, dimension of the rebellion was agitation for syndicalism on the French model. Western radicals had been familiar with the writings of French syndicalists, such as Georges Sorel, for some time, and they had before them the example of the general strikes staged in Sweden in 1909 and Belgium in 1913. The prewar agitation was, however, directly inspired by William Z. Foster who urged Wobblies to begin 'boring from within' the AFL to convert the federation into a revolutionary organization.[90] Syndicalist propaganda of this sort circulated in Winnipeg's north end. The interest that it held for workers in the immigrant ghetto related in part to the IWW presence and to the fact that eastern European itinerants wintered there, but the anarchist tradition among Jews and Russians was undoubtedly important as well.[91] Foster's agitation within the IWW caused Nelson Wobblies to desert the union in 1912 and found the first local of the Syndicalist League of North America. The Vancouver IWW local split on the issue, and dissidents established a local of the league in that city as well.[92] The syndicalists urged radicals to reject political action, 'get inside the labor movement,' and employ the unions to achieve the revolution.[93]

More important was the advocacy of a general strike in support of miners in their long and violent fight against the Vancouver Island coal barons. In August 1913, after riots occurred at Nanaimo, Ladysmith, and Extension, the provincial government despatched troops to the strike zone, and a tremor of bitter indignation passed through the BC labour movement. In Victoria, where the IWW enjoyed comparatively good relations with the trades council, a mass meeting passed a resolution calling for a general strike unless the militia were immediately withdrawn from the Island. The British Columbia Federation of Labor (BCFL) took up the call; its president, Christian Sivertz, declared, 'it is well known that [the capitalists] stand in greater dread of the general strike than any other method that the organized workers have within their means of using.' There was significant support for a general strike, but the all-important Vancouver trades council, because of growing unemployment and a strong SPC influence, refused to act.[94] The advocacy of a general strike continued under the auspices of the Miners' Liberation League which directed labour's campaign to free imprisoned strikers. Wobbly influence was unusually strong in the league. It employed tactics developed by the IWW in the United States, such as parading miners' children through the streets of Vancouver. Bob Gosden and other Wobblies believed that 'a good dose of direct action' promised to be the best means of securing the release of the strikers. IWW influence contributed substantially to the league's call for a general strike.[95] Again because the Vancouver trades council refused to act, a province-wide walkout did not occur. The only workers to strike were stiffs on the Pacific Great Eastern grade who were organized by the IWW.[96]

Developing at the same time as the advocacy of the general strike was a renewed enthusiasm for amalgamation. Led by socialists, who were convinced that the organization of modern industry demanded amalgamation, the BCFL had declared for industrial unionism in 1910. Then the TLC's 1911 convention, which because it was held in Calgary was dominated by western delegates, passed a Vancouver resolution calling upon workers to organize by industry, because craft unions had demonstrated their inability 'to successfully combat the present day aggregations of capital.' TLC bureaucrats were unable to block the western resolution, but the following year, when the convention was safely back in Ontario, an eastern majority returned the congress to Gompersian orthodoxy.[97] While socialist promotion had been basic to the cause before 1912, now Wobbly influence became evident. In August 1912, the Vancouver trades council unanimously passed a resolution endorsing industrial unionism and issued a circular calling upon the labour movement to adopt this form of organization. The Vancouver council contained several influential IWW sympathizers, including Jack Kavanagh the president, and Wobbly doctrines, such as universal union membership, were clearly on the minds of delegates as they voted. In response to the Vancouver circular, trades councils in Victoria, Nelson, and Calgary, all centres where the IWW was influential, endorsed the principle of industrial unionism.[98]

Direct IWW influence figured prominently in the campaign for revolutionary industrial unionism within the United Mine Workers' District 18. The miners of the Crow's Nest Pass had always lacked confidence in business unionism; they elected socialist leaders and were contemptuous of the TLC. But because of a long and essentially unsuccessful strike in 1911, some miners became convinced that the UMW was 'obsolete.'[99] Led by Harry Elmer of Michel, Wobbly miners launched a campaign in which they advocated sabotage, denounced the political orientation of the union's socialist leadership, and derided the 'craft' organization of the UMW. 'To break the chains that hold us,' declared Elmer, 'the workers of the world must organize into one union.'[100] The campaign reached its climax at the 1912 district convention, and although the UMW's socialist leadership beat back the drive, they were forced to make concessions to the Wobblies.[101]

The IWW was not alone in promoting the growth of militant industrial unionism. Despite attacks on the IWW, the Socialist Party of Canada played a role in the phenomenon. From the time of the SPC's inception, the party had tolerated within it a small but sustained anarchosyndicalist tendency, most pronounced in the Kootenays. The tendency was reinforced by the impossiblists' apocalyptic vision of the revolution. A miner wrote, 'when we have an intelligent majority throughout the land ... will it be necessary, will it be sensible, for us to fool and fiddle around with their elections act? ... When you are sufficiently united you won't need to vote for what you want with your master's ballot; you'll just take the world and that's all.'[102] In the years before 1914 members of the SPC, like other radicals, became increasingly interested in the efficacy of the general strike. Even the doctrinaire Vancouver leadership began to perceive a revolutionary dimension to action which mobilized masses of workers. The party's willingness to reconsider tactics clearly resulted from the decline of the SPC after 1910. When its political prospects were diminished by defections and defeats, the party looked to a new means whereby the proletariat could be emancipated. In addition the issue of industrial unionism had been under discussion since 1910. By 1912 dynamic young party members, such as Bill Pritchard and Jack Kavanagh in Vancouver, Joe Knight in Edmonton, and Bob Russell in Winnipeg, were actively promoting industrial unionism. During 1913 SPC propaganda began to advocate the creation of a great international union and use of the general strike.[103] But at this time members of the SPC, even Russell for example, continued to believe that, in a state with a liberal franchise, the ballot was the better means to destroy capitalism.[104]

Perhaps most important in the resurgence of militant industrial unionism in the West during these years were developments in the United Kingdom. After 1910 syndicalists, prominent among whom was Tom Mann, had an important influence on the British labour movement.[105] Many of the workers who continued to emigrate to Canada from the United Kingdom up to 1914 had been exposed to this new propaganda. Bob Russell who arrived in Canada in 1911 was influenced by industrial unionism and syndicalism in his native Glasgow.[106] Western workers took a great interest in the mass strikes of dockers, transport workers, and miners in Britain, and many radicals came to regard direct action as, potentially, a powerful weapon. When in 1913 Mann toured the West preaching syndicalism, he was given an enthusiastic hearing. A Winnipeg worker observed that Mann demonstrated 'great intelligence' in his advocacy of the new tactics and asked 'what better weapon can be found than the strike which comes down to the A.B.C. of showing class lines in society?'[107] The impact of the movement led by Mann was most pronounced in Winnipeg where the British influence was all-important. Arthur Puttee paid the new British militancy the supreme compliment when he observed, 'it will produce as good results as has the success of the Labor party.'[108]

By the beginning of the war the IWW was on the decline in western Canada, its membership falling and its locals disintegrating. This collapse resulted from employer opposition, government repression, and economic depression. Most important, the end of the railway building boom dispersed the construction labour force. These stiffs and others who worked in the woods and on the harvest were the union's only constituency. The IWW's syndicalism was a product of this reality. Exploited by employers, harassed by the state, ignored by trade unions, and excluded from the political process, Wobblies advocated direct action because no viable alternative was open to them. The tactic provided limited relief and vast hope for the wretched workers of frontier camps.

But, like the impossiblism of the SPC, the IWW's syndicalism had considerably less relevance for men and women who did not share this brutal experience. During periods of heightened class tension, urban workers joined the IWW's heroic struggles against corporations and the state, but ordinarily they perceived little solidarity with exploited and alien itinerants. Even at its height the campaign for militant industrial unionism, sparked by the Vancouver Island coal strike and massive unemployment, did not represent any widespread or important subscription to the pragmatic syndicalism of the Wobblies, much less to the classic French system. To most workers who advocated the general strike, it was never more then an enlargement of the strike they knew. Mass action was a means to enforce conventional union demands against unusually strong, or ruthless, opposition, not a means to restructure society. The general strike was an economic weapon, a hefty one certainly, but it was not revolutionary. To the extent that they considered effecting social change, political action remained the more appropriate tactic for most workers. Nonetheless another rebellion by militant industrial unionists had seized, however briefly, the western imagination. The propaganda persisted, and the doctrines of Wobblies, socialists, and British syndicalists gained a much larger constituency at the end of the Great War.

7

Western radicals and the Great War: the first phase

Pacifism and anti-militarism had been an important dimension of the radical movement since its inception. Because these sentiments animated all radicals, the movement was more unified after 1914 than ever before. Socialists and labourites, syndicalists and social democrats joined in a crusade against the war. Their primary object was to encourage working class opposition to Canadian participation in the European conflict. They had some success; indeed, that radicals led the important components of the western labour movement was never more evident. Nonetheless, in August 1914 workers were preoccupied with the serious unemployment which had plagued the region for two years. It was not until mid-1915, when the economy picked up and the demand for labour increased, that they became primarily concerned with the war. By 1916 economic anxieties and hardships produced deep dissatisfaction among workers, and radical labour leaders exploited this discontnet. They had an excellent issue in federal manpower policies which many workers perceived as a threat to trade unions. The fight against registration and later conscription culminated in the radicals' most ambitious political campaign.

The radicals' pacifism and anti-militarism grew out of Marxist internationalism, Christian ethics, and the experience of workers whose strikes had been broken by troops. When the nation began debating the naval question, these sentiments became stronger and more strident. Dixon, a staunch pacifist, declared, 'Canada needs no navy. There is no necessity for the politicians to broaden the basis of their operations by going to sea; they can rob us just as well on dry land.' Radicals insisted that Canada should not develop a military establishment in order to participate in imperial adventures. When Borden proposed a solution to the perplexing national problem, Pettipiece complained, '$35,000,000 could be used in numberless ways, but instead of that we are asked to vote it for the building of murder ships, and then we are asked to send our sons out to be made the target for another fool's bullet.'[1]

As war clouds gathered, radicals attempted to convince the workers that they should not become caught up in the growing national excitement because the working class bore the brunt of war. Socialists and social democrats, following the lead of their German comrade, Wilhelm Liebknecht, argued that European tensions were the product of an international conspiracy of armaments manufacturers. Jack Burrough charged that war fever was fostered by the arms ring: 'to create a demand for their commodities, ... it is necessary that a spirit of hate should imbue the peoples of the different nations in regard to each other.'[2] In 1911 the western-dominated Calgary TLC convention declared that the 'capitalists of the world cause all war' and called for a general strike to prevent the outbreak of hostilities. Then early in 1914 the convention of the BCFL took a strong anti-war line.[3] Most ominous was Puttee's demand that the workers prevent the Canadian government from making any commitments which would entangle the country in European affairs, because the continent was 'a vortex into which any sane people ought to shudder at the prospect of plunging.'[4]

When war came, the reaction of radicals was uniformly negative. Puttee asked, 'from the workers' point of view what quarrel have we with the workers of Germany, or they with us?' To his rhetorical question he answered, 'none, absolutely none.'[5] To Pettipiece, now editor of the *British Columbia Federationist*, organ of the provincial labour federation, the war was a 'miserable muddle' caused by 'certain kings, princes, politicians, financiers and other international scoundrels.'[6] The SPC declared that because 'wars have their origin in the disputes of the international capitalist class for markets ... the struggle in Europe is of no real interest to the international working class.'[7] Wobblies announced that only 'suckers' supported the war effort, and the Vancouver and Edmonton locals expelled members who enlisted.[8] Because of its commitment to the International, because of the unusually strong pacifism of many of its members, and because of its multinational character, the SDP was loudest in its condemnations during the early months of the war. The party's executive immediately inaugurated a propaganda campaign against the war and announced, 'we are indifferent whether our masters are English, American or German capitalists.'[9]

For a time, however, radicals also saw signs of hope in the war. Coming as it did on the heels of world-wide depression, the conflict seemed to represent the death throes of capitalism and, thus, to conform to Marx's grand model. Marxists held this hope most strongly. A Vancouver social democrat wrote, 'the European tragedy now opening up is to be the preliminary act in the world-wide social revolution [and] will usher in an era of peace and transform slaves and their keepers into free and useful citizens.'[10] Even Puttee initially believed that ultimate good would come to the workers as a result of the European holocaust: 'the terrible death roll, suffering and devastation will result in democracy rising in its might and declaring that there will be no more wars.'[11] But hope soon faded, and only the horror remained.

Some radicals initially believed that the International would be able to stop the war, but this hope too soon faded. On the eve of May Day, 1915, Pettipiece observed dryly that celebration of the proletariat's international festival would have to be postponed because 'the workers are all too busy killing each other.'[12] To the SPC the collapse of the International was, in large measure, a vindication of its decision not to affiliate with the organization.[13] A much different reaction came from the SDP. The party 'sorrowfully' admitted that socialists had been 'utopian' to believe that the International could prevent the outbreak of war. But, as Arthur Beech said, simply because 'socialism has projected its ideals farther ahead than its organization,' there were not grounds upon which the doctrine could be 'ridiculed and condemned.'[14]

The initial response of most workers to the war was different from that of the radicals. Photographs of a German cruiser loading scab-dug coal from Vancouver Island in San Francisco harbour did not increase the workers' patriotism. Nor did the entente with Russia, long hated by the British working class.[15] A few unions took explicit anti-war positions. For example, when it met early in 1915, the convention of UMW's District 18 condemned the war and declared that the workers of the world had 'no quarrel whatsoever with one another.'[16] The majority of western workers, however, either accepted the war as a fact of their lives or responded to the country's call by enlisting. Patriotism was undoubtedly the basic motivation for a large number of British immigrants who joined the colours. But men enlisted for other reasons as well. In some cases they were forced to do so by unusually patriotic employers. British Columbia Electric included in the pay envelopes of single men a notice reading, 'Your King and country need you - we don't.'[17] An even greater inducement for enlisting in 1914 and 1915 was 'hunger-scription'; jobless men joined the army in order to feed themselves and their families. A significant number of eastern European labourers, starving on the construction line of the Hudson Bay Railway, enlisted. In Edmonton recruits were served a meal immediately after they underwent their medical examination. A trade unionist self-consciously explained that he might 'just as well fight in Belgium for [my] food as to fight for it in Winnipeg.'[18]

When the conflict in Europe became their major preoccupation, workers manifested an active concern about postwar economic dislocation. Given their recent experience, this fear was natural. The severe depression which followed the Boer War had been burned into the memory of the British working class, and as a result workers expected worse unemployment to follow the war than had preceded it. The potential problem was dramatized in the coal fields of British Columbia and Alberta. Miners became alarmed when low-status immigrants replaced men who had enlisted.[19] Changes in patterns of employment caused by the war also disturbed workers. They uneasily noted the large numbers of women who entered the labour force and became more concerned when Socialists told them that the capitalists would not return to more costly male labour after the war.[20] But the greatest potential threat to the job security of workers was, as Bill Pritchard liked to point out in the editorial columns of the *Clarion*, the veterans. Because returning men could underbid organized workers by the amount of their military pension, they constituted a real threat to trade unions. The problem that returned men represented seemed to be demonstrated when, early in 1916, disabled veterans were used to break a strike of Calgary theatre projectionists. The incident caused grave alarm across the West.[21] By the beginning of 1917 the western labour movement was actively engaged in a search for a means whereby the impact of postwar unemployment might be reduced. But this search did nothing to allay the anxiety of the workers.

Of more immediate concern than postwar unemployment was inflation, mainly the rising cost of food. Costs had been a concern from the beginning. For example, at its first meeting after the declaration of war, the Vancouver trades council viewed with 'grave alarm' the prospect of price increases and demanded that the Borden government prevent these. [22] As it turned out, federal policies intended to control the wartime economy received only criticism from the western labour movement. This is not surprising since food prices increased by 65 per cent between August 1914 and December 1917. [23] By 1916 the labour press was devoting a great deal of attention to uncontrolled inflation. The *Federationist* complained, 'never [was] the price of [necessities] so high, and in comparison never was the purchasing power of the producing class so low as at present.'[24] There was no doubt in the minds of labour leaders as to the cause of the increased prices; it was profiteering. Because Borden and his colleagues refused to regulate the economy as had been done in Britain and Australia, they were guilty of complicity. [25]

Most scholars agree that wages did not keep pace with prices, and a recent study of several occupational groups in Winnipeg demonstrates how precipitous the decline in real wages was for some workers. [26] By 1916 increased prices were causing hardship for workers across the West, and labour leaders began making private representations to government for relief. The Victoria trades council informed Borden that the decline in real wages was 'making it impossible for the worker and his family to exist.'[27] In the summer of 1917 a conference of international unions concluded that Canadian workers were experiencing a 'serious depression of their standard of living occasioned by the increase in the price of necessities of life.'[28]

Inflation naturally resulted in demands for wage increases. In 1915 the Winnipeg trades council, on behalf of the machinists' union, began a campaign to have a fair wage system established in the munitions industry, and this was taken up by other western central bodies. *The Voice* branded as 'clearly an unpatriotic attitude' Borden's reluctance to regulate munitions production. In a blundering attempt at compromise, the federal government made the hated Industrial Disputes Investigation Act applicable to industries which produced war material. Western labour opinion was outraged. The Vancouver trades council charged that by this action Borden had given 'the profit mongers a legislative handicap over those who do the wealth producing.'[29] Significantly the council also denounced the TLC executive's willingness to accept this step, and the *Federationist* warned congress President J.C. Watters that he could not sacrifice the workers' interests to what appeared to be the national interest. [30]

Certainly many workers in western Canada were not prepared to subordinate their wage demands to war necessities. During 1916 inflationary pressures resulted in an increase in trade union membership, which initiated a recovery from the drastic effects of the prewar depression. The following year was characterized by a large number of strikes; time lost was four times greater than in any of the three previous years. More than one million man-days were lost in Canada, and the West accounted for 86 per cent of the total. Major disputes occurred in Vancouver, Calgary, Edmonton, and Winnipeg. But a series of strikes which began late in 1916 in the coal fields of the Crow's Nest Pass resulted in the greatest time loss and best reflected the prevailing militancy.[31] Although the federal government, influenced by the Royal North West Mounted Police, believed that a general strike was imminent and considered taking 'direct steps' to force the men back to work, the strikes were no more than the miners' response to falling real wages.[32]

Industrial tensions could have been eased had there been better communication between the state and the labour movement. In other Allied countries, governments recognized the importance of the trade unions. This was not done in Canada until the last year of the war and then only in a half-hearted fashion. Avoidable blunders were regularly made; for example, recruiting posters did not carry the union label. Borden's great failure was his refusal to invite union leaders into the councils of the nation as they had been in Britain and would be in the United States. Even on those issues which were vital to its interests, labour was ignored. The failure bred resentment. *The Voice* described the slight as 'humiliating.' The *Federationist* demanded a change: 'it's about time the Borden government took the workmen of Canada into its confidence. ... If wage-workers are such an important factor in the war game, why should they not be consulted as to the conduct of national affairs?'[33]

Also disturbing to radical labour leaders was the tendency on the part of many workers to place nation before class. The union members who enlisted, some 26,000 by the end of 1917, became soldiers or veterans first and trade unionists second. This transition was a source of concern to many western leaders. Bill Hoop, the impossiblist organizer of the Winnipeg trades council, observed, 'no matter how "red" you are when the military band passes, the primeval instincts are aroused; a great majority of the men overseas have developed the master class mind.'[34] Even some of those workers who remained at home tended to place the war effort before the objectives of the labour movement. Among this group radicals saw an unfortunate tendency to co-operate with capitalists and warned, 'we must fight the same employers after the war as before.'[35] Since August 1914, the *Federationist* admitted, there had been a 'falling away from the gospel of class activity for class emancipation.'[36]

For a movement which depended upon group consciousness and hoped to achieve class solidarity, this was a development fraught with danger. The *Canadian Annual Review* noted that the rank and file was willing to subordinate 'the cherished fruits of agitation and organization ... to imperative War necessities' but saw no such willingness on the part of trade union leaders.[37] Western leaders were certainly unprepared to forfeit the limited gains which they had made in the past to what others perceived as national priorities. In a 1916 Labour Day message Rigg declared, 'this labor movement is the biggest thing in history; infinitely bigger and more momentous than the great war in Europe.'[38] Western leaders quickly denounced anything that smacked of sacrifice to war necessities. When it learned that the TLC was considering purchasing Victory Bonds, the Vancouver trades council indignantly protested. The Patriotic Fund regularly came under fire. Various central bodies demanded that the Dominion assume responsibility for veterans' and soldiers' dependents because in Puttee's words, 'this is a monopoly country – that the soldiers have defended; therefore let the monopolists pay the wages due.'[39] When the demand for labour began to increase in 1916, the *Federationist* told workers to disregard patriotic considerations and take advantage of their enhanced bargaining position: 'with the number of available men reduced to somewhere near the number of jobs in B.C., the industrial outlook is somewhat brighter than for three years past and no union man left in the province should hesitate to make the best use of this opportunity to regain some of the lost ground. ... Labor should proceed to help itself.'[40]

Early in August 1916, the Borden government passed an Order-in-Council authorizing the appointment of a National Service Board 'with a general power of supervision over recruiting as it affected industries and labour.' R.B. Bennett was named director-general in October, and during the following month supervised the development of plans for an inventory of Canadian manpower. Late in November Bennett announced his intention to 'determine the manner in which men can better serve the nation at this time, whether in a military or industrial capacity.' This was to be achieved by a postal survey in which every male citizen was to supply certain information.[41] The program became known as registration.

These developments alarmed radicals. They regarded registration as a prelude to conscription, and they had been vehemently opposed to the concept of compulsory military service from the beginning of the war. They had watched with a growing sense of alarm the introduction first of registration and then of conscription in Britain. When enlistments began to fall off in 1916 and various schemes were put forward to induce men to join the army, radicals became even more uneasy. The Winnipeg trades council snubbed requests for support from the local Citizen's Recruiting League and District 18's annual convention denounced patriotic firms that pressured their employees to enlist.[42] The intensified recruiting campaign also came in for criticism. 'Big hulking and uncouth ruffians in uniform halting, soliciting and bulldozing people upon the public streets or shallow-pated and impudent creatures in skirts attempting to pin white feathers upon male passersby, are by no means displays calculated to appeal to the patriotism of possible warriors,' lectured Pettipiece.[43] During the spring and summer of 1916 radical labour leaders repeatedly announced that they would not tolerate conscription.

Only when faced with registration were the radicals' objections to the draft completely elaborated and articulated. They feared that military conscription would lead to industrial conscription. The *Federationist* charged that registration was advocated by 'all of those interests that have their fangs of exploitation fastened in the flesh of the workers and that fatten upon the profit sucked from their blood and sweat.' *The Voice* explained, 'a civilian can make a contract ... but not a soldier.'[44] Conscription would result in the destruction of collective bargaining, the very foundation of the trade union movement. In addition radicals charged that 'the government has not shown a disposition to exact from capital sacrifices equal to those demanded from labour,' and insisted on a more equitable distribution of the burdens of war through the conscription of wealth.[45]

Early in December Borden and Bennett undertook a speaking tour to enlist support for registration. The tour, however, aggravated rather than allayed the fears of western workers and only hardened their opposition to registration. In Winnipeg the prime minister and his colleague were given a very cool reception, and *The Voice* lectured that Borden had no right to ask workers to make further sacrifices until he began behaving in a patriotic manner himself. Apparently disturbed by this reception, Bennett wrote J.S. Woodsworth asking for his 'active assistance and co-operation.'[46] Workers in British Columbia were in 'a sullen and critical mood.' When labour leaders met with the prime minister's party in Vancouver, they demanded an assurance that conscription would not follow registration; Borden refused. As a result, the delegation condemned the government.[47] In Calgary Borden and Bennett were rebuffed again; after a meeting with the prime minister on December 18, the Calgary trades council officially denounced Bennett and 'irrational Service.'[48] While the *Federationist* saw in these events 'a veritable rainbow of promise,' H.H. Stevens, the Conservative MP for Vancouver, was alarmed.[49]

During the western tour, and possibly because of labour reaction to it, Borden arranged a meeting with the TLC executive at the end of December. The prime minister explained that registration had been instituted to 'render unnecessary any resort to compulsion.' However, despite demands from the executive, he refused to guarantee that conscription would not be introduced. Borden also rejected the principle of the conscription of wealth, claiming that the existing tax structure ensured an equal distribution of the burdens of war.[50] Despite their apparent failure, the following day the TLC executive recommended that trade unionists complete and return the registration cards and, by implication, endorsed the government plan.[51] This action enraged radical labour leaders. Earlier in the year the congress executive had proposed a general strike to prevent the introduction of conscription. This had been a grievous tactical error because even some of the most conservative elements of the western labour movement had responded favourably to the proposal. Now the congress seemed to be making a humiliating surrender.[52] Increasingly westerners would perceive the TLC's war policy as cowardly and submissive.

The western labour movement refused to adopt the course recommended by the congress executive. Winnipeg led the anti-registration campaign. At a meeting on December 21 the trades council declared itself 'definitely and emphatically' opposed to registration and recommended that workers refuse to sign the cards. The trades council and the SDP established an Anti-Registration League, which immediately began propaganda work. On December 24 the league held a rally which 4000 people attended. The crowd gave the Manitoba director of the National Service Board, 'a very poor hearing' when he attempted to defend registration. But Dixon was cheered when he declared, 'National Service is the first step toward compulsion. ... If there are justice and liberty at home, there will be no need of conscription. Compulsory military service has been defeated in Australia, and it will be in Canada if it is put to a vote.' Then on the second day of the new year an emergency meeting of the Winnipeg trades council was held to consider the TLC executive's action. The meeting reaffirmed the recommendation not to sign the cards and officially censured Watters and his colleagues.[53]

The reaction was the same across the West. The Victoria trades council denounced registration as 'only a prelude to Conscription' and charged that the TLC executive had betrayed the workers.[54] The *Federationist* claimed that Borden had 'pulled the wool over the eyes' of the congress leaders. On January 4 the Vancouver trades council advised workers not to sign the cards because the government had refused to conscript wealth and nationalize basic industries.[55] Joe Knight told the Alberta Federation of Labor's convention that Watters and his colleagues had demonstrated 'their inability to act in accordance with the interests of the working class.'[56] The Calgary trades council declared that it would only support a scheme 'which has for its object the mobilization and use of the Natural Resources and Utilities of this country for the direct benefit of the State.'[57] Even the Regina trades council urged workers to join 'the great fight' against registration, because it was but part of 'a programme designed to place the working power of the nation more completely under the control of that despicable group of men who are now "feasting on the nation's suffering" and "fattening on our soldiers' blood." '[58]

The basic dichotomy in the Canadian labour movement had begun to emerge once again. In eastern Canada the recommendation of the TLC had met with general approval, but in the West it had caused 'severe criticism almost bordering on open revolt.' Watters believed that this reaction had been manufactured by the radicals. He accused McVety, president of the BCFL, of sowing 'the germ of sectional differences in the minds of the workers.'[59] But Watter's analysis was superficial; the radical leaders were a symptom of the basic difference in outlook between East and West. The difference at this point was manifested in the West's reaction to registration. As the opposition to national war policies increased, the dichotomy became more pronounced.

The culmination of the western campaign against registration was the convention of the British Columbia Federation of Labor, which was held at Revelstoke between January 29 and February 1. Delegates officially censured the TLC executive and declared that the workers 'refuse to be party to any arrangement by which the government hope to turn large number of workers over for exploitation to the profiteering manufacturers of this country.' The convention resolved to defend any trade unionist arrested for non-compliance with the terms of registration. Reflecting the temper of the labour movement, the convention elected Joe Naylor, a scarred veteran of Island impossiblism and a violent opponent of the war, as president. In fact, almost all the new officers were socialists. Next the convention turned to political matters. After they had announced their lack of confidence in the Borden government, the delegates enthusiastically passed a Naylor resolution calling for the establishment of a political party by the federation. [60]

The campaign against registration made little impact on the federal government. On May 18, 1917, the prime minister informed the House of Commons that his government would institute conscription. The reaction of western radicals was immediate and violent. On May 25, *The Voice* declared that 'it smacks of Russia, Prussia and Hun-dom at large' and went on to accuse the government of being responsible for the decline in voluntary enlistment: 'if everything had been clean and just and above board at Ottawa there would have been no possible excuse for attempting to inflict conscription on Canadians.' On behalf of the BCFL, Naylor called for resistance: 'fellow slaves, if our masters force us to fight let us fight for our own liberty and cast from our limbs the chains of bondage.' The Alberta executive of the SPC fumed, 'says Premier Borden: "we must fulfill our promise." *Our* promise! Whose promise? Since this atrocious war broke out no opportunity has been given the people to express themselves.' *Robochy Narod*, organ of the Ukrainian social democrats, had no doubt about the workers' opinion: 'if the nation would have to decide the affair of conscription, it would never be instituted in Canada.'[61] Radicals insisted that, because its mandate had run out, the government lacked the constitutional authority to impose conscription and demanded an immediate election.

Although it reflected old fears, the opposition to conscription was characterized by a new strength and a new determination. Radicals claimed that the weight of conscription, which had become necessary only because of government incompetence and corruption, would fall most heavily upon the working class, the class which had already born the greatest burden. The workers would not accept this, and radical labour leaders demanded a more equitable distribution of the burden. This was to be achieved through the conscription of wealth. On May 25, *The Voice* presented what was to become the working definition of wealth conscription: 'What is meant by conscription of wealth is something much different from general taxation. There are many people who have great hoards of cash or liquid assets, hoards so large that they can never spend them all except by insane prodigality. If the state is in danger these hoards are in danger of being lost. If the danger is so great and so impending as to call for conscription of men's living bodies in order to save the country then these hoards of cash and liquid securities should be utilized to pay the cost of the war.'

But labour leaders were opposed to conscription most because they believed that it meant the death of trade unionism. They had always feared that conscription was intended to destroy collective bargaining, and now they believed their worst fears were to be realized. Industrial conscription would be introduced. They were convinced a conspiracy existed between the state and capitalists to kill the trade union movement. Their anxieties were reinforced and increased by demands from many middle and upper class Canadians that the federal government prevent unions from disrupting the war effort by keeping workers at their jobs under military discipline.[62] Although opposition to conscription was primarily economic, it certainly had a doctrinal dimension. Pacifism had not declined in three years. All radicals were profoundly offended by the prospect of the state compelling workers to fight in an imperialistic war. Even Puttee declared, 'we take particular exception to being forced to take active part in any war between sections of the master class in which we would be compelled to shoot down and be shot down by other members of the International Working Class.'[63]

In Vancouver the trades council and the SPC co-operated in the fight against conscription, and this alliance resulted in a vigorous and flamboyant campaign. Arthur Wells, secretary of the BCFL warned, 'in the event of conscription passing, the Federation will ... issue a "down tools" order throughout the entire province.'[64] Despite threats of a general strike, the SPC dominated the Vancouver campaign, and the impossiblists remained primarily committed to political initiatives. The official attitude of the BCFL was that, although active opposition was desirable, it should 'be directed by reason and common sense' and that political action represented the workers' best tactic.[65]

In Winnipeg a broad spectrum of radicals formed an Anti-Conscription League and, with the endorsement of the trades council, launched a propaganda campaign.[66] When the league tried to hold meetings, the speakers were shouted down or attacked and beaten by veterans. Conditions became so explosive that the city police refused the league permission to hold public meetings.[67] The radicals were outraged. Puttee stormed, 'it seems strange and ironical that free speech, the basic stone of democracy, should be imperilled and condemned by those who say that they are fighting to preserve democracy from the attack of an overwhelming autocracy.'[68] Although there was talk of a general strike in Winnipeg, labourites and socialists pushed for political action. Puttee called for a new party composed of 'all those who have always been forced to pay tribute to special privilege and capital.'[69]

The labour movement's truculence in the summer of 1917 alarmed the federal government. Borden and his colleagues, who were coming under increasing pressure because of the workers' militancy, were anxious to improve a situation for which they were in part responsible.[70] Shortly after conscription had been announced, some Conservatives suggested to Borden that the government send a delegation of trade unionists to France to inspect conditions at the front. He accepted the proposal. T.W. Crothers, the minister of labour, believed the delegation 'would make such a report as would tend to reconcile labour in Canada to some of our actions which they are now opposing.' The labour minister submitted the names of possible delegates; not one westerner was included. The delegation was never sent, probably because Arthur Meighen opposed the plan.[71] The government was considering another scheme to gain labour's confidence during the summer. In January, Gideon D. Robertson, a vice-president of the Order of Railroad Telegraphers, had been appointed to the Senate in an unsuccessful attempt to placate the labour movement. Then in response to labour criticism and demands for representation in the government, Borden began considering Robertson for a cabinet post. He was not taken into the government until the late autumn, however, and by that time the small good which the appointment might have done was lost. McVety sneered, 'nobody but a few railroad telegraphers know him.'[72] Despite their concern, then, Borden and his colleagues were unable to quiet the workers' protests, and by the end of summer Bennett admitted that the situation in the West was 'more or less acute.'[73]

Certainly this was the assessment of Canada's various security agencies. Since 1914 these agencies had monitored the radicals' anti-war campaign, and there had been a few cases of repression. But in 1917 the RNWMP, military intelligence, and the press censor began a systematic surveillance of radical organizations; the Regina headquarters of the Police functioned as a clearing-house where dossiers on several hundred western radicals were prepared.[74] This surveillance clearly was the result of two developments in the year, the Russian revolution and the radicals' opposition to conscription. The latter, which demonstrated the workers' militancy, was the more immediate and disquieting. The security agencies' increased interest in radical organizations coincided almost precisely with the beginning of the campaign against compulsory military service. For example, the chief press censor, Ernest Chambers, became much more active. While he admitted that conscription, as a political question, needed to be fully discussed, he believed that 'there is a limit, and when people say that the war is none of our business, they are unquestionably using treasonable expressions which should be stopped.' The government, however, believed that it would be 'disastrous' to suppress any radical paper which attacked conscription.[75] Nonetheless Chambers was deeply disturbed by the editorial policies of all western labour papers. In mid-July he had the offices of *The Messenger*, a violently anti-war sheet published irregularly by the SDP in Victoria, raided by local police and military intelligence forces. By the autumn he had recommended the suppression of the *Federationist* and the *Clarion*.[76] Chambers took these steps because, he said, 'I strongly believe that the developments along extreme Socialistic lines on the part of several newspapers in Canada is due to enemy support.'[77] During the summer of 1917 police officers and military intelligence agents also harassed radicals. But this was only the beginning. The campaign of repression was not fully implemented until after the election of the Union government.

Government war policies dominated the TLC convention when it met in Ottawa late in September. Radical labour leaders from the West did not expect much support from the congress. The 1914 convention had refused to honour the commitment to declare a general strike in the event of war; instead delegates pledged their support to the Empire.[78] From the beginning of the 1917 convention it was apparent that the westerners were in a militant frame of mind and would demand more than the easterners would be prepared to concede. Western delegates believed that a strong stand on conscription was essential, and every resolution advocating organized opposition came from the West. But eastern trade unionists were not prepared to adopt a hard line. When the executive recommended that the congress not oppose the implementation of conscription, the final sectional split was assured. The western delegates considered this policy a complete surrender. Hoop warned, 'if there is no opposition to the Government we have handed over everything bag and baggage to the capitalist class.' Alfred Farmilo, representative of the Alberta Federation of Labor, introduced an amendment to the executive recommendation proposing that 'every effort be made to force the complete conscription of wealth as an essential part of conscription for war purposes, and ... pending the conscription of wealth no support be given to the principle of conscripting men for war purposes.' The Farmilo amendment was defeated 111 to 101. The executive recommendation was carried by a vote of 136 to 106; the minority came 'almost entirely' from the West.[79]

The convention's action was condemned in the West. *The Voice* charged that the TLC had 'side-stepped and compromised.' The *Federationist* cried, 'never has a convention of alleged labor representatives registered a more complete abject surrender to the sinister and baneful influences of political chicanery and reaction.' The organ of the BCFL believed that the convention had demonstrated that 'there is nothing at present in common between the labor movement of the east and that of the west.' It was time, Pettipiece said, that western workers repudiated the 'servile and suicidal' policies of the TLC.[80]

Martin Robin implies that the congress's decision to encourage the formation of the Canadian Labour party postponed the final split in the labour movement by forcing western radicals to forgo direct action for political action.[81] This analysis is difficult to accept. After the September convention, resentment in the West continued to grow, and the leadership became convinced that the differences between the two sections were irreconcilable. For this reason the TLC's decision to encourage political action had no significant effect in the West. But even more important was the fact that westerners needed no prompting from the congress to take political action. Radicals had been urging the workers to challenge Borden politically since the end of January and, before the TLC convention met, had made preparations to run candidates in nearly all the ridings which they would contest in December.[82] If westerners had decided upon political action before the convention, they could hardly have been turned from direct action by the convention's decision. The only two important central bodies which had considered direct action were the British Columbia Federation of Labor and the Winnipeg trades council, and both had rejected immediate use of a general strike before the Ottawa convention met.[83]

By mid-autumn labourites and socialists began campaigning for the December election in seventeen western ridings. In its broad outline and general objectives, the Winnipeg campaign was similar to others across the West. When the trades council announced that its candidates would contest the two newly formed seats of Winnipeg Centre and Winnipeg North, the labourites faced other radicals who were already in the field. During August the SDP had nominated John Queen in Winnipeg North, and the Anti-Conscription League put up S.J. Farmer in Winnipeg Centre. The labourites claimed that these men could not hope to achieve wide support and attempted to fashion a compromise slate. These efforts failed, however, and Puttee and his friends declared that they would nominate R.S. Ward and Dick Rigg to contest Winnipeg Centre and Winnipeg North respectively. Both Queen and Farmer protested this action, but the labourites were adamant. As a result, on November 17 a meeting attended by representatives of all the radical organizations in the city, even the SPC, endorsed Rigg and Ward.[84]

The Laurier-Liberals did not nominate in Winnipeg Centre and Winnipeg North before November 17; on that day they endorsed Rigg and Ward as Laurier's candidates.[85] In fact all labourite candidates on the prairies were endorsed by Laurier. In July Winnipeg labour leaders had been invited to the convention of the prairie Liberals, and, although they did not attend, they were not displeased with the results.[86] By September Laurier realized that the Manitoba Liberals would be forced to 'prepare outside the official organization,' and when he learned that labourites would run in the two Winnipeg ridings, he suggested that his supporters co-operate with them.[87] When the Liberal leader issued his election manifesto, which contained several planks sympathetic to trade unionists, labour acceptance of the proffered help was assured. Fred Dixon told Laurier, 'your opposition to Conscription has encouraged many radicals who had begun to fear that democracy was doomed in Canada.'[88]

The alliance between labourites and Liberals was a marriage of convenience. Laurier's supporters were trying to conduct an election campaign with the remnants of a shattered organization, and they were compelled to capitalize on all opportunities. Winnipeg radicals, for their part, accepted the advantages of Laurier's support and some of the responsibilities. *The Voice* was the only Winnipeg paper to give the Liberal leader a good press, and when he visited the city it printed his speech in full. At the same time, however, the labour candidates realized that it was necessary for them to maintain their independence;

The Voice declared, 'Rigg and Ward do not propose or promise to follow Laurier blindly in the event of his being returned to power.'[89] But such disclaimers did not prevent the SPC from repudiating the labourites for their connection with the Liberals; nor did the disclaimers prevent the *Free Press* from branding Rigg and Ward 'sugar-coated Laurierites.'[90]

Labour's campaign in Winnipeg focused on conscription. Rigg declared, 'I regard human life as the supremely sacred thing and believe that if the state had adopted the policy of the conscription of money, industry and natural resources, there would be absolutely no necessity for the passing and enforcing of any scheme to conscript men.' He demanded the nationalization of 'the natural resources and the essential industries of the country' and a referendum on conscription. Ward warned that workers were compelled to vote against Borden because industrial conscription would be imposed immediately after a Union victory.[91] *The Voice* concentrated on inflation, publicizing the increase in the cost of various items. Puttee charged that the Conservatives had allowed prices to rise 'to swell the bloated purses of profiteers still larger.'[92] The labourites also attempted to appeal to class consciousness. *The Voice* described Rigg as a 'champion of Real Democracy and the rights of the common people' and told workers that they had 'a fight on their hands' to prevent Canada from becoming 'a helpless prey to the piracy of the big capitalists.'[93]

The Unionist campaign skilfully exploited the basic weakness of the radical movement – the workers' lack of class solidarity. Only 'socialists of the Marxian type' were opposed to Borden. Responsible trade unionists favoured a vigorous prosecution of the war, for, as the *Free Press* often noted, 'Mr. Gompers is an out and out win-the-war man.' To convey the impression that the place of patriotic workers was beside Borden, the Unionists employed men long associated with the labour movement in their campaign. The most prominent of these was Salem Bland, who advised workers that the government's war policy offered labour the 'opportunity to throw itself heart and soul into this great struggle for democracy.' There can be no doubt that Bland, whose stature among workers was great, did much to draw moderate trade unionists away from the labour candidates. In response to the appeal to class feeling, M.R. Blake, Unionist candidate in Winnipeg North, declared that there were 'only two classes of voters in this election – loyal and disloyal.' Some speakers charged that supporters of Rigg and Ward were 'anarchists and aliens.'[94] Such tactics caused a worried Puttee to assure readers that Rigg and Ward were completely loyal and to claim that 'Labor is doing its part and will continue to voluntarily do its share.'[95]

All seventeen labourite and socialist candidates were defeated on December 17; the radicals' most ambitious political campaign was a disaster. The only constituencies in which they made respectable showings were those that contained coal fields. Radicals attributed this defeat in large part to the War Time Elections Act. Although the legislation probably had relatively little effect on the outcome of the campaign, the conviction that it did was important. The *Federationist* described the act as 'an achievement beyond compare, an achievement so atrocious, so contemptible, so low, so mean, so vile, so execrable, so repugnant to every principle and concept of common decency, as to preclude the possibility of meeting with the approval of any decent, clean-thinking and well-meaning person in the land.'[96] There can be no doubt about the basic cause of the radical candidates' poor showing. The majority of workers were not prepared to abandon the old parties and vote as a class. Indeed in 1917 this persistent condition was reinforced by the war which convinced many that solidarity must be subordinated to patriotism. The *Federationist* pointed out that less than 3,800 of Vancouver's 10,000 trade unionists had voted for the three radical candidates contesting city ridings. In commenting on the election results Puttee offered the essential analysis: 'Labor must become class conscious before any political success will be ours.'[97]

But perhaps the defeat was more significant than victory could have been. Deteriorating real wages and the spectre of postwar unemployment had alarmed and embittered many workers. Their resentment was compounded by what they perceived as discriminatory government war policies. Thus, even though the majority of workers still refused to abandon the old parties, the popular reaction against registration and conscription clearly demonstrated widespread discontent. In addition substantially different reactions to the federal prosecution of the war had produced a re-emergence of the basic dichotomy in the Canadian labour movement. Western workers would no longer be restrained by the TLC. In September the BCFL convention had decided to employ constitutional means in its campaign to gain recognition for the labour movement in Canadian wartime society and to resort to a general strike only if political initiatives failed. These had now failed. After the 1917 general election radicals would turn increasingly to direct action as a means to gain their objectives. As economic burdens became heavier and class tensions heightened, workers began to listen more readily to this propaganda. Within nine months of the election there were strikes of semi-general proportions in Winnipeg and Vancouver. During the election campaign the *Federationist* made an observation which was to prove prophetic: 'if the constitutional opportunities afforded to press forward the demands of democracy and progress are not seized upon and profited by, the time will come when resort to more deadly and destructive weapons will be made imperative.'[98]

8

Western radicals and the Great War: the second phase

For the western Canadian radical movement, 1918 and the early months of 1919 represented a continuation of the first phase of the war in that the workers' militancy increased to unprecedented levels. The period was also a separate phase because revolutionaries redirected the militancy. Workers were profoundly disturbed by the continuing deterioration in real wages and by the fear - after November the reality - of unemployment. Workers clung to the conviction that they had sacrificed more and suffered more as a result of the war than any other class in society. The trend of rapidly rising union membership persisted during 1918 when the number of organized workers in Canada jumped 21 per cent. Conscious of this increased numerical strength and determined to capitalize on a tight labour market, workers across the West fought for higher wages and improved conditions, unmindful of patriotic appeals. Militancy was also manifested in an unusual solidarity. Beginning in the spring western workers demonstrated an increasing propensity to call general strikes to support beleaguered brothers and to protest encroachments on traditional rights. The penchant for direct action demonstrated a redistribution of power within the radical movement. During the second phase of the war revolutionaries became steadily more influential. Frustrated by the debacle of the general election and inspired by the Russian revolution, they launched a campaign for a militant industrial union which would destroy capitalism.

The militancy of the workers and the avowed aspirations of the revolutionaries ensured that during this turbulent year middle and upper class Canadians and provincial and federal governments would view the western radical movement with fear and alarm. After four years of tremendous tension, it was not difficult to equate opposition to national priorities with incipient treason and to perceive activities that hampered the war effort as the work of an enemy conspiracy. Policemen and politicians, citizens and soldiers associated radicals with enemy aliens; those who counselled actions inconsistent with the nation's values were not regarded as part of Canadian society.

Continuing preoccupations contributed to the workers' militancy. The Mathers commission, established by Borden to inquire into the basis of labour unrest, considered 'the haunting fear of unemployment,' the principal cause.[1] Inflation was probably more important, especially ever-rising food prices. During 1918 the cost of the Department of Labour's 'basket' of staple foods increased 13.5 per cent. Labour leaders and trades councils across the West repeatedly denounced the federal government's failure to control prices. Workers continued to believe they were being victimized by profiteers.[2] The labour movement also continued to fear federal manpower policies. In April the cabinet proclaimed the so-called 'Anti-Loafing Law,' which required all adult males to be engaged in useful work. Then in June the Labour Department initiated a national inventory of manpower. And in October an order-in-council made strikes illegal in a large number of industries; violators of the law were to be drafted. It was hardly difficult for workers to perceive a systematic attack on their unions and a steady push to industrial conscription. The *Federationist* stormed, 'from the time these emissaries of the parasitic class stole the seats at Ottawa they have gradually tightened the screws until today the workers have no rights but are weighed down with everything but iron shackles.'[3]

The operation of the Military Service Act, also contributed to western labour militancy in the last year of the war. Workers continued to resent compulsory military service; to them the draft was anti-democratic. Large numbers of workers applied for exemptions, but radical labour leaders claimed that these applications were routinely rejected.[4] Western workers protested vigorously whenever the Military Service Act affected them directly. At times these protests were violent. Loggers rioted at Big River, Saskatchewan, when military authorities arrived to collect draftees. And Vancouver dockworkers struck when an army policeman challenged a stevedore who was not carrying his registration papers.[5] Some workers literally took to the woods to avoid induction into the army; rag-tag colonies of draft evaders grew up on Vancouver Island, British Columbia's lower mainland, and on the Indian reservations of southeastern Manitoba.[6] In August one of these draft evaders, Ginger Goodwin, a member of the SPC and a leader of the miners' union, was murdered by a Dominion police officer. The western labour movement was outraged.[7]

Radicals took up the cause of conscientious objectors, many of whom had no connection with the labour movement. The *Federationist* complained that under the Military Service Act 'our very thoughts are rationed.' Calgary trade unionists protested what they regarded as unduly harsh sentences imposed by magistrates on conscientious objectors. But the issue caused the greatest excitement in Winnipeg. When, late in January, it was reported that conscientious objectors were being mistreated at Minto Barracks, Fred Dixon protested in the provincial Legislature. William Ivens, a former Methodist minister who was becoming important in the city's radical movement, told a federal cabinet minister that these men should not be treated as 'inhuman fiends worthy of slow torture even unto death.' Anger turned to outrage late in February when David Wells, a carpenter who had refused induction, died in Stony Mountain Penitentiary.[8]

In addition to the burdens of war, a new force agitated western workers – the Russian revolution. Like most Canadians, they had greeted news of the fall of the Romanovs, long regarded as the epitome of oppression, with enthusiasm. As the revolution developed in Russia, the sympathy and approval of radicals increased. In July 1917, *The Messenger* of Victoria observed, 'the Russian situation is all right. The Russian people are displaying marvelous self-control and intelligence. They know what they want and through their council and their Peasants' Congress they are making perfectly plain that they are going to get it.'[9] It was natural, therefore, that events in Russia, even before November 1917, should be held up by radicals as worthy of emulation by Canadian workers. A miner lectured, 'during no revolution that has yet occurred in human history has the red flag of labor been so completely in evidence. ... The supreme command appears to be in the hands of the workers and others who are disciples of democracy and warriors of the social revolution.' For this reason the workers of Petrograd had 'a message of hope' for their comrades in Canada.[10]

During 1917 enthusiasm was tempered by the preoccupation with the anti-conscription fight and, to an extent, by the mechanistic doctrines of the SPC. Initially some socialists considered the struggle in Russia simply another bourgeois revolution. Kingsley, though now out of the party, explained, 'the modern proletariat ... has not yet become a sufficiently powerful factor in the [Russian] state to ensure that the new order shall be dominantly impressed with its aspirations and ideals.' Although events in Russia were encouraging in that they were moving the proletariat towards emancipation, the historical juncture for the inauguration of the co-operative commonwealth had not arrived.[11]

From the very beginning of the revolution in Russia, however, Ukrainian social democrats gave the movement their unqualified support. The collapse of the Romanov dynasty spelled the end of the oppression from which many of them had fled, and the party to which they had belonged was co-operating with the Russian socialists.[12] During the summer of 1917 Ukrainian social democrats were in direct contact with revolutionaries in the Ukraine, and *Robochy Narod* promoted their cause by publishing appeals for funds.[13] A resolution endorsed by a Ukrainian SDP convention held in Winnipeg a few days after the czar's abdication demonstrated the party's attitude: 'We ... extend fraternal greetings to the Russian worker-revolutionaries on the brilliant victory of the revolution over autocratic tsarism and on the downfall of the prison house of nations, which will doubtless bring freedom also to the 30-million strong Ukrainian nation. We are convinced that our Russian comrades will not stop at the changes of the political system of Russia achieved at present but will carry the battle forward to the complete victory of the working people over all their enemies.'[14]

The Bolshevik coup in November 1917 had a profound effect on the western radical movement. It was not, however, the basic departure in the history of Canadian radicalism which Communist historians have claimed. Buck asserts that 'the effect of the [coup] had been like a thunder-clap'; and this seems a valid, if perhaps overstated, characterization. But what other Communists have claimed about Canadian reaction in the months after November 1917 is much more subject to criticism. No workers paraded the streets of western cities to celebrate the news, as Weir claims. Few indeed must have been the miraculous conversions to Communism like the one Smith experienced. Lenin was not the prophet of the new militancy, as Bennett asserts; indeed the Russian revolutionary's theoretical work was virtually unknown in Canada.[15]

Still, there can be no doubt that the Bolshevik coup was a source of inspiration for western Canadian radicals. A handful of obscure revolutionaries had led the workers to power. Labourites, social democrats, Wobblies, and socialists considered this victory the most important event in European working class history since the Paris Commune. They rushed to follow the Bolshevik lead. W.J. Curry, an erudite Vancouver dentist and ardent social democrat, described the coup as 'the greatest single event of this century and probably of all history.' From his death-bed McKenzie wrote, 'the end [of capitalism] is here. ... It is worth three incarnations to live now, better the coming five years than any other full three score and ten.'[16]

After November 1917, Ukrainian social democrats were even more outspoken in their praise of the Russian revolutionaries. In its first issue after the coup *Robochy Narod* declared that the Bolsheviks represented the hope of the international proletariat. Yet, paradoxically, the paper's support of the Bolsheviks grew mainly out of the conviction that they would ensure self-determination for the Ukraine.[17] Following the lead of its powerful Ukrainian language federation, the SDP considered the Bolsheviks a source of hope, and a party convention held at Winnipeg in March 1918 sent greeting to the Soviets.[18] Even the SPC was caught up in the excitement generated by the Bolshevik victory. Though reservations persisted in the party about the possibility of a true proletarian revolution occurring in an economically backward country, these were not pressed in the face of what appeared to be the fulfilment of more important aspects of Marx's teachings. The dominion executive gravely informed the Petrograd Soviet that, after four months of carefully observing its operations, 'we have yet to note an error of tactics or a violation of revolutionary working class principles' – high praise, indeed, from the impossiblists.[19]

In addition to intellectuals, editors, and party leaders, workers across the West were aroused by the Bolsheviks. A labourer from Winnipeg's north end wrote, 'equal rights for men and women, no child labor, no poverty, misery and degradation, no prostitution, no mortgages on farms, no revolting bills for machinery to keep peasants poor till the grave, no sweatshops, no long hours of heavy toil for a meagre existence but an equal opportunity for all, a life made worth living with unlimited possibilities to all, aided by splendid machinery to make [the] earth a real paradise where nothing but happiness can prevail ... this is Bolshevism.'[20] Such zeal increased as the year advanced. By the end of 1918 many workers had become enthralled by events in Russia and sought to learn everything possible about the Bolshevik experiment. Propaganda explaining the soviet system was in great demand. For example, a member of the SPC from Coleman, Alberta, reported, 'in the mine ... the sole topic of conversation both going in and coming out is socialism and Bolshevism.'[21]

The importance of the revolution for radicals was demonstrated by their uses of the Russian experience. In 1918 radicals began to invoke the Bolsheviks to legitimatize their movement. Kingsley justified renewed political initiatives, because 'the blood now courses through [the workers'] veins with new life and they are experiencing thrills of joy and hope, that were unknown to them before the rainbow of promise appeared upon the Russian horizon above the red clouds of ruling class savagery and bloody war.' Even Puttee was prepared to summon up the Russian example when he launched a campaign to establish a new labour party.[22] In March 1918, social democrats renewed their attempts at reconciliation with the SPC and proposed a union 'on the basis of the Bolsheviki programme.' But the impossiblists were no less willing to invoke the new force in support of old policies. When a few SPC locals responded favourably to the SDP initiatives, Chris Stephenson, who had replaced Pritchard as dominion secretary, reminded them that Lenin and Trotsky had denounced socialists who failed to keep rigidly the revolutionary faith.[23] Some radicals rushed to become Bolsheviks. The new self-concept required very little adjustment for members of the SPC and Ukrainian social democrats who had always perceived themselves as the revolutionary vanguard. In 1918 and early 1919 they styled themselves 'Bolsheviks' or 'Reds' and discussed the formation of 'soviets' and 'soldiers and workers councils.'

In part, the Russian revolution represented hope because it held out the promise of peace. Radicals, who were never able to forget their grinding war-weariness, celebrated the Bolshevik coup because they believed that the new government would immediately conclude an armistice. When peace talks began between the Soviet government and the Central Powers, *Robochy Narod* urged the Allies to join them. Lenin's insistence that a treaty be concluded, despite the extravagant demands of the German and Austrian ambassadors, won him the *Federationist*'s nomination for the 1918 Nobel Peace Prize. While the Canadian government and public generally regarded Trotsky's signing of the Treaty of Brest-Litovsk, by which the Soviets concluded peace with the Central Powers, as an act of supreme treachery, radicals considered it the epitome of statesmanship and humanitarianism.[24]

The Bolshevik revolution held a greater promise for radicals, the promise of a fundamental reconstruction of society. In essence hope was the immediate product of the Russian workers' victory. A logger, who had become discouraged after a decade of defeats in the socialist movement, explained, 'the Bolsheviki have rekindled all my old enthusiasm and given me fresh confidence in my class.'[25] Regarded as the natural outcome of the war, the Russian revolution revived and strengthened the conviction that in the European holocaust would be forged the forces which would effect the final emancipation of the proletariat. Forces unleashed by the war had brought down the Romanovs. As these same forces seemed to bear revolution westward, even to Canada, it was not difficult for radicals to believe that the Bolshevik coup had only been the beginning of the time which Marx had taught would come.

In an attempt to capitalize upon the workers' militancy, some radicals began a campaign to establish new labour parties during 1918. In January the BCFL convention called for the formation of a broadly based workers' party, and delegates established the Federated Labor Party (FLP). In March, Puttee and Manitoba's TLC executive fashioned a Winnipeg local of the Dominion Labor Party (DLP). Edmonton trade unionist were politically active during the year, and at the beginning of 1919 the Alberta Federation of Labor began establishing DLP locals in the province.[26] In Alberta and Saskatchewan these parties were composed mainly of labourites, but in British Columbia and Winnipeg, where the radical movement was much more heterogeneous, the parties included an unusually wide spectrum of radical opinion. The FLP contained former members of the SPC such as Kingsley, Pettipiece, and McVety, old social democrats such as Burns, and reformers such as Woodsworth.[27] The Winnipeg DLP was led by Puttee and Harry Veitch, labourites, Fred Tipping, a social democrat, and Fred Dixon, a reformer. Such men constituted an extraordinarily able leadership cadre. The labour parties which emerged in these months were truly a product of the times. The burdens of war and the example of the Russian revolution had made many workers determined to effect significant changes in Canadian life. Recognizing this will, leaders of the labour parties fashioned unusually radical programs.[28]

During 1918 a more vital force in the radical movement was a significant revival of syndicalism. After the prewar agitation, syndicalist propaganda had persisted; consequently the campaign of 1918 and 1919 demonstrated the influence of American Wobblies, British militants, and BC impossiblists. The tendency was also characterized by the conventional imperative of employing more effective tactics. For the revolutionaries who were giving it direction, this new syndicalism represented the most explicit and complete rejection of political action yet made in western Canada. Their attitude grew directly out of the frustrating and bitter experience of the 1917 general election. In 1917 the revolutionaries had chosen to employ constitutional means in their campaign against conscription. But, by passing the War Time Elections Act, an autocratic government had destroyed the democratic process. If the proletariat was to be emancipated, the revolutionaries were obliged to adopt new tactics. The significance of the election was dramatized by the modification in Bill Pritchard's views. In October 1917, he was vehemently upholding the SPC's conventional political line in the pages of the *Clarion*, but by mid-1918 he had become an advocate of direct action. He was not alone. In Winnipeg Bob Russell and Dick Johns regularly insisted that efforts to elect representatives to capitalist legislatures were 'all wrong.'[29] The revolutionaries were also inspired by the One Big Union in Australia, the shop-stewards movement in Britain, and, most important, the Russian revolution. Lenin had used direct action. Would not similar tactics be effective in Canada? After contrasting the dramatic victory of the Bolsheviks with the dismal defeats of Canadian socialists, an Alberta miner concluded 'we want to be using some Russian methods – resolutions don't get us anywhere.'[30]

At the head of the syndicalist tendency was a group of tough-minded, capable young revolutionaries. Some were Jews and Ukrainians who had been trained in the SDP and were now driven by a new zeal.[31] Others, more important for the mainstream of the labour movement, were the second-generation leaders of the SPC, who had been initially inspired by syndicalism in the prewar agitation. Although the party maintained an ambivalent attitude to the syndicalist tendency, some of its most energetic members took a leading role in promoting the new doctrine. While this campaign might seem to constitute a major departure from the SPC line, the change was not as great as might at first appear. Since the years immediately before the war, the party had assigned to the general strike a political role but had persistently claimed that in a state with a liberal franchise the ballot was a superior weapon. Now to many party members the electoral process had failed, and they were prepared to turn to direct action to achieve the revolution. Their essentially simple doctrine, though not fully understood, appealed to a great many workers, and during 1918 they gained real power in the western labour movement. Joe Naylor promoted direct action in the executive councils of the BCFL, and Ernie Winch conducted the same campaign as president of the Vancouver trades council. Joe Knight and Carl Berg, a Wobblie who had joined the SPC, agitated for syndicalism in Edmonton. In Winnipeg, Russell and Johns achieved real power in the trades council. [32]

But if some impossiblists and other revolutionaries advocated direct action as a means of destroying capitalism, it is clear that they had not developed a clear-cut syndicalist doctrine. Indeed, their thought was characterized by a remarkable lack of precision. Walter Head, a miner and member of the SPC, was an exponent of the general strike, yet he applauded the formation of the FLP. [33] A similar fuzziness was typical of the thought of Fred Fix, an influential syndicalist theoretician who had been a member of De Leon's IWW. Although he was an untiring advocate of revolutionary industrial unionism, Fix was apparently never certain what the object of the 'One Great Union' would be. In what was his most important statement on the subject, a speech to the Winnipeg trades council supporting an industrial union resolution prior to the 1918 TLC convention, he assigned to the union a role ancillary to a political party in the class struggle. But then he claimed for it the role of achieving 'a final solution of the Labor problem.' [34] This lack of precision did not prevent workers from responding to the syndicalist propaganda; indeed, the fuzziness may well have promoted the tendency. It seems clear that, while the advocates of direct action were coming to consider the general strike as a political weapon, the workers continued to perceive it as an economic one.

Better than anything else, the willingness to resort to general strikes, almost on the slightest pretext, demonstrated the workers' militancy and the revolutionaries' influence. By the summer of 1918 western trades councils were prepared to issue strike calls whenever they believed the rights of workers were threatened, and the rank and file was ready to 'down tools' in response. During these months, the issue of the general strike was continually before the Vancouver trades council. Led by members of the SPC, Vancouver unionists threatened to declare general strikes in support of a handful of striking laundry girls, workers fired for refusing to purchase Victory Bonds, and striking street railwaymen. Jack Kavanagh had the council's constitution amended to permit collection of a special strike fund, because the times demanded that the workers adopt 'new methods.' [35] The sense of solidarity was not confined to Vancouver. In July trades councils from Victoria to Winnipeg threatened to call out their members unless the federal government met the wage demands of striking postal employees.[36] In October the order-in-council prohibiting strikes produced a similar response.[37]

Workers staged general strikes during the summer of 1918. The first occurred in Winnipeg. Firemen, telephone operators, street railwaymen, teamsters, typographers, freight-handlers, and railroad workers walked out in support of striking civic employees. Winnipeg's economy was disrupted. Alarmed citizens demanded federal intervention, and Senator Gideon Robertson negotiated a settlement which was a clear-cut victory for the civic workers.[38] The Winnipeg fight involved conventional trade union issues; a general strike which took place in Vancouver was purely political. It was a protest against the murder of Ginger Goodwin. On August 2 the great majority of trade unionists refused to work, and the city's economy ground to a halt.[39]

Moderates were on the defensive in those heady summer months. In Vancouver James McVety became isolated in the trades council because he opposed the indiscriminate use of the general strike.[40] More dramatic was the humiliation of Arthur Puttee. While he had worked for a settlement in the civic strike, the editor denounced the new tactics as 'I.W.W. methods.' The criticism offended the trades council, and his old enemies in the SPC led a successful campaign against Puttee and his newspaper. The trades council established the *Western Labor News* and named Ivens, who was sympathetic to the revolutionaries, editor.[41] The power of the most prominent labourite and one of the most effective critics of the SPC in the West had been broken.

As the influence of the moderates declined, the power of the revolutionaries increased. The revolutionaries were exhilerated by the results of the general strikes. Arthur Wells, an editor of the *Federationist*, who was flirting with syndicalism, observed, 'the sympathetic response of thousands of unionists to the call of their striking brothers to come to their aid by also striking is one of the most significant phases of the present situation. It ... shows that the spirit of class solidarity is gaining strength among the workers and affords a most cheering augury for the future.'[42] Certainly the implications of the first general strikes in western Canada were lost on neither the workers nor the revolutionaries. In Winnipeg the workers' determination to defend their fellows had demonstrated that the tactic was effective in fights over bread-and-butter issues. In Vancouver direct action was proven to be a viable form of political protest. By the end of summer workers and revolutionaries considered the general strike their most powerful weapon.

Associated with the syndicalist agitation was a revived commitment to industrial unionism. As they had in earlier industrial crises, western workers perceived the need to establish more powerful organizations. This imperative was demonstrated, for example, by the determination of Winnipeg metal workers to form bigger, stronger unions which could defeat large corporations supported by government.[43] Once again Marxists led the new industrial union campaign. In part they took this action for the conventional reason – because, in Pritchard's words, amalgamation was 'a logical outcome of the developing forces of capitalism.'[44] But the revolutionaries were also motivated by their new commitment to syndicalism, which, to be effective, demanded the formation of organizations through which the proletarian solidarity of the working class could be enforced. The crafts, informed by the reactionary principles of business unionism, could not serve this purpose; therefore they had to be discarded for militant industrial unions which could mobilize masses of workers.[45]

The campaign for industrial unionism was manifested, as it had been in previous rebellions, in attacks upon the power and structure of the internationals and the TLC. In the Crow's Nest Pass, district officers had for some time found it difficult to restrain the rank and file, and by mid-1918 several locals controlled by socialists and Wobblies were in full revolt against the internationals' win-the-war policy. Much the same was true on Vancouver Island. Walter Head condemned increased per capita taxes with which 'a bunch of reactionaries' were buying war bonds. He and Naylor advocated secession from the UMW and the formation of one big union of Canadian miners.[46] The condition of the TLC was a matter much discussed in the Winnipeg trades council in the summer of 1918. Hoop told his colleagues that it was 'a practically useless institution,' because its executive had become 'chloroformed' by the federal government. Encouraged by Johns, Russell, Fix, and others, the council determined to reconstitute the congress on a 'modern and scientific' basis. This was to be achieved through industrial organization. Condemning the craft system as 'organized scabbery,' the council called upon the TLC to lay the foundations for 'one union of all workers ... with the revolutionary goal [of] the taking over of the machinery of production in the interest of society.'[47] The Vancouver council, which had long since declared for industrial unionism, advocated the emasculation of the TLC by making it the creature of provincial federations. This innovation would ensure local autonomy and destroy the power of reactionary international bureaucrats.[48]

The campaign for industrial unionism naturally widened the sectional split which had been developing in the TLC since the outbreak of war. In fact during 1918 tension between East and West had increased because of congress war policies as well. When TLC officials began consulting and co-operating with the federal government, radical western labour leaders were angered. They were outraged when Samuel Gompers delivered a rousing win-the-war speech to Parliament in which he attacked the Bolsheviks as well as the Hun. Westerners believed congress bureaucrats had sold out. The *Federationist* charged, 'assault after assault and encroachment after encroachment has been made upon the Canadian workers by the tools of the dominant interests in the Dominion without an audible protest being heard from those appointed to watch the vulture roost at Ottawa.'[49]

At the Quebec convention the differences between the eastern and western labour movements were never more glaringly apparent. At no previous congress had debate been so bitter. One after another, radical resolutions from the West were defeated on sectional votes. Conscription, relief for conscientious objectors, industrial unionism, Allied intervention in Russia - the convention refused to act on any of these issues.[50] The committee on Officers' Report split for the first time in the congress's history. In a minority report Kavanagh, Russell, and an Alberta miner condemned the executive for its win-the-war policy and charged that Tom Moore, by accepting a seat on the National Registration Board, had 'placed the Trades and Labor Congress of Canada in the position of aiding and abetting the government of this country in curtailing those petty liberties which had been gained only by struggle and sacrifice on the part of those workers who have preceded us.' The eastern majority dutifully upheld the executive.[51] The westerners' defeat was climaxed in the vitally important election of officers. Tom Moore defeated James Watters for the presidency. Even though they had criticized Watters, the westerners supported him because of his British Columbia background and one-time socialism. Moore, an easterner, close friend of Gompers, staunch craft unionist, and outspoken patriot, was despised by western radicals.[52]

The humiliation of the westerners at Quebec produced the deepest division that ever existed in the Canadian labour movement. Western resentment burned hotter because of the widespread conviction that the conservative East had triumphed as a result of machinations between the AFL, international bureaucrats, and the federal government. Western delegates caucused during the convention and decided to hold a meeting to devise a means 'to allow the western unions more clearly and firmly to present their views at the next convention of the Congress.' The westerners agreed that this aim could best be achieved by holding a regional labour conference. The decision did not indicate that a secessionist movement was underway in the autumn of 1918. The initial campaign for the Calgary convention emphasized national unity. In addition the composition of the organizing committee struck at Quebec demonstrated the relatively moderate aims of the majority of westerners at this point. Only Victor Midgley, the secretary, would later take a leading role in the One Big Union. The committee's two other prominent members, David Rees, the West's TLC vice-president, and Ernie Robinson, secretary of the Winnipeg trades council, were labourites who opposed militant industrial unionism.[53] But the final crisis of the war years was to put the revolutionaries in temporary control of the western labour movement, and, as a result, they were able to disrupt the TLC.

Western Canada's middle and upper class feared and resented the workers' militancy. It was unpatriotic. Businessmen and editors denounced strikers as criminals and traitors. During major disputes, such as the general strikes in Winnipeg and Vancouver, committees composed of affluent citizens maintained services abandoned by workers. At times citizens' committees went further. During a strike of Calgary freight-handlers, such a group demanded that 'the men on strike be arrested, placed in Khaki and sent to some point east.'[54] Generally the federal government came under tremendous pressure to curb the workers' militancy and break the power of the radicals.

During the first half of 1918 the war was central to the federal government's policy on radicals. This preoccupation was demonstrated by the investigation of the IWW. Alarmed by the new militancy of their workers, businessmen in Alberta and British Columbia claimed that the western economy was being disrupted by the sinister machinations of the Wobblies. The secretary of the Mountain Lumber Manufacturers' Association, for example, informed Borden that loggers were 'very restless,' as a result of IWW propaganda; if the government were to suppress this agitation, 'we would get 50% more efficiency out of [the workers].'[55] Borden took these charges seriously. Aware of the growing syndicalist tendency, his advisers told him that Wobblies were 'attempting to spread sedition and foment industrial unrest' in the West.[56] Alarm at what was perceived as an IWW menace became confused with the long-standing fear of enemy conspiracies against the war effort. Eugene Fiset, the deputy minister of militia, had 'no doubt whatever' that the Wobblies were 'subsidized by enemy agents.'[57] This confusion is not difficult to understand. Exaggerated accounts of IWW doctrines and activities portrayed them to be completely opposed to the values for which most Canadians believed their country was fighting, and in the charged atmosphere of 1918 dissent was easily construed as treason. In addition, federal officials knew that before the war Wobblies had organized the itinerant eastern European labourers who now, as enemy aliens, embodied the fear of German subversion. Any behaviour among eastern Europeans which was not wholly consistent with Canada's war policy was suspected of being the work of German agents acting through Wobblies. At the end of February Borden told his justice minister, Charles Doherty, that 'I think it exceedingly important that no delay whatever should take place in the investigation of the activities of the I.W.W. in Canada.'[58]

The Dominion Police established a special IWW section which was reinforced by private detectives, immigration agents, and provincial policemen.[59] Investigation tended to reinforce the official association of European immigrants with syndicalism. A few Ukrainian locals of the SDP in Alberta had reasonably close relations with IWW headquarters in Chicago, but secret agents discovered nothing sinister. Intercepted correspondence indicated that the IWW was pleased with the 'good' progress it was making among unskilled workers on the coast, particularly Finns. And RNWMP agents who joined the UMW's Drumheller local encountered a number of Wobblies; the fiery Italian miners boasted that they would have their way or shut down every pit in the country.[60]

Security officials were divided in their evaluation of these findings. Sir Percy Sherwood, commissioner of Dominion Police, did not consider IWW propaganda an important dimension of western militancy. Most of his colleagues disagreed with this analysis. Military intelligence officers in particular urged the government to take a hard line with the IWW and radicals in general. Fiset told E.L. Newcombe, the deputy minister of justice, 'it seems highly desirable that ... prompt measures be taken to crush [the IWW] before it has an opportunity to become fully developed.'[61] Borden's government followed the advice of the hard-liners.

In May the prime minister commissioned C.H. Cahan, a Montreal lawyer, to make a study of radicalism.[62] This step was of fundamental importance, because policies based on Cahan's perception of radicalism were an important factor contributing to the war-end industrial crisis. Instead of viewing labour militancy as the product of German intrigues, he considered it part of a Bolshevik conspiracy. Canadian citizens and officials had been apprehensive about Bolshevism since the beginning of the year, but, in their minds, it had represented a menace ancillary and complementary to that of the enemy. Now, in the last months of the war, Cahan told Borden and his colleagues that Bolshevism was the enemy. Germans did not cease to be feared, but Russians came to be feared as much. Cahan's perception of radicalism was not unique or even original. What is significant about his views is that he encouraged attitudes already developing and led the government to a perception of radicalism which justified the continuation of repressive measures after the war.

Fear of Bolsheviks was the theme of the report which Cahan submitted to the Justice Department in mid-September. 'The Russians, Ukrainians and Finns, who are employed in the mines, factories and other industries in Canada are now being thoroughly saturated with the Socialistic doctrines which have been proclaimed by the Bolsheviki faction of Russia,' he began. Not only did aliens remain the embodiment of the menace, but Cahan gave additional continuity to government fears by implicating the IWW in the Bolshevik conspiracy. Wobblies had prepared the eastern Europeans for revolutionary doctrines, and now there was reason to suspect that IWW organizers had actually been trained in Russia. Cahan believed that it was 'absolutely necessary for the preservation of peace and good order in Canada that [Bolshevik] propaganda should be strictly supervised and controlled.' Therefore, he recommended that Russians, Finns, and Ukrainians be subject to the same regulations as nationals of the Central Powers. 'The Bolsheviki,' he said with ominous simplicity, 'are enemy aliens.' In addition, Cahan recommended the adoption of a much more stringent government security policy. He told Doherty that a number of eastern European radical organizations should be suppressed, that revolutionary propaganda in 'foreign' languages should be prohibited, and that the right of search should be 'widely extended.' Finally, Cahan recommended the establishment of a Directorate of Public Safety to co-ordinate all security operations. [36]

During the first half of 1918, before Allied policy towards Lenin's regime was fully formulated, the Canadian government had been reluctant to take any decisive action against those who were perceived as

Bolsheviks, particularly eastern Europeans, for fear of antagonizing Russia. But now, after the invasion of Russia, there were no such compunctions.[64] Cahan's report, Borden told Doherty, demanded 'immediate and vigorous action.'[65]

In mid-September the Justice Department ordered the Canada Registration Board to make new, more stringent, enemy ordinances applicable to Russians, Finns, and Ukrainians, and the deputy minister of justice suggested that 'perhaps there should be some further special regulations affecting them.'[66] Then, on September 28, Borden's government issued PC2384. The order declared unlawful fourteen radical organizations, the advocacy of violent revolution and meetings held in the languages of countries with which Canada was at war, or Russian, Ukrainian, and Finnish. Most of the organizations suppressed were tiny sects, but the IWW, the SDP, and the Ukrainian Social Democratic Federation, which the government mistakenly believed was a separate party, came under the ban. At the end of the month Cahan was named director of public safety.[67]

Now radicals were regarded with the same official fear as enemy aliens had been since the beginning of the war. Reports in the files of the various security agencies indicate that many radical organizations, certainly all of the large ones, had agents planted in them to search out Bolshevism. Similarly the files demonstrate that the mail of radicals was systematically searched. This practice was a matter of real concern to Chris Stephenson, the dominion secretary of the SPC. He denounced the 'tin horn Bismarcks' who were opening his letters and disrupting the party's propaganda.[68] Western radicals were also profoundly disturbed by raids and arrests of radicals – Naylor and a friend on Vancouver Island, an SPC organizer in the Kootenays, Mrs. Joe Knight in Winnipeg, and a dilettante Wobblie in Saskatoon. 'The time has gone by when the workers ... would sit quiet and allow their fellow workers to be railroaded either over the line or to jail,' warned the Clarion's last edition.[69]

Radicals were most concerned about the censorship of their press. For some time the chief press censor had believed that the Western Clarion and Robochy Narod, the two most revolutionary journals in the West, violated guidelines of conduct issued by his office and warned the editors, Chris Stephenson and Mathew Popovich, that their papers could be suppressed. In May military intelligence officers raided the editorial offices of the Clarion.[70] Stephenson and Popovich defied Chambers' warning and continued to publish revolutionary propaganda, which tended to focus on events in Russia. By mid-summer the press censor was convinced that both papers must be suppressed. Chambers believed that *Robochy Narod* was at the centre of 'a distinct and well organized revolutionary Bolsheviki movement in Canada looking to the overthrow of all established authority and to the introduction into Canada of the chaotic condition of affairs which exists today in Russia.'[71] After PC2384 was issued the federal government prohibited the publication of *Robochy Narod* and the *Western Clarion*.[72]

The press censor was no less concerned about the editorial policies of the *Federationist* and the *Western Labor News*. Security officials were alarmed by the journals' flamboyant propaganda because 'it does not represent the views of the Anglo-Saxon Labour classes.' As militancy increased, the federal government came under increasing public pressure to suppress the two papers. For example, one of Ivens's former Methodist colleagues told Chambers that the editor of the *Western Labor News* 'is the cause of much of the Labor trouble in [Winnipeg] and the West.'[73] In the early autumn Chambers warned Ivens and the directors of the *Federationist* that, unless they restricted pacifist and revolutionary articles, their papers would be outlawed. Anxious to maintain their propaganda, the radicals nominally accepted these restrictions.[74] But in the autumn of 1918 it was impossible for any western radical paper to improve, so far as security officials were concerned. Chambers continued to receive complaints that the *Federationist* and the *Western Labor News* were publishing Bolshevik propaganda. Virtually every federal security agency recommended the suppression of the two papers. The government did not act. In the charged atmosphere of the last months of 1918, Borden and his colleagues were reluctant to risk a confrontation with the Winnipeg trades council and the British Columbia Federation of Labor.[75]

Radicals expected restrictions on civil liberties to end with the end of the war. During October they protested arrests, raids, and censorship, but in an unusually restrained manner probably because they were reluctant to incur prosecution. By mid-autumn Canadians generally believed the war would soon be over. Radicals waited. But, because of the federal government's official attitude to Bolshevism, their expectation that civil liberties would be restored after the armistice was not fulfilled. Indeed censorship became more stringent. In a most provocative move, Chambers proscribed all the publications of Charles H.

Kerr and Company of Chicago, the main source of propaganda literature for the western radical movement.[76] After the middle of November, radicals' protests against the restriction of civil liberties became
noisy and threatening. 'During the past four years ... the master class
has never lost an opportunity to cripple the mentality of the slave and
to rivet the chains of serfdom more firmly on his limbs; the government of Canada is the most autocratic in the Empire and the most ig-
norànt on the planet,' charged the *Federationist*. It went on to warn
that unless Borden and his colleagues showed 'some glimmer of sanity,
we are likely to have serious trouble.'[77]

Now radicals launched a counter-attack. The campaign was led by
members of the SPC who were convinced that civil liberties must be
restored if the movement were to survive. Russell told Stephenson 'it
is up to us to use every weapon we can lay hands on to offset the dirty attempts to put us under.'[78] In part radicals were determined to
counter-attack because they recognized that workers bitterly resented
the orders-in-council and realized that a fight would increase their
militancy even more. Kavanagh introduced a resolution in the Vancouver trades council declaring that the workers would 'use every
available weapon' to end censorship; it passed unanimously. Across
the West workers' meetings denounced the restriction of civil liberties;
from tiny locals in mining camps and powerful central bodies such as
the Alberta Federation of Labor, protests went to Ottawa. The storm
reached its height late in December at the great rallies at the Walker
Theatre in Winnipeg and the Empress Theatre in Vancouver. At the
Vancouver meeting, Pritchard was cheered when he pledged, 'we will
say what we like; we will think what we like and we will write what
we like in our own interests.'[79] This was precisely what radicals did.
In the first weeks of 1919 impossiblists defiantly founded five journals across the West. With cause, Chambers regarded the foundation
of these papers as a direct challenge to the federal government's program of press censorship.[80] But the new journals were only one dimension of the radical counter-attack. Led by the revolutionaries, the
trades council in Victoria, Vancouver, Regina, and Winnipeg and the
Alberta Federation of Labor threatened general strikes to force the
federal government to restore civil liberties.[81]

Radicals were also outraged by Canadian participation in the Siberian expedition. Their exhilaration over the Bolshevik victory increased
in the chaotic months at the end of the war. Radical journals seemed
to publish every favourable account of the new order in Russia; this

was especially true of new papers, such as *The Red Flag* of Vancouver and *The Soviet* of Edmonton, the columns of which were devoted almost exclusively to accounts of the Bolsheviks' good works. Part of the campaign in support of Lenin and his comrades took the form of minimizing or dismissing accounts of revolutionary atrocities. For example, Kingsley told a Victoria audience, 'I don't care what the Bolsheviks are doing to ... the capitalistic gang and the bourgeoisie, if they shoot every land baron and every general without an army, ... not one person would have lost his life compared to the thousands who lost theirs under the Czar.'[82]

Radicals considered the Bolsheviks the sovereign authority in Russia, and intervention was, therefore, nothing more than international brigandage. The expedition was an imperialistic adventure; in its last issue the *Clarion* charged that the invasion demonstrated 'the insatiable hunger on the part of enterprising capitalists to make profitable investments and to exploit undeveloped territories and backward people.' More important, French, British, American, and Canadian troops were in Siberia to destroy the revolution before it could spread – 'gendarmes of the Counter Revolution,' *The Red Flag* called them.[83] This purpose was intolerable. The revolution marked 'the inception of the new order in Russia based on industrial democracy,' lectured the *Federationist*, and 'the workers in Russia should be allowed to work out their own salvation according to the methods they thought most advantageous.'[84] The Alberta Federation of Labor, the Victoria trades council, and the meetings at the Walker and Empress theatres demanded the withdrawal of Canadian troops.[85] The campaign against the Siberian expedition went beyond passing resolutions. Radicals attempted to disrupt the loading of munitions in Vancouver and to encourage troops committed to the operation to desert. But, although these activities caused the government concern, they were unsuccessful.[86]

Opposition to the Siberian expedition dramatized the radicals' conviction that the Bolsheviks were heralds of a new order and that their revolution had to be protected, as an example to other workers. The hope, renewed by the Bolshevik coup, that the war would spark a global revolution burst forth after November 1918. In addition to events in Russia, radicals were stirred by revolution in Germany, incipient rebellion in Australia, and political unrest in Britain. With the end of the war workers had entered a new phase of their history; the great crusade for democracy, instead of having ended, had begun.

Marxists were exhilarated by the conviction that the historical juncture for the revolution was imminent; Arthur Wells announced, 'in this age and generation it has been decreed by all the economic forces on the planet that the working class shall henceforth be the only class in human society, that the useless element shall be transformed from parasites into producers.' Labourites were inspired by a less cosmic faith, their belief in the workers' inherent good sense which would ensure a new humane order in which men were of supreme worth. [87]

As more and more men lost their jobs, as veterans returned to swell the ranks of the unemployed, as postwar economic chaos grew, a consensus emerged that a restoration of prewar society was inconceivable. Radicals demanded a new order, not a reconstruction of the old. 'Reconstruct a system of wage-slavery! Perpetuate your class bondage! Make the world safe for mansions and shacks, for private parks and slums, for millionaires and paupers, for $10,000 poodles and underfed children!' stormed Joe Knight. But even the manifesto of the Saskatoon DLP could declare, ' "Reorganization" rather than "reconstruction" of society is essential. There must be ... something new.' [88]

If there was agreement that society must be reorganized, there was disagreement on the extent of change and the means whereby it was to be achieved. Revolutionaries advocated destruction of the wage system by direct action. Labourites adhered to their faith that major reforms in society could be affected through the political process. A power struggle developed. Labourites fought revolutionaries for control of the labour movement. For example, the Winnipeg trades council was the scene of bitter conflict between Russell and Johns and members of the DLP, such as Ernie Robinson and James Winning. [89] The mood of the workers was such that most were inclined to embrace the more radical doctrine. The victories in the summer of 1918 had demonstrated the effectiveness of the general strike. Ironically the revolutionaries' influence in the labour movement was also increased by the federal government's anti-Bolshevik policy. When their federation was outlawed and their newspaper was banned, the Ukrainian social democrats' propaganda was disrupted; in order to gain other means of access and communication, they closed ranks with the largely British labour movement. Inspired by the Bolsheviks, the Ukrainian social democrats were natural allies for the members of the SPC who were advocating syndicalism. [90] The revolutionaries were never able to dominate the entire western labour movement. Though influential, they were held in check by labourites in Saskatoon, Regina, and Edmonton. But by the beginning of 1919 the revolutionaries had gained control of District 18, the miners' unions of Vancouver Island, and the trades councils in Winnipeg and Vancouver. When in January Russell boasted 'we are fast knocking hell out of the Labor Party,' he might well have been describing conditions in all key centres of the western labour movement. [91]

From their place of power the revolutionaries launched a crusade to convert the labour movement to the gospel of militant industrial unionism. Using his position as secretary of the western conference committee, Midgley, with the assistance of Russell and Johns in Winnipeg, Burg and Knight in Edmonton, and Kavanagh, Naylor, Pritchard, Wells, and Winch in British Columbia, worked to win a syndicalist victory at the Calgary conference. Immediately he returned from the TLC convention, Midgley inaugurated the campaign. [92] It had two purposes. One was to break the power of labourites in important western centres. [93] The second purpose was to 'pack' the conference with 'reds.' By January Knight felt able to express the hope that 'we might be able to turn it into an S.P. Convention.' [94]

The effects of the campaign became apparent early in the new year. The results of the mid-January convention of the Alberta Federation of Labor delighted the revolutionaries. As chairman of the resolutions committee, Knight submitted and saw passed a number of radical motions, several of which were parachuted into the convention by the Vancouver trades council. The two most important resolutions called for the establishment of one big union and for the creation of machinery for the effective prosecution of general strikes. [95] In February delegates to District 18's annual convention took a similar line. After condemning the Siberian expedition and press censorship, they endorsed militant industrial unionism. [96] At the March convention of the BCFL, Pritchard and Kavanagh led the syndicalist attack on craft unionism and political action; both revolutionaries emphasized the workers' need to adopt new tactics in their struggle against capitalism. Although members of FLP were prepared to accept the validity of industrial unionism, they insisted that the workers must also continue their fight on the political field. The convention went overwhelmingly for militant industrial unionism, however, by advocating an organization 'to embrace all the workers' which could enforce its demands through direct action. [97]

The Western Labour Conference, held in Calgary in March, was the forum in which western workers expressed their anger, frustration, and bitterness. Dominated and directed by the revolutionaries, it was the most radial convention ever held in western Canada. It was also the swan song of the Socialist Party of Canada; Calgary would be the last western conference controlled by the brilliant revolutionaries of that organization. The first order of business, submitted by the Resolutions Committee which was chaired by Kavanagh, called for 'the abolition of the present system of production for profit.' This resolution was passed unanimously and without debate. The convention then sent 'fraternal greetings to the Russian Soviet government, the Spartacans in Germany and all definite working class movements in Europe and the world.'[98] Familiar grievances were rehearsed. Delegates passed resolutions demanding the cessation of censorship, the release of political prisoners, and the withdrawal of troops from Siberia; they threatened a general strike on June 1 if their demands were not met.[99]

The most important aspect of the convention, however, was the triumph of militant industrial unionism. The West's sense of alienation from the TLC was even greater in March 1919 than it had been in the previous October. In this atmosphere the convention easily passed a BCFL resolution, calling for a referendum on the proposition that western unions bolt the internationals and form 'an industrial organization of all workers.'[100] Then the convention unanimously endorsed a resolution, introduced by Kavanagh and seconded by Pritchard, urging the workers to abandon the practice of 'lobbying parliament for palliatives which do not palliate' and to enforce their demands 'by virtue of their industrial strength.' The syndicalist tendency which had been developing since the general election of 1917 was made explicit when the convention voted to table an Alberta Federation of Labor resolution, which recommended 'a homogenous political party' for the working class. Kavanagh expressed the new revolutionary gospel when he told the delegates, 'any time the workers imagine they can emancipate themselves through the gas houses of this or any country, they have another think coming.' But the revolutionaries were members of the SPC, and they were unable to escape entirely the political indoctrination of their party. They did not declare the general strike the only means whereby the revolution could be achieved. Indeed the exact function of the general strike in the class struggle was ambiguous. Kavanagh recalled the SPC's earliest considerations of direct action when he defended the general strike with the claim that 'any act taken by a class in defence of its own interests is political action.'[101] The climax of the conference came when Johns, chairman of the Policy Committee, introduced a series of seven resolutions which set out the machinery by which the One Big Union (OBU) would be organized.[102] It would unify all workers in a single union which could achieve its purposes, economic or political, through general strikes. The OBU was to be the embodiment of proletarian solidarity.

The labourites did not put up a strenuous fight against the revolutionaries at Calgary. The only vocal opponents of the syndicalist tendency were a handful of obscure delegates from Alberta, where a commitment to political action remained strong. None of the prominent Winnipeg labourites was even at the conference. And members of the FLP, such as David Rees, James McVety, and William Trotter, who had fought the revolutionaries at the BCFL convention remained silent at Calgary. Although convinced that direct action would ultimately prove disastrous, labourites were apparently impressed by the enthusiastic response of a large and representative convention to militant industrial unionism, and they allowed the revolutionaries to lead the western labour movement, for a time.

The Calgary conference gave the revolutionaries the responsibility of establishing the OBU; the central organizing committee comprised Pritchard, Knight, Johns, Midgley, and Naylor. With Vancouver as the centre of operations, they launched an energetic and effective propaganda campaign. The committee distributed ballots on the questions of secession and the June 1 general strike, solicited funds, circulated literature, staged rallies in western cities, and despatched agitators, notably Knight and Naylor, to mining camps. 'The old-fashioned and obsolete craft union ... has outlined its usefulness,' proclaimed the *One Big Union Bulletin*; 'by organizing the workers according to the industry in which they work ... it becomes possible to get united action at any time along any line condusive to those workers' welfare.'[103]

In areas that had traditionally been important to the radical movement, workers massed under the OBU's red banner. The *British Columbia Federationist* informed unionists affiliated with the BCFL that the Calgary conference had brought 'the organized labor movement into line with the development of capitalistic society and made preparation to form an organization that would be of use during the transition period from capitalism to a system of production for use instead of for profit.' The trades councils in Vancouver and Victoria voted overwhelmingly to endorse the OBU and to contribute funds to the central organizing committee. A similar response came from loggers, who were flooding into an OBU union directed by Pritchard, and from the miners on Vancouver Island and in the Kootenays.[104] In District 18 coal miners enthusiastically joined in the western rebellion against the internationals, and within weeks of the Calgary convention, the District Executive Board agreed 'to fall in line with the One Big Union.'[105] In Winnipeg the *Western Labor News* promoted the cause of the OBU, and the trades council provided financial support for the organizational campaign. The enthusiastic response of the city's workers to OBU propaganda convinced Russell that 'Winnipeg is solid for [the] Industrial Union.'[106]

There was opposition to the campaign for militant industrial unionism. In Edmonton labourites and craft unionists united and within weeks of the Calgary convention initiated an offensive which left the revolutionaries reeling. The *Edmonton Free Press*, apparently established to counteract OBU propaganda, indulged in a red-baiting campaign which would have been worthy of any Citizen's Committee. Late in April the trades council purged affiliates which had declared for the OBU, a move which was heartily applauded by TLC leaders.[107] Nor did labourites retire from the field even in the most radical centres. In District 18 Rees led a fight to preserve the UMW. In Vancouver McVety led members of the FLP and supporters of the internationals in a fight to cripple the secessionist movement and to prevent the OBU gaining control of union funds.[108]

The opposition was largely ineffective. Militant industrial unionism was too compelling for the majority of workers engaged by the apparently simple concept that a great industrial union could control the economy and, if necessary, the state. Highly skilled and highly paid craft unionists tended to remain aloof from the rebellion. Similarly the relatively conservative workers in Alberta and Saskatchewan cities tended to be loyal to the TLC. In the referendum at Calgary the vote went against secession 840 to 724. By May the locations of the most substantial support for the OBU were clear. The 5100 members of the UMW in Alberta voted overwhelmingly to join the rebellion. British Columbia's 5500 organized loggers endorsed militant industrial unionism by a ratio of nine to one. But the phenomenon was not restricted to the usual centres of revolutionary propaganda. The fragmentary data available indicate that Winnipeg workers voted overwhelmingly in favour of secession from the TLC. Three out of four Vancouver trade unionists endorsed the OBU, swelling its following by some 10,200 men and women, probably about 75 per cent of the city's organized workers.[109] As spring passed into a long hot summer, the western labour movement's most extensive and radical rebellion against craft unionism and the eastern-dominated TLC was fully under way.

By the beginning of 1919 the workers' militancy and the radicals rhetoric caused the uneasiness felt by many Canadians as a result of long years of war and revolution in Europe to turn to alarm. Canada experienced a red scare. Western newspapers published lurid accounts of, what the Winnipeg *Free Press* called, the 'orgy of cruelty and bestiality' in Russia and uncritical reports of radical activities in the United States, such as the Seattle general strike.[110] Many employers, who were confronted by the militant labour movement, were convinced that it was led by men who were 'permeated with ... socialistic and anarchistic theories.'[111] All radicals were perceived by the middle and upper classes as violent revolutionaries, as Bolsheviks; it became necessary, therefore, to suppress them. The federal government received warnings and expressions of concern from across the West. A Vancouver clergyman told the press censor, 'Bolshevism is something we may have to reckon with in this City before long.'[112]

Some affluent citizens now engaged in, or more often encouraged, direct attacks on radicals. Since the general election campaign of 1917 citizens' and veterans' groups had been threatening violent repression of pacificists and strikers. Now these groups began an active campaign against the radical movement. Perceiving radicals as enemy aliens and encouraged by employers, returned men, with too much time on their hands, became the shock troops in the battle to preserve Canadian society. Veterans led by officers and aided by business and civic leaders disrupted radical meetings in Victoria, Vancouver, Edmonton, and Calgary.

The worst violence flared in Winnipeg. Prominent citizens' traditional fears of north end immigrants had increased during the war, and now these heightened anxieties were compounded by the radicalization of the labour movement. Military intelligence officers learned that 'a select body of men' was forming a vigilante organization which would carry out the 'systematic kidnapping of the leading Socialists [and make] liberal use of tar and feathers.'[113] Prominent Winnipegers urged veterans to save the city. On January 26 a mob of returned men prevented the SPC from holding a memorial service for Karl Liebnecht and Rosa Luxemburg. In the two days of rioting that followed, soldiers attacked companies employing Europeans, beat suspected enemy aliens in the streets, and sacked the German Club. Radicals felt their wrath, too. Veterans hunted Sam Blumenberg throughout the north end and wrecked his wife's dry cleaning shop. At SPC headquarters, the mob threw records and literature from the windows, beat suspected socialists (who were promptly arrested by watching police) and then, lighting the party's red flags, paraded the streets as they burned.[114] Winnipeg's dailies, and the middle and upper class opinion which they represented, applauded the veterans' rampage.

Instead of being disturbed by the lawless behaviour of some veterans, federal officials were clearly relieved and gratified. For some time the security agencies had feared that the returned men would be radicalized, and when they appeared to come out against the so-called Bolsheviks, Ottawa's anxieties were allayed. The willingness of government officials, including Borden,[115] to permit and even encourage vigilantes to harass and coerce radicals demonstrated that the latter were regarded as outlaws, in the classic sense of the term. Because they aimed to destroy society, it was legitimate for society to protect itself by whatever means it could, even to the extent of putting radicals beyond the protection of the law. 'I am firmly convinced,' Chambers told John Bayne Maclean, the publisher, 'that, [unless] the real solid sensible people of the country take into their own hands the active combating of this Bolshevist propaganda, we run the risk of reaching, within measurable time, the conditions which at present prevail in Russia.'[116]

By the beginning of 1919 the security agencies were convinced that a revolution was imminent in the West. In part they reached this conclusion because of the unrest among the workers and the fiery pronouncements of the radicals. But federal officials were also persuaded that the western ferment was in part a conspiracy hatched in Moscow. Cahan, for example, believed that he could trace the spate of resolutions denouncing the orders-in-council and the Siberian expedition to a circular issued late in November by the dominion executive of the SPC and then back to sinister forces in Chicago, financed, according to the United States Department of Justice, by the Bolsheviks. 'Never before in our political history has the Government of one country inaugurated so widespread and persistent a propaganda to bring about internal revolution in an enemy country as that which is now being carried on in the United States and Canada,' Cahan told the minister of justice.[117] The RNWMP and the military prepared to suppress revolution in western Canada. For the first time the Mounted Police moved into British Columbia, and the commissioner instructed his officers to infiltrate the province's radical movement. The army conducted an inventory of troops in western Canada, and the chief of the General Staff ordered his commanders to develop contingency plans for the outbreak of civil disorder.[118]

Although members of the federal cabinet were alarmed by developments in western Canada after the end of the war, they initially rejected their security adviser's recommendations to step up the attack on radicals. The ministers feared that increased repression would produce more unrest. The Western Labor Conference changed this attitude. In the opinion of government members, the revolutionaries' victory seemed to vindicate the security officials' worst fears. After the Calgary conference the adjutant general of the Canadian Army told a brother officer that 'the Government has "got the wind up" properly over the unrest in [the West].'[119] This condition was best demonstrated when the cabinet requested that Borden, who was in Paris, arrange to have a British cruiser call at Victoria and Vancouver. His colleagues informed the prime minister that 'Bolshevism has made great progress among the workers. ... Plans are being laid [in British Columbia] for revolutionary movement.' The presence of a British warship and its crew would have a 'steadying influence' on the workers. Borden rejected the proposal, because he regarded the rebellion as a purely domestic matter in which British forces should have no part.[120] Although the cruiser was never dispatched, the incident demonstrated the government's state of mind. Members of the federal cabinet now believed that the OBU crusade was an incipient revolution. In the event of any insurgency by workers, all the powers of the state would be used to smash the radical challenge.

At the end of the Great War many Canadians recognized a need for social change, but generally this necessity was construed as no more than reform. Few Canadians were committed to a fundamental reconstruction of society. Middle and upper class citizens – and the federal government which continued to protect their interests – were determined to conserve the constituted order, and they feared that workers were no less determined to effect change on the Russian scale. Considering the tragic experience of four war years, the revolutionary ferment in Europe and the extraordinary militancy of the working class, the Red Scare is understandable. To perceive a conspiracy in the campaign to 'pack' the Calgary Conference hardly requires paranoia. Revolutionaries persistently proclaimed their intention to destroy industrial capitalism, and by preparing to stop them, the federal government was only taking them at their word.

Western workers manifested a unique mentality. During 1918, in addition to the social realities of war, new preoccupations substantially compounded their discontent. Most workers were outraged by the suspension of civil liberties which they believed was intended to deprive them of all constitutional means of protest. And many were captivated by the dramatic events in Russia, a fascination which increased as the year advanced. By the early months of 1919 workers in western Canada had developed a greater degree of class consciousness than they had ever manifested in the past, or would in the future. Their mood was such that the power of labourites had steadily eroded. Early in 1918 the advocates of reform and political action had been able to establish vigorous labour parties; by early 1919 the labourites had been swept aside by the tide of militant industrial unionism. The apparent simplicity of syndicalism appealed to workers. They understood the structure and nature of unions, and the proposition that mass strikes, by men and women organized in one big union, could force major concessions from corporations and the state by totally disrupting the economy seemed valid. Experience taught them that only the most limited and gradual amelioration could be achieved through political action. But victories in 1918 persuaded workers that general strikes were expeditious and effective. Because they insisted on immediate change, workers embraced militant industrial unionism and transferred the leadership of their movement to the doctrine's advocates. The Western Labour Conference consummated the revolutionaries' victory. At Calgary two radical tendencies fused. Industrial unionism, to which workers had been committed for some time, became the vehicle for the socialist transformation of society. Never had revolutionaries possessed more potential power. Most of the workers who joined the rebellion against craft unions, callous employers, and an oppressive state did not intend to destroy capitalism. The revolutionaries who founded the One Big Union did.

Western Canadian society was polarized.

9

Epilogue

Winnipeg was the centre of the industrial crisis which shook the nation in the early summer of 1919. On May 15 the city's economy was paralyzed by a general strike. United by a common sense of grievance at economic hardship and political repression, some 25,000 men and women struck in sympathy with the embattled workers of the city's building and metal trades.[1] The basic issue in the general strike was the metal workers' demand for collective bargaining. Because of their recent experience and because of the revolutionaries' propaganda, the workers were confident that their massive strength would inevitably defeat the employers and force them to recognize unions. But the general strike had another objective which was only vaguely formulated and partially articulated. The *Western Labor News* persistently emphasized that the workers were fighting for 'A Living Wage.' Victory would result in power on the job but also power to eliminate burdensome social and economic conditions. 'The worker must get a more equitable share of the wealth of the world,' James Winning, president of the trades council, told a meeting of the Labour Church, 'and this strike [has] already demonstrated the ability of the worker to get his, if he would consolidate his forces. Withdraw your labour power from the machine ... and at once profits cease.'[2]

The tremendous solidarity which had been developing among workers since the end of 1917 caused thousands to rally in support of their Winnipeg comrades. The trades councils in Brandon, Calgary, Vancouver, and Victoria issued circulars calling for general strikes in sympathy with the Winnipeg workers. The challenge of the ruling class to the basic principle of collective bargaining was 'a national question,' declared the *Federationist*.[3] The radical centres of the region, those

areas where support for the OBU was strongest, responded enthusiastically to the calls for sympathetic strikes. In District 18 a walkout was
already under way, but the miners made it clear that they supported
the Winnipeg workers. Early in June almost 10,000 workers in Vancouver struck, and later in the month they were joined by trade unionists in other BC cities and by interior loggers. Even relatively conservative trade unionists joined the fight. Sporadic strikes flared in
Saskatchewan. And workers in Calgary and Edmonton staged sympathetic strikes, despite opposition by leading craft unionists. This
great sympathetic response across the West was, in Joe Knight's opinion, a 'living demonstration of the solidarity of labor.'[4]

Although the general strikes were non-violent, they became the focus of popular and official fears about Bolshevism. Middle and upper
class westerners believed the strikes to be an incipient revolution. And
they resolved to fight the red menace to the finish. The federal government aligned itself completely with the middle and upper classes.
Borden and his colleagues were convinced that the strikes were the
product of a revolutionary conspiracy, the first campaign of the One
Big Union. The prime minister considered the OBU a syndicalist organization, which would attempt to restructure society by the use of
general strikes.[5] Consequently the federal government was determined
to smash the revolutionaries and their industrial union.

No evidence exists to link the Winnipeg general strike directly to
the emerging OBU, and the historians who have studied the sympathetic
strikes agree that the basic issue was, indeed, collective bargaining.
Nonetheless both the OBU and the general strikes were manifestations
of a single pattern of militancy. Certainly the revolutionaries perceived a critical relationship between their emerging organization and
events in Winnipeg. Johns believed that, if the solidarity of the western working class won the fight, the success of the OBU would be assured.[6] Many western radicals had long since declared themselves Bolsheviks. For a year security officials had been telling Borden and his
colleagues that Bolsheviks were hatching a revolutionary conspiracy
in the West, and during the early months of 1919 the flamboyant
rhetoric of the OBU campaign had appeared to confirm these claims.
How many times had Knight or Naylor or Kavanagh or Russell announced that the wage system would be destroyed by a general strike?
The federal government, and many other Canadians, had grounds for
fearing that a revolution was beginning in Winnipeg.

Winnipeg was the key. There the strikes had begun; there the largest number of workers were out; and there dislocation was greatest. Consequently, the major effort to disrupt the rebellion had to be made in the city. 'Winnipeg is fighting the fight for the whole of Western Canada,' said the commissioner of the RNWMP.[7] Municipal and provincial authorities adopted a hard line with the strikers, but the federal government led the fight. Gideon Robertson attempted to create the first break in the strikers' solidarity by driving postal employees back to work. The minister of labour also intervened in mediation efforts to ensure an award unfavourable to the metal workers. And the army and the RNWMP made massive preparations to combat insurrection. By the beginning of June, Borden and his colleagues decided to take more direct action to end the general strikes. On June 6 the House of Commons quickly passed an amendment to the Immigration Act which allowed for the deportation of British-born immigrants. Four days later Parliament approved amendments to the Criminal Code which broadened the definition of sedition. Federal authorities in the city were now better armed to deal the strike a lethal blow.

Almost from the time the crisis began, there had been calls for the arrest of strike leaders, and late in May the Justice Department's agents in Winnipeg had begun preparing cases against men such as Ivens. On June 17 six strike leaders, including Russell and Ivens, and two OBU propagandists, Johns and Pritchard, were arrested by the RNWMP. The arrests were a shattering blow to the already faltering resistance of the workers. Deprived of their most vigorous leaders, they staggered through the riots of Bloody Saturday and capitulated on June 26. The ruthless determination of the federal government to crush the OBU had intimidated the workers and broke their will to carry on the fight.

For Winnipeg workers the general strike was a complete failure. And their sense of defeat was transmitted to strikers in other western cities who began to drift back to work at the end of June. Across the West, but especially in Winnipeg and Vancouver, workers paid heavily for defeat. Triumphant employers established open shops and blacklists. In Winnipeg unions in the contract metal shops, where the general strike began, collapsed, and civic employees signed no-strike pledges. Men returning to work on the Vancouver docks were forced, literally, to tear up their union cards and sign 'yellow dog' contracts.

The campaign against the revolutionaries was not suspended after June 1919. In fact it intensified. Only OBU leaders were arrested in connection with the general strikes; craft unionists who had taken a leading role in the fight went unmolested by the RNWMP. Borden and his colleagues clearly staged the Winnipeg strike trials to disrupt and discredit the OBU. International craft unions joined the fight to smash the western rebellion. TLC organizers emphasized that the tactics advocated by the revolutionaries had been disastrous. For example, the *Edmonton Free Press* asserted that, as a result of the sympathetic strikes, 'organized labour has been led into a most uncomfortable position ... and may have sacrificed some prestige and confidence that required years in the building.'[8] Because employers and public officials perceived the TLC as the responsible and legitimate representative of labour, corporations and the state co-operated with the internationals. The most blatant collusion occurred in District 18 where support for the OBU was strong. The Western Coal Operators' Association granted large wage increases to the United Mine Workers, and the federal government passed an order-in-council requiring miners to join the international.[9]

The One Big Union was the principal victim of the repressive campaign. The OBU was officially established at a convention held at Calgary in mid-June 1919, a time when it was clear that the general strikes were failing. Gone was the revolutionary rhetoric which had characterized the conference held three months earlier in the same city. The preamble of the OBU's constitution was remarkably mild. It demonstrated that the union would concentrate on the economic needs of the workers and leave the class struggle in temporary abeyance. Initially the OBU made impressive gains. By the end of 1919 workers in the traditional radical centres had affiliated with the union, which claimed over 40,000 members.[10] But during 1920 the OBU began to collapse. Prosecution, then imprisonment, deprived the union of three of its most dynamic leaders: Russell, Johns, and Pritchard. The vigorous counter-attack of the TLC was even more damaging. Calgary, Edmonton, Regina, and Saskatoon remained bastions of craft unionism. BC workers surrendered to the internationals. And the power of the OBU was broken in Winnipeg. The One Big Union, the grandest expression of militant industrial unionism, soon became a caricature of the revolutionaries' ambitions.

Repression compounded ideological confusion among revolutionaries. The Social Democratic party, which never really recovered from proscription, disintegrated when members of its constituent federations took different roads to Utopia.[11] Ukrainians and Finns joined the emerging Communist movement, and British social democrats drifted into labour parties. The Socialist Party of Canada struggled unsuccessfully to resume operations which had been disrupted during and after the general strikes. Then a controversy over affiliation with the Third International began to rack the party. The SPC collapsed when a majority of party members became Communists. By the early twenties both of the prewar revolutionary parties were effectively dead.

But the institutional disarray of the revolutionary organizations was less important than the changed attitude of the workers. They were disillusioned by the outcome of the general strikes. The strikes were not engineered by the emerging OBU, and historians have demonstrated that the various strike committees were not dominated by revolutionaries. Nonetheless, the general strike was certainly the revolutionaries' tactic. For almost a year they had insisted that industrial unions prepared to stage mass strikes would be invincible. A significant proportion of the western labour movement accepted this proposition. In 1919 for the first time – and to a remarkable degree – revolutionaries forged a constituency which included not only workers in class-polarized British Columbia but also prairie cities. This phenomenon occurred, in part, because an extraordinary solidarity existed in the labour movement, in part, because revolutionaries abandoned their abstruse propaganda in favour of tactics which appeared feasible to workers. But the general strikes failed. The revolutionaries' tactics were unsound, their rhetoric hollow. Because they had never fully explored the implications of their syndicalism, the revolutionaries led the workers to disaster. The dimensions of defeat were such that they could not escape the consequences.

Before 1919 the appeal of revolutionary propaganda had been restricted because ordinarily few workers were sufficiently class conscious to be engaged by the vision of capitalism's destruction. Even coal miners and construction stiffs demanded programs related to the present. Generally men and women perceived ill-defined, futuristic utopias as less relevant than immediate relief from the ravages of industrial capitalism. Nonetheless the working class solidarity which had developed by early 1919 represented the greatest opportunity for significant social change ever to occur in Canada. And revolutionaries who despised the present failed to inaugurate a better future. The disaster did not create the workers' scepticism of millenial doctrines, but it certainly consummated that persuasion. The two radical tendencies which fused at Calgary were almost completely discredited. Workers turned their backs on militant industrial unionism and rejected revolutionary doctrines.

The outcome of the general strikes resolved the tension in the western radical movement and thereby ended its first phase. Labourites had been waiting in the wings since the Calgary conference, their organizations intact and their credibility unimpaired. No longer confronted with antagonistic tendencies as well as a hostile political system, labourism dominated western radicalism in the twenties.[12] There was, of course, real continuity - in personnel, in institutions, in character, and in doctrines - between the two phases of the movement separated by the events of 1919. Labourites built from their established constituency in prairie cities. The process of incorporating BC radicals into labour parties was substantially facilitated by the political tactics of the SPC. And the revolutionaries' propaganda helped to ensure that workers in British Columbia remained the most militant in the Canadian labour movement. Similarly rebels left a heritage. The massive state repression of the last industrial union crusade engraved into the collective memory of the working class a residual solidarity, a tradition labourites used to legitimize their every action.

In terms of constituency, tactics, and ideology, the predominant radical tendency represented the fulfilment of the philosophy which the reformers had advocated since the run of the century. Labourites acted on their conviction that the most effective political parties were inclusive, those that contained all progressive workers. Consequently their constituency was broad, incorporating men and women once divided by experience and ideology. Coal miners from Vancouver Island and trade unionists from Regina built parties with similar ideals. In Winnipeg middle class reformers whose critique of industrial capitalism was inspired by Henry George not Karl Marx worked shoulder to shoulder with former social democrats. The composition of these parties ensured that they would be gradualistic and pragmatic. Labourites sought election to municipal councils, provincial legislatures, and Parliament in order to campaign for reform. They never allowed their immediate political prospects to be impaired by some theoretical commitment to the co-operative commonwealth. In Vancouver, where impossiblism had once reigned supreme, the labour party fought for school lunches and free text books. During the twenties moderation became the hallmark of the workers' political movement. J.S. Woodsworth emerged as the region's most influential radical; his commitment to social change was derived from Methodism, not Marxism, and was significantly more temperate and humane than earlier western socialism.

Labourism passed the acid test of the pragmatic British tradition.[13] During the twenties workers dissatisfied with Canadian society sought reform by supporting labour parties, and those parties enjoyed greater political success than ever before. Saskatchewan labourites made a doctrine peculiarly well-suited to their relatively conservative constituency the foundation of working-class political action in the province. Through co-operation with farmers, the Dominion Labor party of Alberta, which had never really been inspired by the militancy of 1918 and 1919, achieved a vitality characteristic of no prewar organization. For the first time in two decades labourites, not revolutionaries, were the political representatives of BC workers. In Winnipeg the legacy of the general strike reinforced earlier traditions and established the north end as one of the safest radical seats in the nation. Labourites won municipal office in cities across the West. In elections held in each of the four provinces early in the decade, labour parties scored significant victories. And in 1921 workers in Calgary and Winnipeg sent William Irvine and J.S. Woodsworth to the House of Commons.

In any case labourism was politically appropriate to the twenties. The decade was one of relative quiescence for workers across the continent. For westerners this attitude was, in part, the result of sheer exhaustion. To sustain the militancy and solidarity of 1919 would have been impossible, and the decline was substantially accelerated by the bad beating workers had taken. More important the quiescence was a function of improved social conditions. In the most basic terms, workers enjoyed a higher standard of living; with the decline in immigration, real wages steadily increased during the decade. At the same time, the Great War, reconstruction, and popular unrest had resulted in a new social climate. Many Canadians refused to return to the heyday of predatory entrepreneurs and the *laissez-faire* state. They insisted upon reform, essentially increased state involvement in the economy to eliminate the harshest aspects of industrial capitalism and to guarantee certain minimum standards of life for all Canadians. Consequently during the twenties federal and provincial social policies mitigated the worst aspects of the Boom.

Not only were the objectives of labourism appropriate to the workers' quiescence, but they could be accommodated within the new social climate. Shared by men and women across the country, these aspirations became the source of a new social democratic movement that Woodsworth and his associates began to build in the late twenties. Labourites addressed themselves to deficiencies in society which were becoming increasingly apparent to Canadians. Yet labourism's tactics and ideology were not incompatible with the nation's orderly and moderate political culture.

Notes

CHAPTER 1

1 *Fifth Census of Canada* (1911), Vol. III, Table XI
2 M.C. Urquhart and K.A.H. Buckley, *Historical Statistics of Canada* (Toronto, 1965), 398 and 407; *Canadian Forestry Statistics, Revised 1959* (Ottawa, 1960), 32-3; and *Canadian Mineral Statistics 1886-1956* (Ottawa, 1957), 105-12
3 Quoted in Michael Bliss, *A Living Profit: Studies in the Social History of Canadian Business, 1883-1911* (Toronto, 1974), 15-16
4 Margaret A. Ormsby, *British Columbia: A History* (Toronto, 1964), 305-9; and Martin Robin, *The Rush for Spoils: The Company Province 1871-1933* (Toronto, 1972), 49-86
5 Quoted in Robin, *Rush for Spoils*, 85
6 J.M.S. Careless, 'Aspects of Urban Life in the West, 1870-1914,' in A.W. Rasporich and H.C. Klassen, eds, *Prairie Perspectives 2: Selected Papers of the Western Canadian Studies Conferences, 1970, 1971* (Toronto, 1973), 26 and 30; and A.F.J. Artibise, 'The Urban Development of Winnipeg, 1874-1914,' PHD thesis, University of British Columbia, 1971, 26
7 *The People's Voice*, June 16, 1894; and *The Voice*, May 19, 1899, and Jan. 5, 1900
8 *The Trade Unionist*, Sept., 1908; *Victoria Daily Colonist*, March 3, 1901; and Paul A. Phillips, *No Power Greater: A Century of Labour in British Columbia* (Vancouver, 1967), 28 and 41
9 *The Bond of Brotherhood*, June 5, 1903; and Lorne Thompson, 'The Rise of Labor Unionism in Alberta,' unpublished study, 1965, 77-88
10 W.J.C. Cherwinski, 'The Trade Union Movement in Saskatchewan,' PHD thesis, University of Alberta, 1972, 11

11 *The Voice*, Jan. 17, 1902
12 *The B.C. Workman*, July 22, 1899
13 Canada, *Sessional Papers*, 1904, Vol. XXXVIII, No. 13-36A, 'Evidence Taken Before the Royal Commission to Inquire into Industrial Disputes in the Province of British Columbia,' 240-6 and 411 and Phillips, *No Power Greater*, 7
14 *Western Clarion*, Oct. 6, 1906 and Oct. 13, 1906; and *Sessional Papers*, 1904, 'Evidence Royal Commission [on] BC,' 74-85 and 454
15 H.C. Pentland, 'A Study of the Changing Social, Economic and Political Background of the Canadian System of Industrial Relations,' prepared for Task Force on Labour Relations, 1968, 24-6
16 J.M.S. Careless, 'The Development of the Winnipeg Business Community, 1870-1890,' *Transactions of the Royal Society of Canada*, Series IV, Vol. VIII (1970), 240-54; and David Jay Bercuson, *Confrontation at Winnipeg: Labour, Industrial Relations and the General Strike* (Montreal, 1974), 51-2
17 Bercuson, *Confrontation at Winnipeg*, 9-21
18 *The Voice*, Aug. 4, 1911
19 British Columbia Provincial Library, Royal Commission on Labour, 1914, Typescript Proceedings, Vol. II, 12; and Public Archives of Canada [PAC], Laurier Papers, Vol. 543, Cameron to Laurier, Nov. 6, 1908
20 Edith Lorentsen and Evelyn Wollmer, 'Fifty Years of Labour Legislation in Canada,' in A.E. Kovacs, ed., *Readings in Canadian Labour Economics* (Toronto, 1961), 95-101; *The Voice*, Feb. 5, 1904; and H.F. Underhill, 'Labour Legislation in British Columbia,' PH D thesis, University of California at Berkeley, 1935, passim and 277
21 BC Royal Commission on Labour, Proceedings, Vol. III, 283, and Vol. I, 72-7
22 *The Voice*, June 18, 1908, and Feb. 6, 1914
23 Underhill, 'Labour Legislation in BC,' 26-42; C.J. McMillan, 'Trade Unionism in District 18, 1900-1925; A Case Study,' MBA thesis, University of Alberta, 1969, 79; and John Hedley, *The Labor Trouble in Nanaimo District* (NP, ND), 3-4
24 BC Royal Commission on Labour, Proceedings, Vol. II, 143-56
25 F.L. Hoffmann, 'Fatal Accidents in Coal Mining,' *Bulletin of the Bureau of Labour* (Washington, 1910), 658-9 and 671; and McMillan, 'Trade Unionism in District 18,' 79
26 *District Ledger*, Jan. 14, 1911; and BC Royal Commission on Labour, Proceedings, Vol. IV, 220
27 Donald Avery, 'Dominion Control over the Recruitment and Placement of Immigrant Industrial Workers in Canada, 1890-1918,' paper read to The Conference on Canadian Society in the Late Nineteenth Century, Montreal, 1975, 35

28 Laurier Papers, Vol. 186, Kirby to Blackstock, Jan. 31, 1901
29 *The Voice*, March 24, 1899; and Laurier Papers, Vol. 116, Mortimer to Laurier, June 23, 1899
30 *The Voice*, June 16, 1899; and McMillan, 'Trade Unionism in District 18,' 44
31 Phillips, *No Power Greater*, 162; H.K. Ralston, 'The 1900 Strike of Fraser River Sockeye Salmon Fishermen,' MA thesis, University of British Columbia, 1965, 134-41; and *The Western Wage-earner*, May, 1910
32 *Western Socialist*, Jan. 24, 1903
33 Laurier Papers, Vol. 470, Sivertz to Laurier, July 29, 1907
34 *The Voice*, Aug. 3, 1906
35 Ibid., Oct. 18, 1907
36 *The Bond of Brotherhood*, Nov. 14, 1903; *The Trade Unionist*, April, 1908; and *The Voice*, Aug. 4, 1899
37 BC Royal Commission on Labour, Proceedings, Vol. I, 157
38 Pentland, 'Changing Social, Economic and Political Background of Industrial Relations,' 72; S.M. Jamieson, *Times of Trouble: Labour Unrest and Industrial Conflict in Canada, 1900-66* (Ottawa, 1968), 66; H.D. Woods and S. Ostry, *Labour Policy and Labour Economics in Canada* (Toronto, 1962), 398-400; and Harry Sutcliffe and Paul Phillips, 'Real Wages and the Winnipeg General Strike: An Empirical Investigation,' unpublished study, 9
39 *The Bond of Brotherhood*, June 19, 1903; *The Voice*, March 8, 1907; and *British Columbia Federationist*, Nov. 22, 1912
40 *Solidarity*, March 22, 1913; and PAC, Frontier College Papers, Vol. 17, Graham to Fitzpatrick, Sept. 17, 1913
41 Edmund Bradwin, *The Bunkhouse Man* (2nd ed.; Toronto, 1972), 63-75; Frontier College Papers, Vol. 14, Perry to Fitzpatrick, 1912; and *The Evening Empire*, Aug. 24, 1912
42 BC Royal Commission on Labour, Proceedings, Vol. VII, 53; and BC, Provincial Board of Health, *Fourteenth Annual Report* (1912), 12-13; *Sixteenth Annual Report* (1914), 6; and *Eighteenth Annual Report* (1915), 9-12
43 Public Archives of British Columbia [PABC], BC Provincial Police Records, Superintendent's Incoming Correspondence, Tete Juane Cache, File 21, Beyts to Campbell, July 31, 1912; and W. Lacey Amy, 'Snaring the Bohunk,' *The Railroad and Current Mechanics*, XVII (May, 1913), 279-84
44 *District Ledger*, June 25, 1910; and *Industrial Worker*, Feb. 15, 1912
45 *District Ledger*, April 22, 1911
46 BC Royal Commission on Labour, Proceedings, Vol. IV, 132-46
47 *Canada Year Book 1932* (Ottawa, 1932), 103
48 A.F.J. Artibise, 'An Urban Environment: The Process of Growth in Winnipeg 1874-1914,' *Historical Papers*, 1972, 119-24; and Artibise, 'Urban Development of Winnipeg,' 338-61

49 *The Voice*, June 9, 1911
50 *The Bond of Brotherhood*, Jan. 9, 1904; and *The Voice*, Dec. 24, 1897
51 Mancur Olson, 'Rapid Growth as a Destabilizing Force,' *Journal of Economic History*, XXIII (1962), 530-1
52 *Industrial Union Bulletin*, Nov. 23, 1907
53 *Sessional Papers*, 1904, 'Evidence Royal Commission [on] BC,' 131
54 *The Voice*, Aug. 2, 1907

CHAPTER 2

1 No attempt is made here to discuss pre-socialist political initiatives; for a detailed account see T.R. Loosmore, 'The British Columbia Labor Movement and Political Action, 1879-1906,' MA thesis, University of British Columbia, 1954, 19-87
2 *The B.C. Workman*, July 1, 1899; and Paul W. Fox, 'Early Socialism in Canada,' in J.H. Aitchison, ed., *The Political Process in Canada* (Toronto, 1963), 81-2
3 W.A. Pritchard to the author, Feb. 24, 1972; Interview with Pritchard, Aug. 16-18, 1971; and *Western Clarion*, Jan. 12, 1907
4 *Appeal to Reason*, July 29, 1899; and October 20, 1900; and Canada Dept. of Labour Library, R.C. Clute, 'Royal Commission on Mining Conditions in British Columbia,' (typescript, 1899), Appendix D
5 *Appeal to Reason*, March 31, 1900. For Wayland see Howard H. Quint, 'Julius Augustus Wayland, Pioneer Socialist Propagandist,' *Mississippi Valley Historical Review*, XXXV (1949), 585-606
6 William Bennett, *Builders of British Columbia* (Vancouver, ND), 38-9; University of British Columbia, Special Collections Division, Vancouver Trades and Labor Council Minutes, June 2, 1896; and July 16, 1897; and Paul Phillips, *No Power Greater: A Century of Labour in British Columbia* (Vancouver, 1967), 31. For Debs see Ray Ginger, *The Bending Cross* (New Brunswick, NJ, 1949).
7 *Appeal to Reason*, June 4, 1898; and June 18, 1898
8 Ibid., Sept. 17, 1898; and State Historical Society of Wisconsin, Socialist Labor Party of America Papers, National Executive, Incoming Correspondence, Moore to Kuhn, Sept. 29, 1898; and Bennett, *Builders of British Columbia*, 135
9 *The People*, Jan. 1, 1899; and Nov. 12, 1899
10 Ibid., April 9, 1899; and November 12, 1899
11 D.K. McKee, 'Daniel De Leon: A Reappraisal,' *Labor History*, I (Fall, 1960), 264-97; and Charles M. White, 'The Socialist Labor Party, 1890-1903,' PHD thesis, University of Southern California, 1959, passim

12 *The People*, Feb. 19, 1899; May 7, 1899; Nov. 12, 1899; and June 30, 1900
13 SLP Papers, Socialist Trades and Labour Alliance, Local No. 250, Vancouver, Minutes, June 4, 1899; and *The People*, April 9, 1899
14 SLP Papers, Vancouver STLA, Minutes, July 26, 1899; Aug. 9, 1899; Aug. 16, 1899; and Sept. 27, 1899
15 Ibid., Feb. 25, 1900; and *The People*, March 4, 1900
16 *The People*, Jan. 28, 1900
17 Bennett, *Builders of British Columbia*, 137
18 *The People*, Sept. 17, 1899; and Oct. 15, 1899; and *The Daily News-Advertiser*, May 15, 1900
19 *Citizen and Country*, Dec. 2, 1899; *Appeal to Reason*, Feb. 3, 1900; and *The People*, May 20, 1900
20 *The People*, May 20, 1900
21 This view is well supported by contemporary opinion; for example Ernest Burns and Frank Rogers, who took part in these events, believed that the USLP was a 'Kangaroo' party. (University of British Columbia, Special Collections Division, Angus McInnes Collection, Vol. 53-1, interview with Ernest Burns and *The Daily News-Advertiser*, May 15, 1900)
22 *Citizen and Country*, July 13, 1900; and *The Independent*, July 7, 1900
23 *Citizen and Country*, July 13, 1900
24 Bennett (*Builders of British Columbia*, 137) claimed that McClain was the first socialist to contest a Canadian election; in fact the SLP had nominated candidates earlier in Ontario.
25 *The Independent*, May 26, 1900; June 2, 1900; and June 9, 1900
26 *Citizen and Country*, June 15, 1900
27 *The People*, July 14, 1900
28 *The Independent*, June 16, 1900; and *Appeal to Reason*, June 30, 1900
29 *The Coming Nation*, May 27, 1899; *Citizen and Country*, July 8, 1899; and *The People*, Nov. 12, 1899
30 *Appeal to Reason*, Jan. 28, 1899; *The Coming Nation*, May 27, 1899; and *The People*, Nov. 12, 1899
31 *Citizen and Country*, March 11, 1899; and May 6, 1899
32 Ibid., Feb. 2, 1900
33 University of British Columbia, Special Collections Division, International Union of Mine, Mill and Smelter Workers' Records, Vol. 157, Kelly to Shilland, Aug. 21, 1901; and *Citizen and Country*, May 13, 1899; April 6, 1900; and May 4, 1900
34 *Citizen and Country*, Dec. 2, 1899
35 Mine, Mill Records, Vol. 157, Circular from Kelly, June, 1901; G. Weston Wrigley, 'Socialism in Canada,' *International Socialist Review*, I (May, 1901), 687; and *Lardeau Eagle*, June 27, 1900

36 *Lardeau Eagle*, Sept. 19, 1901; and *Citizen and Country*, June 1, 1900
37 *Citizen and Country*, Aug. 17, 1900; Oct. 5, 1900; and Oct. 12, 1900; and Bennett, *Builders of British Columbia*, 137
38 *The Independent*, March 2, 1901; and *The Socialist*, July 14, 1901
39 *The Socialist*, July 7, 1901; and Aug. 18, 1901
40 Ibid., June 30, 1901; July 21, 1901; and Sept. 29, 1901
41 Ibid., June 30, 1901; and Sept. 8, 1901
42 Ibid., Sept. 29, 1901
43 Wrigley, 'Socialism in Canada,' 686; and *The Socialist*, Oct. 20, 1901
44 *The Socialist*, Oct. 20, 1901
45 Because it was at times a pejorative in a controversy not yet finished, the term 'impossiblist' was used only reluctantly in this study. It is, nonetheless, a word which seems to characterize particularly well a major tendency within the socialist movement, and is employed descriptively and without any prejudicial connotation.
46 *Lardeau Eagle*, Feb. 13, 1902
47 Ibid., and *The Socialist*, Sept. 1, 1901
48 *The Socialist*, Jan. 19, 1902; and Pritchard to the author Sept. 26, 1971
49 *The Voice*, May 29, 1908; *The People*, Dec. 25, 1898; and June 25, 1899; and SLP Papers, National Executive, Incoming Correspondence, Everett to Kuhn, May 19, 1899
50 *The People*, Oct. 8, 1899; Oct. 15, 1899; and Aug. 25, 1900
51 Interview with Pritchard, Aug. 16-18, 1971; and Pritchard to the author, Sept. 26, 1971
52 *Lardeau Eagle*, March 20, 1902; and Pritchard to the author, Sept. 26, 1971
53 *The Socialist*, May 18, 1902
54 *The Independent*, Oct. 5, 1901; and Nov. 9, 1901
55 For the fishermen's strike see H.K. Ralston, 'The 1900 Strike of Fraser River Sockeye Salmon Fishermen,' MA thesis, University of British Columbia, 1965, 105-75; and Phillips, *No Power Greater*, 34-7; and for the miners' strike see chap. 3.
56 Canada *Sessional Papers*, 1904, Vol. XXXVIII, No. 13-36A, 'Evidence Taken Before the Royal Commission to Inquire into Industrial Disputes in the Province of British Columbia,' 209
57 *Victoria Daily Colonist*, Jan. 12, 1902; and *The Socialist*, Dec. 1, 1901
58 *Lardeau Eagle*, Nov. 21, 1901; Jan. 23, 1902; and Jan. 30, 1902
59 Loosmore, 'BC Labor Movement and Political Action,' 173-6; *Western Socialist*, Oct. 18, 1902; and Feb. 21, 1903; and *Western Clarion*, Jan. 12, 1907
60 *Victoria Daily Colonist*, March 2, 1903; and *Western Socialist*, Feb. 7, 1903
61 Mine, Mill Records, Vol. 158, Lipsett to O'Neal, Oct. 23, 1901; and Vol. 157, O'Neal to Parr, ND; and Foley et al. to Shilland, Nov. 21, 1901

62 Ibid., Vol. 156-3, O'Neal to Parr, Dec. 27, 1901; and Wilkes to Parr, Jan. 7, 1902; and Vol. 157, O'Neal et al. to Shilland, Nov. 28, 1901; and Parr to Shilland, Jan. 10, 1902
63 *Miners' Magazine*, Feb., 1902
64 Mine, Mill Records, Vol. 157, Wilkes to Shilland, March 6, 1902
65 *The Independent*, April 19, 1902; and May 10, 1902; and Bennett, *Builders of British Columbia*, 138
66 *The Independent*, April 19, 1902; and *Victoria Daily Colonist*, April 20, 1902
67 *Canadian Socialist*, July 19, 1902; and Aug. 2, 1902. In the spring of 1902 Pettipiece sold the *Eagle*, and G. Weston Wrigley moved *Citizen and Country* to Vancouver where they jointly edited a new party organ. First called the *Canadian Socialist*, the name was changed to the *Western Socialist* when Wrigley dissolved the partnership in the autumn. In the spring of 1903 the latter paper merged with the *Clarion*, a Nanaimo socialist paper, to become the *Western Clarion*.
68 Ibid., July 12, 1902; and July 26, 1902; and *Miners' Magazine*, Aug., 1902
69 Mine, Mill Records, Vol. 157, circular from Moyer, June 14, 1902; and *Miners' Magazine*, Oct., 1902
70 *Western Socialist*, Oct. 11, 1902
71 Ibid., and *The Socialist*, Oct. 26, 1902
72 *Sessional Papers*, 1904, 'Evidence Royal Commission [on] BC,' 645
73 *Western Socialist*, Jan. 24, 1903; Jan. 31, 1903; and Feb. 7, 1903; and *Western Clarion*, May 28, 1903; June 4, 1903; and July 3, 1903
74 *Sessional Papers*, 1904, 'Evidence Royal Commission [on] BC,' 315
75 *Western Socialist*, Feb. 7, 1903; Feb. 28, 1903; March 27, 1903; and April 24, 1903; and *Western Clarion*, July 10, 1903
76 Phillips, *No Power Greater*, 42; *Western Socialist*, Jan. 24, 1903; and Vancouver Trades Council Minutes, Feb. 19, 1903; and May 7, 1903
77 For the ALU rebellion see chapter 3.
78 *The Voice*, July 3, 1903
79 Mine, Mill Records, Vol. 155-4, Dougherty to McDonald, June 26, 1903; and Vol. 158, Dougherty to Shilland, June 13, 1903
80 *Western Socialist*, April 10, 1903; and *Western Clarion*, May 26, 1903; and June 26, 1903
81 *Western Clarion*, Oct. 8, 1903; and Oct. 29, 1903
82 G. Weston Wrigley, 'Another Red Spot on the Socialist Map,' *International Socialist Review*, IV (December, 1903), 398-400
83 Ibid., 401 and *Western Clarion*, Oct. 8, 1903
84 *Western Clarion*, Sept. 17, 1903; Oct. 8, 1903; Dec. 19, 1903; and July 2, 1904

85 Ibid., Oct. 8, 1903; June 18, 1904; June 25, 1904; and Sept. 10, 1904; and *Miners' Magazine*, Oct. 22, 1903
86 *Western Clarion*, Oct. 15, 1903
87 Wrigley, 'Another Red Spot on the Socialist Map,' 400-1 and *Western Clarion*, Sept. 11, 1903; Nov. 28, 1903; and Dec. 12, 1903

CHAPTER 3

1 For the WFM in the United States see Vernon H. Jensen, *Heritage of Conflict: Labor Relations in the Nonferrous Metals Industry up to 1930* (Ithaca, 1950), 1-159; John H.M. Laslett, 'Syndicalist Socialism and the Western Federation of Miners,' *Labor and the Left: A Study of Socialist and Radical Influences in the American Labor Movement, 1881-1924* (New York, 1970), 241-86; and Melvyn Dubofsky, *We Shall Be All: A History of the Industrial Workers of the World* (Chicago, 1969), 19-87.
2 F.W. Howay, W.N. Sage, and H.F. Angus, *British Columbia and the United States: The North Pacific Slope from Fur Trade to Aviation* (Toronto, 1942), 274-86 and Canada Dept. of Labour Library, R.C. Clute, 'Royal Commission on Mining Conditions in British Columbia,' typescript, 1899, 23 (hereafter cited Clute, 'Report')
3 Canada Dept. of Labour Library, R.C. Clute, 'Royal Commission on Mining Conditions in British Columbia: Evidence,' typescript, 1899, passim (hereafter cited Clute, 'Evidence')
4 Clute, 'Report,' 16; and Clute, 'Evidence,' 432 and passim. The records of the Sandon local of the WFM contain a large number of transfer cards from American locals. (University of British Columbia, Special Collections Division, International Union of Mine Mill and Smelter Workers' Records, Vols. 151 and 158)
5 Clute, 'Report,' 374; Clute, 'Evidence,' 724 and passim
6 Clute, 'Report,' 149 and Appendix D; and Mine, Mill Records, Vol. 157, Haywood to Shilland, Dec. 26, 1902
7 Clute, 'Report,' 148; PAC, RCMP Records, RG 18, A-1, Vol. 141-580, Galt to Laurier, Sept. 17, 1897; and Clute, 'Evidence,' 510
8 Mine, Mill Records, Vol. 157, Woodside to Shilland, Oct. 14, 1901; Laurier Papers, Vol. 139, Kirby to Gooderham, Feb. 6, 1900; King Papers, Vol. 3, King to Mulock, Nov. 18, 1901; and *Miners' Magazine*, Sept., 1901. This issue contains an account of the struggle by Frank Woodside, secretary of the Rossland local.
9 *Miners' Magazine*, July, 1901
10 Ibid., May, 1902; Mine, Mill Records, Vol. 155-4, 'A Plain Statement,' July 12, 1901; and *Labour Gazette*, II, 363

11 Mine, Mill Records, Vol. 158, O'Neal to Shilland, Dec. 12, 1902; and Vol. 157, Circular from Haywood, Aug. 9, 1903; *American Labor Union Journal*, Jan. 15, 1903; and *Miners' Magazine*, March, 1901; May, 1901; and Sept., 1901

12 Mine, Mill Records, Vol. 155-4, Deposition of J. Edward Irving, July 29, 1901; and Deposition of Edward Pavier, ND

13 Mine, Mill Records, Vol. 155-4, Rossland Miners' Union Resolutions, July 3, 1901 and ND

14 Ibid., Vol. 156-3, Boyce to Wilkes, July 17, 1901

15 Ibid., Vol. 155-4, Haywood to Woodside, Sept. 6, 1901

16 Ibid., Vol. 155-4, Haywood to Woodside, Aug. 13, 1901; and circular from Seman et al., April 15, 1903

17 Laurier Papers, Vol. 202, Blackstock to Laurier, July 12, 1901; and *Miners' Magazine*, Dec., 1901

18 *Miners' Magazine*, Oct., 1901; and Mine, Mill Records, Vol. 157, Woodside to Shilland, Oct. 25, 1901

19 Mine, Mill Records, Vol. 155-4, Boyce to Woodside, Nov. 26, 1901; and Vol. 157, Woodside to Shilland, Nov. 14, 1901. The case dragged through the courts until 1906 when the union, all its avenues of appeal exhausted, was forced to give up its hall to pay damages. For full documentation on the court action see Mine, Mill Records, Vol. 155-4.

20 *Labour Gazette*, II, 364; *Miners' Magazine*, Nov., 1901; Mine, Mill Records, Vol. 156-3, Laurier to Parr, Nov. 22, 1901; and *Lardeau Eagle*, Jan. 16, 1902

21 *Labour Gazette*, II, 364; and *Miners' Magazine*, Feb., 1902

22 King Papers, Vol. 3, King to Harper, Nov. 18, 1901; and King to Mulock, Nov. 18, 1901

23 Mine, Mill Records, Vol. 156-3, Woodside to Parr, Jan. 29, 1902; and Feb. 23, 1902; *Victoria Daily Colonist*, Jan. 12, 1902; and *Miners' Magazine*, Oct., 1901

24 *Citizen and Country*, April 6, 1900; and Clute, 'Report,' Appendix D

25 Canada *Sessional Papers*, 1904, Vol. XXXVIII, No. 13-36A, 'Evidence Taken Before the Royal Commission to Inquire into Industrial Disputes in the Province of British Columbia,' 33 and 72; and *Lardeau Eagle*, Oct. 10, 1901

26 *Miners' Magazine*, Oct., 1901

27 For the convention see chap. 2.

28 *Miners' Magazine*, August, 1902. For the campaign see chap. 2.

29 *Sessional Papers*, 1904, 'Evidence Royal Commission [on] BC,' 29 and 30; and *Western Socialist*, Jan. 24, 1903

30 Laslett, 'Syndicalist Socialism and the WFM,' 253-7; Dubofsky, *We Shall Be All*, 71-6; and *Miners' Magazine*, Dec., 1900; and Feb., 1901

31 *Sessional Papers*, 1904, 'Evidence Royal Commission [on] BC,' 33

32 *Western Socialist*, March 13, 1903; and April 10, 1903; and *The Bond of Brotherhood*, Oct. 3, 1903
33 *Western Clarion*, May 19, 1903
34 It is interesting to note that Bakes was the only Canadian ever to attend a convention of the Second International; he represented the Vancouver trades council at the 1904 session. (University of British Columbia, Special Collections Division, Vancouver Trades and Labour Council Minutes, June 16, 1904)
35 *Sessional Papers*, 1904, 'Evidence Royal Commission [on] BC,' 37-59
36 *American Labor Union Journal*, April 23, 1903; and *The Independent*, Feb. 21, 1903
37 *American Labor Union Journal*, July 30, 1903
38 Mine, Mill Records, Vol. 157, Moyer to Shilland, Oct. 20, 1902; and Vol. 158, McLean to Shilland, Nov. 19, 1902
39 *American Labor Union Journal*, Nov. 27, 1902; and Mine, Mill Records, Vol. 158, McDonald to Shilland, Nov. 19, 1902; and O'Brien to McDonald, Dec. 31, 1902
40 *American Labor Union Journal*, March 19, 1903; and TLC *Proceedings*, 1902, 38
41 *Sessional Papers*, 1904, 'Evidence Royal Commission [on] BC,' 784
42 Mine, Mill Records, Vol. 157, Baker to Shilland, April 10, 1903; and *Sessional Papers*, 1904, 'Evidence Royal Commission [on] BC,' 452-6 and 475
43 TLC *Proceedings*, 1902, 56-7; and *Western Socialist*, Sept. 6, 1902; and Feb. 14, 1903
44 D.A. Orr, 'The Western Federation of Miners and the Royal Commission on Industrial Disputes in 1903 with Special Reference to the Vancouver Island Coal Miners' Strike,' MA thesis, University of British Columbia, 1968, 113-7; *Sessional Papers*, 1904, 'Evidence Royal Commission [on] BC,' 319-21 and *The Independent*, May 24, 1902
45 *The Voice*, Sept. 8, 1899; May 2, 1902; and Feb. 20, 1903
46 Ibid., June 13, 1902; and Feb. 13, 1903; Canada, *Sessional Papers*, Vol. XXXVII, No. 36a, 1903, 'Report of the Royal Commission on Industrial Disputes in the Province of British Columbia,' 8; and TLC *Proceedings*, 1903, 10
47 *Victoria Daily Colonist*, Dec. 14, 1902; *The Independent*, March 28, 1903; and *Sessional Papers*, 1903, 'Report Royal Commission on BC,' 8
48 *Western Socialist*, April 3, 1903; and April 17, 1903
49 *Sessional Papers*, 1903, 'Report Royal Commission on BC,' 8-21; *Sessional Papers*, 1904, 'Evidence Royal Commission [on] BC,' 531; *The Voice*, March 6, 1903; and *The Independent*, March 21, 1903
50 *The Independent*, March 14, 1903
51 *Sessional Papers*, 1903, 'Report Royal Commission on BC,' 13-21

52 *Railway Employees' Journal*, June 11, 1903; Vancouver Trades Council Minutes, May 16, 1903; and *The Bond of Brotherhood*, May 30, 1903
53 *Western Clarion*, June 2, 1903; and *Western Socialist*, April 10, 1903
54 *Sessional Papers*, 1903, 'Report Royal Commission on BC,' 11 and 25
55 *Western Socialist*, March 27, 1903
56 *Sessional Papers*, 1903, 'Report Royal Commission on BC,' 10; and *The Bond of Brotherhood*, Sept. 12, 1903
57 William Bennett, *Builders of British Columbia* (Vancouver, ND) pp. 63-4; and *Western Clarion*, May 12, 1903
58 *Sessional Papers*, 1903, 'Report Royal Commission on BC,' 27-9
59 *Western Socialist*, March 27, 1903; *The Independent*, April 18, 1903; and Vancouver Trades Council Minutes, March 5, 1903
60 *American Labor Union Journal*, April 30, 1903
61 *Railway Employees' Journal*, July 2, 1903; and *The Bond of Brotherhood*, July 10, 1903
62 Laurier Papers, Vol. 252, Ross to Laurier, Feb. 17, 1903; and Vol. 259, Mulock to Laurier, April 4, 1903
63 Canada, *House of Commons Debates*, April 3, 1903, 946-51. Socialists charged that Smith had initiated the investigation to weaken the SPBC and thus regain some of his past political strength. See, for example, John Mortimer's letter to *The Voice*, March 18, 1904.
64 Laurier Papers, Vol. 259, Mulock to Laurier, April 4, 1903
65 *Sessional Papers*, 1903, 'Report Royal Commission on BC,' 15-16 and 27
66 Ibid., 39
67 Ibid., 66-8
68 *Sessional Papers*, 1904, 'Evidence Royal Commission [on] BC,' 475, 523 and 755
69 *American Labor Union Journal*, March 19, 1903
70 Robert H. Babcock, *Gompers in Canada: A Study in American Continentalism Before the First World War* (Toronto, 1975), 103-4
71 Ibid., 78
72 Vancouver Trades Council Minutes, Feb. 5, 1903; March 19, 1903; and April 3, 1903; and TLC *Proceedings*, 1903, 32
73 *The Independent*, April 4, 1903; and May 30, 1903; and *Sessional Papers*, 1904, 'Evidence Royal Commission [on] BC,' 690
74 *The Independent*, May 23, 1903; and June 20, 1903
75 *Victoria Daily Colonist*, July 12, 1903
76 *Western Clarion*, July 17, 1903; and *Victoria Daily Colonist*, June 21, 1903; and July 12, 1903
77 *American Labor Union Journal*, July 30, 1903; and *Victoria Daily Colonist*, Aug. 9, 1903

78 *Victoria Daily Colonist*, July 12, 1903; July 19, 1903; Aug. 9, 1903; and Aug. 23, 1903

79 Ibid., Aug. 9, 1903; and Babcock, *Gompers in Canada*, 134-5

80 TLC *Proceedings*, 1903, 31; and *American Labor Union Journal*, Sept. 3, 1903

81 *The Independent*, Aug. 8, 1903; and *American Labor Union Journal*, Sept. 10, 1903

82 TLC *Proceedings*, 1903, 10, 29, and 51; and *The Voice*, Oct. 16, 1903. Approval was qualified because the recommendations of the Report were somewhat ambiguous and could have been taken to include all international unions.

83 *Victoria Daily Colonist*, July 12, 1903

84 *The Bond of Brotherhood*, Dec. 19, 1903

85 *Victoria Daily Colonist*, Dec. 27, 1903; and Jan. 17, 1904

86 Vancouver Trades Council Minutes, Sept. 5, 1906

87 Dubofsky, *We Shall Be All*, 75; *Victoria Daily Colonist*, Feb. 7, 1904; and Mine, Mill Records, Mahoney to Shilland, Dec. 20, 1903

88 *American Labor Union Journal*, June 18, 1903

CHAPTER 4

1 *Western Socialist*, April 24, 1903; and *Western Clarion*, May 7, 1903; May 9, 1903; Nov. 5, 1903; Aug. 19, 1905; and Jan. 6, 1906

2 *Western Clarion*, Jan. 28, 1905

3 Jessie Wallace Hughan, *American Socialism of the Present Day* (New York, 1912), 238-9

4 *Western Clarion*, May 27, 1911; and Oct. 5, 1912; *The Voice*, June 17, 1910; and interview with W.A. Pritchard, Aug. 16-18, 1971

5 *Western Clarion*, Feb. 15, 1908; July 18, 1908; and July 18, 1914

6 Ibid., April 30, 1910.

7 Interview with Pritchard, Aug. 16-18, 1971

8 *Western Clarion*, Jan. 26, 1909

9 *Socialism and Unionism* (Vancouver, ND), 6; and *Manifesto of the Socialist Party of Canada*, 3rd ed., (Vancouver, ND), 28

10 *Western Clarion*, March 21, 1908

11 Ibid., Oct. 20, 1906; and Dec. 1, 1906

12 Ibid., March 18, 1905; and April 22, 1905

13 Ibid., April 30, 1910

14 Ibid., July 15, 1905; and March 3, 1906

15 Pritchard to the author, April 12, 1972; *The Voice*, Nov. 8, 1907; *The Trade Unionist*, July, 1908; and *Western Clarion*, March 31, 1906; and Dec. 24, 1910

16 Interview with Pritchard, Aug. 16-18, 1971; and *British Columbia Federationist*, April 20, 1912
17 *Western Clarion*, Aug. 19, 1905; and *The Trade Unionist*, July, 1908
18 *Socialism and Unionism*, 10; and *Manifesto of the SPC*, 29
19 Interview with Pritchard, Aug. 16-18, 1971; University of Toronto, Special Collections Division, Woodsworth Memorial Collection, Transcript of Interview of J. Harrington by P. Fox and Transcript of Interview of Al Farmilo by Fox and *The Voice*, April 6, 1906
20 Jack Place, *Record of J.H. Hawthornthwaite: Member for Nanaimo City in the Local Legislature* (Nanaimo, ND) 5-10; *The Voice*, March 17, 1911; and University of British Columbia, Special Collections Division, Angus McInnis Collection, Vol. 53-8, John McInnis to Steves, Sept. 20, 1958
21 *Western Clarion*, March 31, 1906
22 Ibid., March 9, 1907; and Oct. 24, 1908; and interview with Pritchard, Aug. 16-18, 1971
23 *Western Clarion*, June 29, 1907; and *The Voice*, Feb. 16, 1906
24 *Western Clarion*, March 16, 1907; May 2, 1908; June 25, 1908; June 5, 1909; and Oct. 2, 1909. Hughan, an American socialist, claimed that even the members of the SPA whom she called 'revolutionists' only regarded violence as a vague possibility and paid very little attention to it in their propaganda [*American Socialism of the Present Day*, 115]
25 *The Voice*, July 30, 1908; and *Western Clarion*, Feb. 24, 1906; and Feb. 26, 1910
26 *The Voice*, April 26, 1908; *Western Clarion*, June 17, 1911; and *District Ledger*, Nov. 27, 1909
27 *The Voice*, July 30, 1909
28 Ibid., Oct. 5, 1906; Nov. 2, 1906; and Oct. 9, 1908
29 Interview with Pritchard, Aug. 16-18, 1971
30 Ronald Grantham, 'Some Aspects of the Socialist Movement in British Columbia, 1898-1933,' MA thesis, University of British Columbia, 1942, 174; and Pritchard to the author, Feb. 15, 1972
31 *Western Clarion*, April 14, 1906; and Woodsworth Memorial Collection, interview of Harrington by Fox
32 Alex Paterson, 'S.P. of C. Notes,' undated manuscript; *Western Clarion*, July 31, 1903; and Nov. 9, 1912; and Angus McInnis Collection, Vol. 53-4, Faulkner to Steeves, March 5, 1959
33 *The Voice*, Dec. 17, 1909; and Sept. 20, 1910; *Weekly People*, Oct. 7, 1905; *Industrial Worker*, Feb. 15, 1912; and William Bennett, *Builders of British Columbia* (Vancouver, ND), 139
34 *Western Clarion*, June 11, 1910

35 *The Voice*, Nov. 29, 1907

36 Interview with Fred Tipping, May 3, 1971; and *The Voice*, April 2, 1909

37 *The Trade Unionist*, Jan., 1909; and *District Ledger*, April 5, 1913

38 *District Ledger*, Oct. 21, 1910; and Dec. 9, 1911; and *The Trade Unionist*, Aug., 1908

39 *District Ledger*, Feb. 13, 1909

40 Ibid., Aug. 19, 1911

41 *The Voice*, Nov. 15, 1907; Dec. 27, 1907; and May 1, 1908

42 *District Ledger*, March 13, 1909; March 20, 1909; and April 24, 1909

43 *Western Clarion*, April 22, 1911

44 University of British Columbia, Special Collections Division, Vancouver Trades and Labor Council Minutes, Oct. 19, 1911; Interview with Pritchard, Aug. 16-18, 1971; Woodsworth Memorial Collection, Transcript of Interview of Harrington by Fox and Angus McInnis Collection, Vol. 53-17, 'Ambrose Tree: Old S.P.C. member,' ND

45 *The Western Wage-earner*, June, 1910; and Vancouver Trades Council Minutes, June 16, 1910

46 *Miners' Magazine*, Feb. 15, 1906; Aug. 9, 1906; and Nov. 29, 1906; and University of British Columbia, Special Collections Division, International Union of Mine, Mill and Smelterworkers' Records, Vol. 157, McKenzie to Shilland, April 11, 1910; and Shilland to Matheson, ND

47 E.W.D., 'A New Figure,' *International Socialist Review*, IX (May, 1909), 920

48 British Columbia Provincial Library, Royal Commission on Labour, 1914, Typescript Proceedings, Vol. III, 159-62

49 For a detailed description of the party's electoral fortunes see Grantham, 'Aspects of Socialist Movement in BC,' 45-53

50 Dan Sproul, 'The Situation in British Columbia,' *International Socialist Review*, X (Feb., 1910), 741

51 *Nanaimo Free Press*, Jan. 7, 1907; and Jan. 12, 1907

52 *Western Clarion*, March 16, 1907

53 *District Ledger*, Oct. 21, 1910

54 *Nanaimo Free Press*, Jan. 7, 1907

55 Place, *Record of Hawthornthwaite*, 3; Vancouver Trade Council Minutes, Jan. 7, 1904; and Mine, Mill Records, Vol. 158, Bambury to Shilland, Jan. 30, 1904

56 Place, *Record of Hawthornthwaite*, 3-6

57 *District Ledger*, June 4, 1910

58 F. Blake, *The Proletarian in Politics* (Vancouver, ND), 11-16; *District Ledger*, Nov. 26, 1910; and Feb. 3, 1912

59 *Western Clarion*, May 11, 1907

60 Ibid., Sept. 17, 1910; and Oct. 8, 1910
61 *The Voice*, Aug. 10, 1906; and Oct. 4, 1907
62 Ernie Chisick, 'The Development of Winnipeg's Socialist Movement, 1900 to 1915,' MA thesis, University of Manitoba, 1972, 54n; Transcript of Interview of Jacob Penner by Roland Penner and *Western Clarion*, Dec. 28, 1907
63 *The Voice*, May 10, 1907
64 *Western Clarion*, Nov. 16, 1907; Dec. 7, 1907; and Dec. 28, 1907. Stechishin, who had been a member of the SPA, was mistaken when he claimed that autonomous national units existed in the American party; these were not officially established until 1910 [David A. Shannon, *The Socialist Party of America: A History* (Chicago, 1967), 44].
65 *Western Clarion*, Nov. 16, 1907; and Jan. 4, 1908
66 Ibid., May 30, 1908; and John Weir, 'The Flaming Torch,' undated manuscript, 9-10
67 *Western Clarion*, Jan. 4, 1908; Feb. 22, 1908; and Aug. 8, 1908
68 Quoted in Howard Palmer, 'Nativism in Southern Alberta, 1880-1920,' MA thesis, University of Alberta, 1971, 125
69 *Western Clarion*, March 28, 1908; and July 31, 1909; and *The Voice*, May 8, 1908
70 *Western Clarion*, July 31, 1903
71 Interview with Pritchard, Aug. 16-18, 1971; and Pritchard to the author, Nov. 15, 1971. Pritchard's statement, of course, says as much about the British comrades as it does about the Europeans.
72 *Western Clarion*, May 30, 1908; and Feb. 14, 1915
73 Transcript of Interview of Jacob Penner by Roland Penner
74 Interview with Pritchard, Aug. 16-18, 1971; Pritchard to the author, Oct. 25, 1971; Woodsworth Memorial Collection, Transcript of Interview with Harrington by Fox and *Western Clarion*, Jan. 16, 1909
75 Woodsworth Memorial Collection, Transcript of Interview with Lefeaux by Fox
76 *The Voice*, April 10, 1908. The practical political implications of this sectarianism are discussed in chap. 5.
77 *Western Clarion*, Nov. 28, 1908
78 Interview with Pritchard, Aug. 16-18, 1971; and *Western Clarion*, Dec. 17, 1910
79 Pritchard to the author, April 12, 1972; and interview with Pritchard, Aug. 16-18, 1971
80 Sproul, 'Situation in British Columbia,' 742; and *Western Clarion*, Oct. 30, 1909
81 Daniel Bell, *Marxian Socialism in the United States* (Princeton, 1967), 82-6

82 *Western Clarion*, April 15, 1905; and Feb. 12, 1910; and *The Voice*, April 15, 1910
83 *Western Clarion*, March 18, 1905; and Jan. 1, 1910
84 Ibid., Sept. 8, 1906
85 Ibid., March 18, 1911
86 *The Trade Unionist*, Dec., 1908
87 *The Voice*, May 22, 1908; and *Western Clarion*, Feb. 20, 1909
88 *The Voice*, Feb. 11, 1910; and *Western Clarion*, March 18, 1911
89 *The Voice*, Oct. 9, 1908; G. Weston Wrigley, 'Kier Hardie Impeached,' *International Socialist Review*, IX (March, 1909), 723-6; and *The Trade Unionist*, Nov., 1908
90 *Western Clarion*, April 15, 1905; and July 1, 1905
91 *The Voice*, Sept. 18, 1908; interview with Pritchard, Aug. 16-18, 1971; and Angus McInnis Collection, Vol. 53-4, Faulkner to Steeves, March 5, 1959
92 *The Voice*, June 1, 1906; and Place, *Record of Hawthornthwaite*, 5
93 *Western Clarion*, Jan. 11, 1908; A.M. Simons, 'The Western Clarion,' *International Socialist Review*, X (Aug., 1909), 279; and Angus McInnis Collection, Vol. 53-4, Faulkner to Steeves, March 5, 1959
94 *The Voice*, March 18, 1910
95 *L'Internationale Ouvrière & Socialiste: Rapports soumis au Congrès Socialiste Internationale de Stuttgart* (Bruxelles, 1907), 76
96 *Western Clarion*, Aug. 7, 1909; and Wrigley, 'Hardie Impeached,' 723-6. Obviously stung, Hardie told Arthur Puttee, 'the humor of this is delightful; ... it is only Kingsley and the dogmaridden junta which meets on the other side of the Rockies which discover heresy in the British movement' (*The Voice*, Dec. 17, 1909].
97 *The Voice*, Sept. 20, 1910; Oct. 7, 1910; and Nov. 25, 1910
98 *Western Clarion*, Aug. 21, 1909
99 Transcript of interview of Jacob Penner by Roland Penner
100 George Lichtheim, *Marxism* (London, 1961), 278-300; *Western Clarion*, July 24, 1909; and *The Voice*, Aug. 13, 1909
101 Jacob Penner, 'Recollections of the Early Socialist Movement in Winnipeg,' *The Marxist Quarterly*, 2 (Summer, 1962), 27
102 *The Voice*, March 13, 1908
103 Ibid., July 29, 1910; Interview with Tipping, May 2, 1971; and Weir, 'Flaming Torch,' 10
104 *The Voice*, July 29, 1910
105 *Western Clarion*, Sept. 25, 1909
106 Penner, 'Recollections,' 26; William Kolisnyk, 'In Canada Since the Spring of 1898,' *Marxist Review* (Jan.-Feb., 1961), 37; and Vera Lysenko, *Men in Sheepskin Coats: A Study of Assimilation* (Toronto, 1947), 118-9

107 Interview with Tipping, May 3, 1971
108 *District Ledger*, Oct. 28, 1910; and *Western Clarion*, Sept. 25, 1909
109 *Western Clarion*, April 9, 1910; and May 21, 1910
110 Ibid., April 9, 1910; and Weir, 'Flaming Torch,' 10-11
111 *The Voice*, Sept. 3, 1909; June 3, 1910; June 10, 1910; and July 29, 1910. For the details of the incident see Chap. 5.
112 *The Voice*, Oct. 14, 1910; and *District Ledger*, Sept. 17, 1910; and Oct. 28, 1910
113 *Western Clarion*, April 16, 1910; and Angus McInnis Collection, Vol. 53-1, 'Interview with Ernest Burns'
114 *British Columbia Federationist*, Aug. 2, 1912; and Sept. 7, 1912
115 *Western Clarion*, May 6, 1911; and May 20, 1911
116 Donald Avery, 'Foreign Workers and Labour Radicalism in the Western Canadian Mining Industry: 1900-1919,' paper read before the Western Canadian Urban History Conference, Winnipeg, 1974, 19
117 *The Voice*, April 28, 1911; and Dec. 22, 1911; and transcript of interview of Jacob Penner by Roland Penner. For the SDP see Chap. 5.
118 *Western Clarion*, March 9, 1912

CHAPTER 5

1 *The People's Voice*, Sept. 29, 1894; and Dec. 22, 1894
2 Laurence V. Thompson, *Robert Blatchford: Portrait of an Englishman* (London, 1951), 82-101; and Henry Pelling, *The Origins of the Labour Party, 1880-1900* (London, 1954), 169-71
3 *The People's Voice*, Dec. 1, 1894; Oct. 12, 1895; Dec. 19, 1896; and April 23, 1896; and *The Voice*, May 13, 1898; Jan. 27, 1899; and Dec. 13, 1901
4 *The People's Voice*, June 16, 1894; Dec. 29, 1894; April 27, 1895; and Oct. 17, 1896; and *The Voice*, May 13, 1898
5 *The People's Voice*, Sept. 12, 1896
6 Ibid., Sept. 29, 1894; and March 9, 1895
7 Ibid., March 2, 1895
8 Ibid., April 18, 1896
9 Ibid., Feb. 15, 1896; and March 7, 1896; Pelling, *Origins of the Labour Party*, 127; and *The Voice*, Dec. 8, 1899; and Jan. 11, 1901
10 *The Voice*, March 10, 1899; May 19, 1899; June 2, 1899; and June 28, 1899
11 *Manitoba Free Press*, June 5, 1899; and A.R. McCormack, 'Arthur Puttee and the Liberal Party: 1899-1904,' *Canadian Historical Review*, LI (June, 1970), 144-6
12 PAC, Sir Charles Tupper Papers, Tupper to Macdonald, May 10, 1899

13 *The Voice*, Jan. 12, 1900
14 Ibid., Jan. 17, 1900; Jan. 19, 1900; and Jan. 24, 1900
15 It is possible to cite specific examples of this process of class identification within the Liberal party. For instance, Isaac Campbell, a staunch Siftonite, could not bring himself to vote for Puttee and gave his support to Martin. But John Appleton who considered himself a 'representati[ve] liberal' loyal to Sifton, had strong connections with the city's labour movement, and he supported Puttee [PAC, Sir Clifford Sifton Papers, Vol. 77, Campbell to Sifton, Jan. 18, 1900; and Appleton to Sifton, Aug. 2, 1900; and *The Voice*, Feb. 9, 1900].
16 McCormack, 'Puttee and the Liberal Party,' 153-6
17 *The Voice*, Nov. 9, 1900
18 *The People*, May 1, 1899; and *The Voice*, Dec. 21, 1899
19 *The Voice*, April 24, 1903; July 24, 1903; Nov. 13, 1903; and Dec. 4, 1903
20 Ibid., Nov. 15, 1901; and Dec. 27, 1901
21 Ibid., March 14, 1902; March 21, 1902; and March 28, 1902
22 Ibid., Nov. 14, 1902
23 Ibid., Feb. 6, 1903; July 10, 1903; and Nov. 27, 1903
24 *Citizen and Country*, July 13, 1900; *Western Clarion*, Sept. 17, 1903; G. Weston Wrigley, 'The Recent Canadian Elections,' *International Socialist Review*, V (Jan., 1905), 400; and *The Voice*, Nov. 28, 1902
25 McCormack, 'Puttee and the Liberal Party,' 157-9
26 PAC, Sir Wilfrid Laurier Papers, Vol. 286, Dafoe to Laurier, Oct. 16, 1903
27 Sifton Papers, Vol. 140, Dafoe to Sifton, Nov. 13, 1903
28 Ibid., Vol. 154, Bole to Sifton, April 14, 1904; and *The Voice*, Nov. 18, 1904
29 Sifton Papers, Vol. 154, Bole to Sifton, Feb. 13, 1904; and *Manitoba Free Press – News Bulletin*, Jan. 2, 1904
30 *Manitoba Free Press – News Bulletin*, Oct. 8, 1904
31 *The Voice*, Nov. 4, 1904
32 Ibid., Dec. 30, 1904; and Oct. 19, 1906
33 Ibid., July 14, 1911
34 Ibid., Aug. 15, 1913
35 Ibid., Dec. 28, 1906
36 Ibid., July 19, 1907; Oct. 1, 1909; and March 8, 1912. The British Labour party was, by no means, as unified as Puttee preferred to believe [Henry Pelling, *A Short History of the Labour Party*, (London, 1965), 21-5].
37 *Western Clarion*, Oct. 6, 1906; April 25, 1908; and July 30, 1910
38 *The Voice*, Oct. 12, 1906; Feb. 19, 1909; Aug. 27, 1909; and Feb. 27, 1914
39 David Jay Bercuson, *Confrontation at Winnipeg: Labour, Industrial Relations and the General Strike* (Montreal, 1974), 11-17

40 *The Voice*, Sept. 7, 1906; and Oct. 5, 1906
41 Ibid., Oct. 12, 1906
42 TLC *Proceedings*, 1906, 80-7
43 *The Voice*, Sept. 7, 1906; Oct. 5, 1906; Oct. 19, 1906; Nov. 15, 1906; and Jan. 4, 1907
44 Ibid., Oct. 26, 1906
45 Ibid., April 19, 1907
46 Richard Allen, *The Social Passion: Religion and Social Reform in Canada, 1914-28* (Toronto, 1971), 15
47 Ibid., 10; and interview with Fred Tipping by the author, May 3, 1971
48 Kenneth McNaught, *A Prophet in Politics: A Biography of J.S. Woodsworth* (Toronto, 1959), 40-52; G.N. Emery, 'The Methodist Church and the "European Foreigners" of Winnipeg: The All People's Mission, 1889-1914,' paper read before the Manitoba Historical Society, 1972, 13-35; and *The Voice*, Nov. 10, 1911
49 Interview with Tipping, May 3, 1971
50 *The Voice*, Nov. 30, 1906; and Dec. 7, 1906
51 Ibid., Dec. 14, 1906
52 *Western Clarion*, Feb. 15, 1908; and Oct. 30, 1909; and *The Voice*, Nov. 13, 1908
53 *The Voice*, Feb. 15, 1907; Feb. 22, 1907; March 1, 1907; and March 8, 1907; and *Western Clarion*, March 28, 1907
54 *The Voice*, June 12, 1908
55 *Western Clarion*, March 7, 1908; *The Voice*, Aug. 2, 1907; and March 6, 1908; and *Manitoba Free Press*, July 27, 1907
56 *The Voice*, March 6, 1908
57 Ibid., May 8, 1908; and June 26, 1908
58 McNaught, *Prophet in Politics*, 53-5; and *The Voice*, May 2, 1910
59 *The Voice*, Jan. 28, 1910; and *Western Clarion*, April 2, 1910
60 *The Voice*, May 13, 1910; and M.S. Donnelly, *The Government of Manitoba* (Toronto, 1963), 47. The MLP was the first radical party in which Woodsworth was active.
61 *Western Clarion*, May 14, 1910; and July 30, 1910
62 Ibid., March 12, 1910
63 *The Voice*, June 3, 1910; and June 10, 1910
64 Ibid., June 10, 1910; June 17, 1910; June 24, 1910; and July 1, 1910; and Public Archives of Manitoba, F.J. Dixon Papers, circular from Dixon, July 6, 1910
65 Laurier Papers, Vol. 692, Dixon to Laurier, Sept. 23, 1911; interview with Tipping, May 3, 1971; and *Manitoba Free Press*, July 6, 1910

66 *The Voice*, July 8, 1910; and *Western Clarion*, July 16, 1910; July 23, 1910; and July 30, 1910

67 *The Voice*, July 8, 1910; and July 29, 1910; *Western Clarion*, Sept. 13, 1910; and Nov. 9, 1912; and interview with Tipping, May 3, 1971

68 Jacob Penner, 'Recollections of the Early Socialist Movement in Winnipeg,' *Marxist Quarterly* (Summer, 1962), 29-30; Jacob Penner, 'Reminiscences of Early Labor-Farmer Elections,' undated manuscript, 4; and *The Voice*, Oct. 28, 1910; and April 7, 1911

69 Interview with Tipping, May 3, 1971; and *The Voice*, Nov. 24, 1911

70 *The Voice*, Oct. 28, 1910; and Jan. 24, 1913

71 Ibid., June 19, 1914

72 Interview with Tipping, May 3, 1971; transcript of interview of Jacob Penner by Roland Penner; and *The Voice*, Oct. 28, 1910; Oct. 30, 1914; and April 16, 1915

73 Interview with Tipping, May 3, 1971; *The Voice*, April 15, 1912; and July 12, 1912; and University of Toronto, Special Collections Division, Woodsworth Memorial Collection, Transcript of Interview of David Orlikow by Paul Fox

74 *The Voice*, Feb. 21, 1913; and interview with Tipping, May 3, 1971

75 *District Ledger*, Dec. 30, 1911; and *Cotton's Weekly*, Aug. 21, 1913

76 John Weir, 'The Flaming Torch,' undated manuscript, 13; and interview with Tipping, May 3, 1971

77 *The Voice*, May 19, 1911; and Aug. 25, 1911

78 Interview with Tipping, May 3, 1971; Leo Heaps, *The Rebel in the House: The Life and Times of A.A. Heaps, M.P.* (London, 1970), 4; and *The Voice*, Sept. 18, 1914

79 *The Voice*, Oct. 18, 1912; Jan. 31, 1913; and March 7, 1913

80 Ibid., Jan. 31, 1913; and Feb. 28, 1913

81 Chisick, 'Development of Winnipeg's Socialist Movement,' 103-4; *The Winnipeg Daily Tribune*, Dec. 13, 1913; and *The Voice*, Dec. 19, 1913

82 *The Voice*, June 12, 1914; and Chisick, 'Development of Winnipeg's Socialist Movement,' 110-11

83 *The Voice*, July 10, 1914; and Dixon Papers, Watt to Dixon, July 10, 1914

84 *The Voice*, Feb. 16, 1912; April 24, 1914; and May 8, 1914; Dixon Papers, Bland to Dixon, July 1, 1914; Stubbs to Dixon, July 9, 1914; and 'Candidates supporting the Liberal Policy'; *Manitoba Free Press*, July 6, 1914; and July 8, 1914; and Roy St. George Stubbs, 'F.J. Dixon,' *Prairie Portraits* (Toronto, 1954), 101

85 *The Voice*, July 17, 1914

86 Interview with Tipping, May 3, 1971; *Western Clarion*, June 6, 1914; and July 4, 1914; and *Manitoba Free Press*, July 8, 1914

87 *The Voice*, July 3, 1914; and July 17, 1914; and Dixon Papers, Watt to Dixon, July 10, 1914
88 Interview with Tipping, May 3, 1971
89 *The Voice*, March 19, 1915; and July 2, 1915
90 *Manitoba Free Press*, Aug. 6, 1915; and Aug. 7, 1915; *Western Clarion*, Aug., 1915; and *Winnipeg Daily Tribune*, Aug. 7, 1915
91 *The Voice*, July 16, 1915
92 Ibid., July 16, 1915; July 23, 1915; and July 30, 1915
93 *Western Clarion*, Jan. 2, 1915; Aug., 1915; and Sept., 1915
94 *The Voice*, Aug. 13, 1915; *Winnipeg Daily Tribune*, Aug. 9, 1915; *Manitoba Free Press*, Aug. 7, 1915; and Chisick, 'Development of Winnipeg's Socialist Movement,' 128-9

CHAPTER 6

1 It is interesting to note that the most widely accepted explanation of the term Wobbly ascribes it to a Chinese restaurateur in Calgary who mispronounced IWW as 'Eye Wobbly Wobbly' [Steward H. Holbrook, 'Wobbly Talk,' *American Mercury*, (Jan. 1926), 62].
2 Melvyn Dubofsky, *We Shall Be All: A History of the Industrial Workers of the World* (Chicago, 1969), 76-80
3 *Miners' Magazine*, April 27, 1905; and Dec. 6, 1906; *Proceedings of the Second Annual Convention of the Industrial Workers of the World*, 1906, 132; and *Official Proceedings of the Fifteenth Annual Convention of the Western Federation of Miners*, 1907, 645
4 *Official Proceedings of the Thirteenth Annual Convention of the Western Federation of Miners*, 1905, 233-4 and 245; *Miners' Magazine*, March 9, 1905; and *Voice of Labor*, May, 1905
5 Dubofsky, *We Shall Be All*, 81-7
6 *Proceedings of the First Convention of the Industrial Workers of the World*, 1905, 287, 510, and 546
7 *Miners' Magazine*, Feb. 15, 1906
8 *Miners' Magazine*, Feb. 15, 1906; and *Industrial Union Bulletin*, March 16, 1907; Aug. 24, 1907; and Sept. 14, 1907
9 *Industrial Union Bulletin*, Nov. 16, 1907
10 *Weekly People*, Oct. 7, 1905; and Oct. 14, 1905
11 *Industrial Union Bulletin*, Dec. 7, 1907
12 *Weekly People*, Aug. 4, 1906
13 *Industrial Union Bulletin*, Sept. 14, 1907; and Nov. 9, 1907
14 *Official Proceedings of the Fifteenth Annual Convention of the Western*

Federation of Miners, 1907, 612 and 690; *Miners' Magazine*, Aug. 9, 1906; and Aug. 23, 1906; and *Industrial Union Bulletin*, July 20, 1907

15 *Proceedings of the Second Annual Convention of the Industrial Workers of the World*, 1906, 132-8 and 256-7. Dubofsky and Joseph R. Conlin have demonstrated that such a simplistic view does not reflect the realities of the controversy [*We Shall Be All*, 110-15 and *Bread and Roses Too: Studies of the Wobblies* (Westport, 1969), 53].

16 *Official Proceedings of the Fifteenth Annual Convention of the Western Federation of Miners*, 1907, 492-5; 610-38; 641-7; 656-61; 690-1; and 700-1; and *Proceedings of Third Annual Convention: Industrial Workers of the World: Official Report No. 8* (1907), 5

17 *Industrial Union Bulletin*, April 20, 1907; June 1, 1907; May 23, 1908; and Oct. 10, 1908; and *Weekly People*, March 21, 1908; and Nov. 7, 1908

18 Wayne State University, Labour History Archives, E.W. Latchem Collection, 'Some Vitally Important Background Information,' ND, 1-2. For the itinerants see A. Ross McCormack, 'The Blanket-stiffs: Itinerant Railway Construction Workers in Canada, 1896-1914,' NFB/National Museum Visual History Set, 1975

19 *Industrial Union Bulletin*, Feb. 27, 1909

20 *Industrial Worker*, June 11, 1910; Sept. 14, 1911; Nov. 23, 1911; and July 4, 1912; *Solidarity*, Sept. 19, 1914; and *I.W.W. Strike Bulletin*, Oct. 12, 1912

21 Wayne State, IWW Records, GEB Minute Book, Sept. 25, 1907; *Industrial Worker*, May 7, 1910; and May 14, 1910; and Myrtle Bergen, *Tough Timber: The Loggers of B.C. – Their Story* (Toronto, 1967), 21-7

22 *Labour Organizations in Canada*, 1912, 112 and 119; *Ninth Census of Canada* (1951), Vol. X, Table 62; and *Labour Gazette*, XIV, 113

23 *I.W.W. Strike Bulletin*, Oct. 12, 1912; and *Industrial Worker*, June 24, 1909; and Oct. 31, 1912

24 *Industrial Union Bulletin*, Aug. 17, 1907; and *Industrial Worker*, Oct. 24, 1912; and Nov. 28, 1912; and *The Voice of the People*, May 7, 1914

25 *Industrial Union Bulletin*, Nov. 2, 1907

26 PAC, RCMP Records, A-1, Vol. 343-602, Primrose to Perry, Sept. 28, 1907; and Vol. 465-326, Callow 'Crime Report,' May 3, 1914

27 *Solidarity*, Oct. 21, 1911; Wayne State, H.E. McGucken, 'Recollections of a Wobbly,' ND, 43 and British Columbia Provincial Library, Royal Commission on Labour, Proceedings, Vol. V, 106

28 *Industrial Union Bulletin*, July 13, 1907

29 *Industrial Worker*, Aug. 12, 1909; and University of British Columbia, Special Collections Division, IWW Records, Local 322 Account Book

30 *Industrial Union Bulletin*, Dec. 7, 1907; and UBC, IWW Records, Library Catalogue

31 *British Columbia Federationist*, Nov. 28, 1913; and *Industrial Worker*, May 14, 1910

32 *Industrial Worker*, June 19, 1913

33 Dubofsky, *We Shall Be All*, 146-70; and Conlin, *Bread and Roses Too*, 8-35

34 Philip S. Foner, *History of the Labor Movement in the United States: The Industrial Workers of the World, 1905-1917* (New York, 1965), 159. For French Syndicalism see F.F. Ridley, *Revolutionary Syndicalism in France: The Direct Action of its Time* (Cambridge, 1970); and Peter N. Stearns, *Revolutionary Syndicalism and French Labor: A Cause without Rebels* (New Brunswick, NJ, 1971).

35 *Solidarity*, July 22, 1911

36 *Industrial Union Bulletin*, March 14, 1908; *Industrial Worker*, Sept. 23, 1909; July 6, 1911; and Dec. 7, 1911; and *Solidarity*, July 1, 1911; July 22, 1911; and Aug. 12, 1911

37 *Industrial Worker*, June 8, 1911; and Nov. 2, 1911; Agnes C. Laut, *Am I My Brother's Keeper: A Study of British Columbia's Labor and Oriental Problems* (Toronto, 1913), 7; and BC Royal Commission on Labour, Proceedings, Vol. 5, 108

38 *Solidarity*, July 15, 1911; and *Industrial Worker*, June 29, 1911

39 Wayne State, IWW Records, Vol. 145, File 28, Latchem, 'Yellow Socialists and Red Communists,' ND, 1

40 Laut, *Brother's Keeper*, 16; *Industrial Worker*, May 20, 1909; and *Solidarity*, March 22, 1913

41 Dubofsky, *We Shall Be All*, 173-4; Conlin, *Bread and Roses Too*, 74; *Solidarity*, Sept. 17, 1910; and *Industrial Worker*, Sept. 28, 1911

42 Carleton H. Parker, 'The Casual Laborer,' in *The Casual Laborer and Other Essays* (New York, 1920), 80; PAC, Immigration Records, Vol. 486-752149-1, MacGill to Scott, Feb. 12, 1912; *Labour Gazette*, XII, 538; and *British Columbia Federationist*, Jan. 6, 1912

43 *Industrial Worker*, Jan. 25, 1912; and Immigration Records, Vol. 485-752149-1 MacGill to Scott, Jan. 25, 1912

44 *The Province*, Nov. 25, 1911; Immigration Records, Vol. 486-752149-1, MacGill to Scott, Feb. 12, 1912; *British Columbia Federationist*, Feb. 5, 1912; and PAC, DND Records, Vol. 6517, HQ 363-24-1, Wadmore to Adjutant General, Feb. 3, 1912

45 *Western Clarion*, Feb. 3, 1912 and DND Records, Vol. 6517, HQ 363-24-1, Stewart to Wadmore, Feb. 5, 1912

46 *Industrial Worker*, Feb. 15, 1912; and *The Province*, Feb. 12, 1912

47 Immigration Records, Vol. 486-752149-1, Rodgers to Scott, Feb. 8, 1912; and MacGill to Scott, Feb. 12, 1912; *The Province*, Feb. 2, 1912; and McGuckin, 'Recollections of a Wobbly,' 40-2

48 *Industrial Worker*, Feb. 22, 1912
49 *The Province*, Jan. 30, 1912; Feb. 12, 1912; and Feb. 20, 1912; *The Sun*, Feb. 14, 1912; and Immigration Records, Vol. 486-752149-1, MacGill to Scott, Feb. 15, 1912
50 *Industrial Worker*, March 7, 1912
51 RCMP Records, A-1, Vol. 426-286, McKenzie to Borden, April 29, 1912; *Solidarity*, Sept. 16, 1911 and BC Provincial Police Records, Superintendent's Incoming Correspondence, Yale District, File 6-2, MacNair to Campbell, May 13, 1912 [the latter collection will be hereafter cited BCPP-IWW].
52 *Solidarity*, Nov. 11, 1911
53 *Industrial Worker*, April 11, 1912; and May 30, 1912; *The Sun*, April 2, 1912; and *Kamloops Standard*, April 9, 1912
54 *Industrial Worker*, April 4, 1912; and April 18, 1912; *Solidarity*, April 13, 1912; Wayne State, IWW Records, Vol. 24-17, Moreau to Thompson, Feb. 20, 1967; and March 8, 1967; *The Sun*, April 4, 1912; and *Kamloops Standard*, April 9, 1912
55 *The Province*, April 8, 1912; and BCPP-IWW, File 5-1, Smith to Campbell, April 1, 1912
56 BCPP-IWW, File 5-1, Burr to Campbell, March 30, 1912; *Industrial Worker*, April 4, 1912; and Agnes C. Laut, 'Revolution Yawns,' *Illustrated Technical World*, Vol. 18 (May, 1913), 135-6
57 Donald Avery, 'Canadian Immigration Policy and the "Foreign" Navvy,' *Historical Papers*, 1972, 152; and BCPP-IWW, File 5-1, Smith to Campbell, April 2, 1912
58 BCPP-IWW, File 5-1, Smith to Campbell, April 14, 1912; and April 16, 1912; and File 6-2, 'Translation of circular in Italian language issued from the office of the I.W.W. at Savona,' April 10, 1912; and Campbell to Bowser, April 15, 1912
59 PABC, Attorney General's Records, Vol. 2570-16-12, White to Bowser, April 1, 1912; *The Province*, April 2, 1912; and *The Kamloops Standard*, April 30, 1912
60 BCPP-IWW, File 6-2, Goucher to Bowser, April 13, 1912; and *Edmonton Journal*, April 13, 1912
61 BCPP-IWW, File 6-2, Bowser to Campbell, April 16, 1912
62 *British Columbia Federationist*, June 22, 1912
63 *Industrial Worker*, May 23, 1912; and May 30, 1912; and BCPP-IWW, File 5-1, Campbell to Cox, April 21, 1912; and File 6-2, Hannay to Campbell, May 8, 1912; and Dunwoody to Campbell, May 10, 1912
64 *The Kamloops Standard*, May 3, 1912; *Solidarity*, June 15, 1912; and *British Columbia Federationist*, Aug. 2, 1912

65 BC Provincial Police Records, Superintendent's Incoming Correspondence, AG Files, Campbell to Bowser, April 27, 1912; and Bowser to Campbell, May 30, 1912

66 Dubofsky, *We Shall Be All*, 162-3; and Conlin, *Bread and Roses Too*, 103-5

67 *Industrial Worker*, June 15, 1911; Nov. 30, 1911; and Feb. 8, 1912; and *Solidarity*, July 15, 1911

68 Herbert G. Gutman, 'Work, Culture, and Society in Industrializing America, 1815-1919,' *The American Historical Review*, 78 (June, 1973), 573-4

69 *Industrial Worker*, April 18, 1912; and July 4, 1912

70 Ibid., June 19, 1913

71 Ibid., March 13, 1913; March 27, 1913; April 17, 1913; April 24, 1913; May 1, 1913; May 15, 1913; and July 3, 1913. The term sabotage was coined from *sabot*, a clumsy wooden shoe.

72 *Labour Gazette*, XIII and XIV

73 *Solidarity*, Oct. 10, 1914; and *The Voice of the People*, Feb. 5, 1914

74 Laurier Papers, Vol. 695, Turnbull, 'Re Un-employed in Edmonton, 1913-14'; *Edmonton Daily Bulletin*, Jan. 17, 1914; and *Edmonton Capital*, Jan. 16, 1914

75 *The Voice of the People*, Feb. 12, 1914; *Western Clarion*, Feb. 28, 1914; *Edmonton Daily Bulletin*, Feb. 2, 1914; and *Edmonton Capital*, May 20, 1914

76 *Edmonton Capital*, May 15, 1914; and May 16, 1914

77 *Edmonton Daily Bulletin*, Feb. 5, 1914; and *The Voice of the People*, Oct. 22, 1914

78 RCMP Records, A-1, Vol. 487-348

79 *Industrial Worker*, Oct. 24, 1912; and *The Voice*, Sept. 26, 1913

80 Robert H. Babcock, *Gompers in Canada: A Study in American Continentalism Before the First World War* (Toronto, 1974), 163-4; *Industrial Union Bulletin*, Aug. 17, 1907; Foner, *Industrial Workers of the World*, 231; and *Industrial Worker*, June 11, 1910

81 *Solidarity*, Aug. 27, 1910; and *Industrial Worker*, Nov. 2, 1911

82 *The Prince Rupert Optimist*, Nov. 25, 1910; and Samuel Gompers, *Seventy Years of Life and Labor* (New York, 1925), Vol. 1, 424-5

83 *Industrial Worker*, Aug. 12, 1909; April 27, 1911; and Oct. 12, 1911

84 *British Columbia Federationist*, May 20, 1912; and *Western Clarion*, Oct. 23, 1909; and July 18, 1914

85 *Industrial Worker*, July 1, 1909; and July 8, 1909; and *Solidarity*, Dec. 16, 1911

86 *Industrial Worker*, Dec. 19, 1912

87 *Solidarity*, March 11, 1911; George Hardy, *Those Stormy Years* (London,

1956), 28; Wayne State, IWW Records, Vol. 145-28, Latchem, 'Yellow Socialists and Red Communists,' 82; and McGuckin, 'Recollections of a Wobbly,' 41

88 Babcock, *Gompers in Canada*, 139; William Bennett, *Builders of British Columbia* (Vancouver, ND), 41; H.A. Logan, *Trade Unions in Canada* (Toronto, 1948), 300; and Paul Phillips, *No Power Greater: A Century of Labour in British Columbia* (Vancouver, 1967), 46

89 PABC, Attorney General's Records, Vol. 6046-16-12, McVety to Bowser, July 17, 1912; and RCMP Records, A-1, Vol. 487-348, Gavell to Rowan, Aug. 4, 1914

90 Dubofsky, *We Shall Be All*, 223-5

91 *The Agitator*, April 1, 1911. For north Winnipeg anarchism see Immigration Records, Vol. 513-800111, Ashdown to Oliver, April 9, 1908; and Rudolph Rocker, *The London Years*, trans. by J. Leftwich (London, 1956), 233-5

92 *Solidarity*, Dec. 2, 1911; and May 23, 1914; *The Agitator*, May 15, 1912; and *The Syndicalist*, Jan. 15, 1913

93 *The Syndicalist*, Feb. 15, 1913; and June 1, 1913

94 *British Columbia Federationist*, Aug. 22, 1913; and Sept. 12, 1913; and University of British Columbia, Special Collections Division, Vancouver Trades and Labor Council Minutes, Sept. 4, 1913

95 *British Columbia Federationist*, Dec. 12, 1913; Jan. 2, 1914; Jan. 16, 1914; and Feb. 13, 1914; and Hardy, *Those Stormy Years*, 51-2

96 Vancouver Trades Council Minutes, Jan. 15, 1914; and *The Voice of the People*, Nov. 13, 1913

97 Phillips, *No Power Greater*, 50; and TLC *Proceedings*, 1911, 73-4; and 1912, 82

98 Vancouver Trades Council Minutes, Aug. 15, 1912; and Oct. 17, 1912; *Industrial Worker*, Aug. 29, 1912; and *British Columbia Federationist*, Nov. 15, 1912; and Nov. 22, 1912

99 *District Ledger*, Jan. 13, 1912

100 Ibid., Feb. 10, 1912; and Feb. 24, 1912

101 Ibid., Feb. 24, 1912; March 3, 1912; and April 30, 1912; and *Industrial Worker*, March 14, 1912

102 Dan Sproul, 'The Situation in British Columbia,' *International Socialist Review*, X (Feb., 1910), 743; and *Western Clarion*, Dec. 11, 1909

103 *Western Clarion*, March 29, 1913; and Sept. 27, 1913

104 *Bulletin* [IAM, Winnipeg], June, 1914

105 Henry Pelling, *A History of British Trade Unionism* (London, 1965), 135-43

106 David J. Bercuson, 'The Roots of the One Big Union: A Study of Western Canadian Syndicalism,' paper read before the convention of the Canadian Historical Association, Edmonton, 1975, 4-5

107 *Western Clarion*, Dec. 20, 1913
108 *The Voice*, March 8, 1912

CHAPTER 7

1 *The Voice*, April 15, 1910; and *British Columbia Federationist*, Jan. 24, 1913
2 *Western Clarion*, Aug. 2, 1913; and *The Voice*, Feb. 7, 1913
3 TLC *Proceedings*, 1911, 74; and *Labour Gazette*, XIV, 954
4 *The Voice*, Dec. 13, 1912
5 Ibid., Aug. 7, 1914
6 *British Columbia Federationist*, Aug. 7, 1914
7 *Western Clarion*, Aug. 15, 1914; Oct. 24, 1914; and Nov. 21, 1914
8 *Solidarity*, Oct. 10, 1914; and Wayne State, IWW Records, Vol. 113-15, 'United States vs. Haywood, Et Al,' 8757-8
9 Interview with Tipping, May 3, 1971; Leo Heaps, *The Rebel in the House: The Life and Times of A.A. Heaps MP* (London, 1970), 10; and *The Voice*, Aug. 28, 1914; and Oct. 2, 1914
10 *Western Clarion*, Aug. 15, 1914; *Voice of the People*, Sept. 10, 1914; and *British Columbia Federationist*, Aug. 28, 1914
11 *The Voice*, Aug. 14, 1914
12 *British Columbia Federationist*, April 30, 1915
13 *Manifesto of SPC*, [4th ed.], 4-5; Pritchard to the author, Dec. 27, 1971; and *Western Clarion*, Oct. 24, 1914
14 *The Voice*, Feb. 12, 1915; April 2, 1915; and April 30, 1915
15 Ibid., Sept. 11, 1914; and *British Columbia Federationist*, Oct. 30, 1914
16 Glenbow Foundation, Archives Division, Records of the United Mine Workers of America, District Executive Board Minutes, Nov. 7, 1914; and *British Columbia Federationist*, Feb. 26, 1915
17 William Bennett, *Builders of British Columbia* (Vancouver, ND), 76
18 RCMP Records, A-1, Vol. 490-396, Cuthbert to Fortescue, July 13, 1915; *Western Clarion*, Jan. 2, 1915; and *The Voice*, Aug. 7, 1914
19 *British Columbia Federationist*, June 9, 1916; and RCMP Records, A-1, Vol. 490-433, McNiven to Acland, June 23, 1915
20 *The Voice*, Dec. 1, 1916; *British Columbia Federationist*, Oct. 8, 1915; Feb. 18, 1916; and Dec. 8, 1916; and Public Archives of Manitoba [PAM], T.C. Norris Papers, Rigg to Norris, April 28, 1916
21 *The Voice*, April 28, 1916
22 University of British Columbia, Special Collections Division, Vancouver Trades and Labor Council Minutes, Aug. 6, 1914
23 *Labour Gazette*, XVIII, 48

24 *British Columbia Federationist*, Oct. 20, 1916
25 *The Voice*, Oct. 20, 1916
26 H.D. Woods and S. Ostry, *Labour Policy and Labour Economics in Canada* (Toronto, 1962), 398-400; H.C. Pentland, 'A Study of the Changing Social, Economic and Political Background of the Canadian System of Industrial Relations,' prepared for the Task Force on Labour Relations, 1968; and J.H. Sutcliffe and Paul Phillips, 'Real Wages and the Winnipeg General Strike: An Emperical Investigation,' unpublished study, 1972
27 Borden Papers, Vol. 68, McVety to Stevens, April 15, 1916; Norris Papers, Rigg to Norris, Nov. 18, 1916; and Dec. 12, 1916; and University of Victoria, Special Collections Division, Victoria Trades and Labor Council Minutes, Nov. 29, 1916
28 *Labour Organizations In Canada*, 1917, 38-9
29 David Jay Bercuson, *Confrontation at Winnipeg: Labour Industrial Relations and the General Strike* (Montreal, 1974), 35-9; *The Voice*, Dec. 17, 1915; and *British Columbia Federationist*, May 5, 1916
30 *British Columbia Federationist*, April 28, 1916
31 *Labour Gazette*, XVIII, 98-118; and C.J. McMillan, 'Trade Unionism in District 18, 1900-1925: A Case Study,' unpublished MBA thesis, University of Alberta, 1969, 124-32
32 Borden Papers, Vol. 213, Plessis to Blount, Jan. 24, 1917; and Borden to Crothers, Feb. 3, 1917; and *The Voice*, May 4, 1917; and May 18, 1917
33 *The Voice*, Nov. 26, 1915; and *British Columbia Federationist*, Dec. 22, 1916
34 *Labour Organizations in Canada*, 1917, 18; and TLC *Proceedings*, 1917, 149
35 *British Columbia Federationist*, June 1, 1917
36 Ibid., Oct. 6, 1916
37 *Canadian Annual Review*, 1917, 416-17
38 *The Voice*, Sept. 1, 1916
39 *British Columbia Federationist*, June 2, 1916; and *The Voice*, Sept. 24, 1915
40 *British Columbia Federationist*, Aug. 11, 1916
41 *Canadian Annual Review*, 1916, 325-8
42 *The Voice*, March 17, 1916; and *British Columbia Federationist*, March 3, 1916
43 *British Columbia Federationist*, May 5, 1916
44 Ibid., Oct. 27, 1916; and *The Voice*, Dec. 29, 1916
45 *The Voice*, Dec. 29, 1916
46 Ibid., Dec. 15, 1916; and PAC, J.S. Woodsworth Papers, Vol. 31, Bennett to Woodsworth, Dec. 21, 1916
47 *Canadian Annual Review*, 1916, 332; and *British Columbia Federationist*, Dec. 22, 1916

48 Borden Papers, Vol. 68, Young to Borden, Dec. 22, 1916; and *Alberta Federation of Labor, Proceedings Fourth Annual Convention* (1917), 8-14

49 *British Columbia Federationist*, Jan. 12, 1917; and Borden Papers, Vol. 68, Stevens to Borden, Dec. 22, 1916

50 Borden Papers, Vol. 68, 'Executive of Trades Labor Council' to Borden, Dec. 21, 1916 and Borden to Watters, et al. Dec. 27, 1916

51 *Labour Organizations in Canada*, 1916, 39-40

52 *British Columbia Federationist*, April 28, 1916

53 *The Voice*, Dec. 22, 1916; Dec. 29, 1916; and Jan. 5, 1917

54 Victoria Trades Council Minutes, Dec. 20, 1916; and Jan. 9, 1917

55 *British Columbia Federationist*, Jan. 5, 1917

56 *Alberta Federation of Labor, Proceedings of Fourth Annual Convention*, (1917), 41

57 Saskatchewan Archives Board, Regina Trades and Labor Council, Correspondence, Young to Regan, Jan. 6, 1917

58 Ibid., circular from 'Resolution Publicity Committee,' Jan. 10, 1917

59 *Labour Organizations in Canada*, 1916, 45-6; *British Columbia Federationist*, Jan. 12, 1917; and Jan. 26, 1917; and *The Voice*, Jan. 5, 1917

60 *British Columbia Federationist*, Feb. 2, 1917; and Paul A. Phillips, *No Power Greater: A Century of Labour in British Columbia* (Vancouver, 1967), 67

61 *The Voice*, May 25, 1917; *British Columbia Federationist*, June 1, 1917; RCMP Records, A-1, Vol. 537-393, 'No Conscription'; and PAC, Records of the Secretary of State's Dept., Chief Press Censors Files, Vol. 144-A-1, Coulter to Chambers, July 21, 1917

62 Borden Papers, Vol. 213; this box contains a number of letters to Borden which advocate the industrial conscription feared by the labour movement.

63 *The Voice*, June 15, 1917

64 *British Columbia Federationist*, June 1, 1917; and June 8, 1917

65 Ibid., June 1, 1917; and Pritchard to the author, Feb. 5, 1972

66 *The Voice*, June 1, 1917; and June 22, 1917

67 Ibid., June 8, 1917; and June 22, 1917; and Transcript of Interview of Jacob Penner by Roland Penner

68 Chief Press Censors' Files, Vol. 144-A-1, Coulter to Chambers, July 26, 1917; *Western Clarion*, Sept., 1917; and *The Voice*, July 6, 1917

69 Interview with Tipping, May 3, 1971; and *The Voice*, June 15, 1917

70 Borden Papers, Vol. 213, Wood to Borden, May 16, 1917; and Borden to Curtiss, May 25, 1917

71 Ibid., Vol. 219, Grain to Borden, May 30, 1917; McGillicuddy to Borden, June 2, 1917; Borden to Crothers, June 10, 1917; Crothers to Borden, June 13, 1917; and Meighen to Borden, June 23, 1917

72 TLC *Proceedings*, 1917, 36; Borden Papers, Vol. 182, Godfrey to Borden, July 6, 1917; and *British Columbia Federationist*, Nov. 9, 1917

73 Borden Papers, Vol. 82, Bennett to Clark, Sept. 1, 1917

74 The registers to the Commissioners' Records contain pages of entries for 'personal history files,' but these dossiers are not on deposit at the PAC, if they still exist.

75 Chief Press Censor's Files, Vol. 279-7-1, Chambers to Reid, June 24, 1917; and Vol. 279-7, Mulvey to Chambers, June 9, 1917

76 Ibid., Vol. 279-7-2, Tweedale to Chambers, July 17, 1917; Vol. 272, Chambers to Scott, Oct. 29, 1917; and Vol. 279-1, Chambers to Burrell, Nov. 19, 1917

77 Ibid., Vol. 272, Chambers to Hindmarch, Nov. 26, 1917

78 TLC *Proceedings*, 1914, 15-16 and 129

79 Ibid., 1917, 43 and 142-4; and *British Columbia Federationist*, Sept. 28, 1917

80 *The Voice*, Sept. 21, 1917; and *British Columbia Federationist*, Sept. 28, 1917

81 Martin Robin, *Radical Politics and Canadian Labour, 1880-1930* (Kingston, 1968), 131-3

82 *The Voice*, Aug. 17, 1917; Woodsworth Papers, Vol. 31, 'Scrapbook'; and *British Columbia Federationist*, Sept. 7, 1917

83 *British Columbia Federationist*, Sept. 7, 1917; and *The Voice*, Sept. 28, 1917

84 *The Voice*, Aug. 31, 1917; Sept. 14, 1917; Oct. 19, 1917; and Nov. 16, 1917; and *Manitoba Free Press*, Nov. 12, 1917; and Nov. 19, 1917

85 Laurier Papers, Vol. 716, Donovan to Laurier, Nov. 15, 1917; and Vol. 717, Knott to Laurier, Nov. 21, 1917

86 *The Voice*, July 20, 1917; and Aug. 10, 1917

87 Laurier Papers, Vol. 713, Laurier to Chevrier, Sept. 15, 1917; and Vol. 715, Laurier to Donovan, Oct. 29, 1917

88 *The Voice*, Nov. 9, 1917; and Laurier Papers, Vol. 716, Dixon to Laurier, Nov. 7, 1917

89 *The Voice*, Nov. 23, 1917

90 *Western Clarion*, Jan., 1918; and *Manitoba Free Press*, Dec. 10, 1917

91 *The Voice*, Nov. 30, 1917

92 Ibid.

93 Ibid., Dec. 7, 1917

94 *Manitoba Free Press*, Nov. 20, 1917; Nov. 27, 1917; Dec. 4, 1917; and Dec. 17, 1917; and Victoria College, Salem Bland Papers, Vol. 10, Crerar to Bland, Dec. 22, 1917

95 *The Voice*, Dec. 14, 1917

96 Ibid., Oct. 5, 1917; TLC *Proceedings*, 1917, 63; and *British Columbia Federationist*, Nov. 30, 1917
97 *British Columbia Federationist*, Dec. 21, 1917; and *The Voice*, Jan. 4, 1918
98 *British Columbia Federationist*, Nov. 9, 1917

CHAPTER 8

1 *Royal Commission on Industrial Relations, Report*, Supplement to *Labour Gazette*, XIX (July), 6-7
2 *Royal Commission on Industrial Relations, Report*, 8-9; *Labour Gazette*, XVIII, 1131; and *The Voice*, Feb. 22, 1918
3 *Labour Gazette*, XVIII, 378-9; *Canadian Annual Review*, 1918, 490; PC 2525, Oct. 11, 1918; and *British Columbia Federationist*, June 7, 1918
4 *British Columbia Federationist*, May 24, 1918
5 Ibid., Jan. 18, 1918; Jan. 25, 1918; Feb. 1, 1918; and Feb. 8, 1918
6 University of British Columbia, Special Collections Division, Angus McInnis Collection, Vol. 53-17, 'Ambrose Tree: Old S.P.C. member' and Vol. 53-13, 'Tom O'Connor'; interview with W.A. Pritchard, Aug. 16-18, 1971; interview with Fred Tipping, May 3, 1971; transcript of interview of Jacob Penner by Roland Penner; and *The Origin of the One Big Union: A Verbatim Report of the Calgary Conference 1919* (Winnipeg, ND), 26-7
7 William Bennett, *Builders of British Columbia* (Vancouver, ND), 77; Angus McInnis Collection, Vol. 34-4, 'Proceedings at Inquest on the body of Albert Goodwin,' July 31, 1918; *British Columbia Federationist*, Aug. 2, 1918; and *Western Clarion*, Aug., 1918
8 *British Columbia Federationist*, April 19, 1918; and July 19, 1918; *The Voice*, Jan. 25, 1918; and Borden Papers, Vol. 238, Ivens to Crerar, Feb. 25, 1918; and Robinson to Borden, April 8, 1918
9 *British Columbia Federationist*, April 27, 1917; and *The Messenger*, July, 1917
10 *British Columbia Federationist*, May 4, 1917
11 Ibid., May 18, 1917; *Western Clarion*, May, 1917; and interview with Pritchard, Aug. 16-18, 1971
12 William Rodney, *Soldiers of the International: A History of the Communist Party of Canada, 1919-1929* (Toronto, 1968), 15; and John Weir, 'The Flaming Torch,' undated manuscript, 15-16
13 Chief Press Censor's Files, Vol. 144-A-1, 'Central Committee U.S.D.R.P. and Workmen's Gazette' to 'Canada Executive Committee of the U.S.D.P.,' Sept. 23, 1917
14 Weir, 'Flaming Torch,' 16

15 Tim Buck, *Lenin and Canada* (Toronto, 1970), 15-19; A.E. Smith, *All My Life* (Toronto, 1949), 43-4; Weir, 'Flaming Torch,' 15; Bennett, *Builders of British Columbia*, 141; and transcript of interview of Jacob Penner by Roland Penner

16 *British Columbia Federationist*, Jan. 25, 1918; and Feb. 1, 1918; and *Western Clarion*, Feb., 1918

17 Weir, 'Flaming Torch,' 16; and Chief Press Censor's Files, Vol. 144-A-1, Tartak to Chambers, May 10, 1918

18 Transcript of interview of Jacob Penner by Roland Penner; and *The Voice*, March 15, 1918

19 *Western Clarion*, March, 1918; April, 1918; and July, 1918; and Pritchard to the author, Dec. 27, 1971

20 *Western Labor News*, Aug. 9, 1918

21 PAM, Winnipeg General Strike Trials Collection, The King vs R.B. Russell, Beattie to Stephenson, Nov. 24, 1918

22 *British Columbia Federationist*, Feb. 1, 1918; *The Voice*, March 5, 1918; and Woodsworth Memorial Collection, transcript of interview of James Aiken by Paul Fox. For the labour parties established in 1918, see below.

23 *The Voice*, March 15, 1918; and *Western Clarion*, March, 1918; and Sept., 1918

24 Chief Press Censor's File, Vol. 144-A-1, Tartak to Chambers, May 10, 1918; and *British Columbia Federationist*, Jan. 18, 1918; and March 29, 1918

25 *British Columbia Federationist*, April 12, 1918

26 Ibid., Feb. 1, 1918; and Feb. 8, 1918; *The Voice*, Jan. 4, 1918; Jan. 25, 1918; and March 16, 1918; W.R. Askin, 'Labour Unrest in Edmonton and District and Its Coverage by the Edmonton Press: 1918-1919,' MA thesis, University of Alberta, 1973, 39, 58

27 It is misleading to assert, as do Steeves and Robin, that the SPC split on the issue of the FLP; Kingsley, Pettipiece, and McVety had not been active in the party for some time [D.G. Steeves, *The Compassionate Rebel: Ernest E. Winch and his Times* (Vancouver 1960), 37; and Martin Robin, *Radical Politics and Canadian Labour 1880-1930* (Kingston, 1968), 150].

28 W.J.C. Cherwinski, 'The Trade Union Movement in Saskatchewan,' PHD thesis, University of Alberta, 1972, 241; *The Voice*, June 7, 1918; and *British Columbia Federationist*, March 15, 1918

29 *Western Clarion*, Oct., 1917; interview with Pritchard, Aug. 16-18, 1971; and *The Voice*, May 3, 1918

30 *Western Clarion*, Oct., 1917; and The King vs Russell, Beattie to Stephenson, Feb. 27, 1919

31 *Western Clarion*, June, 1918; and *The Voice*, May 17, 1918

32 *British Columbia Federationist*, Feb. 1, 1918; and Feb. 8, 1918; Steeves, *Compassionate Rebel*, 36-8; Askin, 'Labour Unrest in Edmonton,' 54-5; and PAC, R.A. Rigg Papers, Murray to Rigg, May 28, 1918

33 *British Columbia Federationist*, Jan. 11, 1918; and March 29, 1918

34 Interview with Tipping, May 3, 1971; and *Western Labor News*, Sept. 17, 1918; and Oct. 14, 1918

35 *British Columbia Federationist*, July 15, 1918; July 12, 1918; and Oct. 18, 1918

36 Ibid., Aug. 16, 1918; University of Victoria, Special Collections Division, Victoria Trades and Labor Council Minutes, July 29, 1918; Glenbow Foundation, Archives Divisions, United Mine Workers of America Records, District 18 Executive Board Minutes, July 26, 1918; Saskatchewan Archives Board, Regina Trades and Labor Council Records, Sambrook to Churton, July 30 1918; and *Western Labor News*, Aug. 2, 1918

37 *British Columbia Federationist*, Oct. 25, 1918; UMW Records, District 18 Executive Board Minutes, Oct. 30, 1918; Regina Trades Council Records, Robinson to Sanbrook, Oct. 28, 1918; and Sanbrook to Robinson, Nov. 5, 1918; and *Western Labor News*, Oct. 11, 1918 and Oct. 25, 1918

38 David Jay Bercuson, *Confrontation at Winnipeg: Labour, Industrial Relations and the General Strike* (Montreal, 1974), 58-65

39 Paul A. Phillips, *No Power Greater: A Century of Labour In British Columbia* (Vancouver, 1967), 73-4

40 *British Columbia Federationist*, July 15, 1918

41 *The Voice*, May 10, 1918; May 17, 1918; June 7, 1918; and June 21, 1918; and *Western Clarion*, June, 1918

42 *British Columbia Federationist*, May 24, 1918

43 Bercuson, *Confrontation at Winnipeg*, 67-8

44 Interview with Pritchard, Aug. 16-18, 1971

45 The King vs Russell, Stephenson to Beattie, Nov. 30, 1918; and Beattie to Stephenson, Feb. 6, 1919; and *Western Labor News*, Sept. 17, 1918; and Oct. 14, 1918

46 C.J. McMillan, 'Trade Unionism in District 18, 1900-1925: A Case Study,' MBA thesis, University of Alberta, 1969, 126; RCMP Records, A-1, Vol. 550-128, Zaneth to Horrigan, Oct. 14, 1918; and *British Columbia Federationist*, March 15, 1918; and Oct. 18, 1918

47 *Western Labor News*, Aug. 23, 1918; and Aug. 30, 1918

48 *British Columbia Federationist*, Aug. 9, 1918

49 *The Voice*, May 3, 1918; and *British Columbia Federationist*, April 19, 1918; and May 10, 1918

50 TLC *Proceedings*, 1918, 33, 114, 129-31 and 138-9

51 Ibid., 121 and 125
52 Ibid., 122; *Western Labor News*, Sept. 20, 1918; and *British Columbia Federationist*, Oct. 11, 1918
53 *Labour Organizations in Canada*, 1918, 65-6; *Western Labor News*, Oct. 4, 1918; and *British Columbia Federationist*, Oct. 25, 1918
54 RCMP Records, A-1, Vol. 565-505, Horrigan to Perry, Oct. 21, 1918
55 Borden Papers, Vol. 104, Poole to Borden, Feb. 11, 1918
56 Ibid., Robertson to Rowell, Feb. 20, 1918; and RCMP Records, A-1, Vol. 550-129, Horrigan to Wilson, Feb. 9, 1918
57 DND Records, Vol. 2553-2102, Fiset to Newcombe, July 23, 1918
58 Borden Papers, Vol. 104, Borden to Doherty, Feb. 23, 1918
59 Ibid., Cawdron to Doherty, May 23, 1918; and Immigration Dept. Records, File 917093, Scott to Cawdron, April 13, 1918
60 Borden Papers, Vol. 104, Cawdron to Doherty, March 19, 1918; and May 25, 1918; DND Records, Vol. 2553-2102, Hardy to Karrio, May 27, 1918; and RCMP Records, A-1, Vol. 550-128, Zaneth to Horrigan, Sept. 29, 1918
61 DND Records, Vol. 2553-2102, Sherwood to Gwatkin, Aug. 27, 1918; and Fiset to Newcombe, Aug. 26, 1918
62 Borden Papers, Vol. 104, Borden to Cahan, May 19, 1918
63 PAC, Justice Dept. Records, 1918-934, Cahan to Doherty, Sept. 14, 1918
64 Chief Press Censor's Files, Vol. 144-A-1, Chambers to Coulter, May 14, 1918; and Chambers to Davis, Sept. 6, 1918
65 Borden Papers, Vol. 104, Borden to Cahan, Sept. 17, 1918
66 Justice Dept. Records, 1918-2021, Newcombe to DeWolf, Sept. 16, 1918. In August the regulation of enemy aliens had been made more stringent by requiring all persons over sixteen years of age to register (PC 1908, Aug. 5, 1918).
67 Borden Papers, Vol. 104, Cahan to Borden, Oct. 21, 1918
68 The King vs Russell, Stephenson to Beattie, Nov. 30, 1918; Regina Trades Council Records, Stephenson to Baldwin, Jan. 1, 1919; and *The Red Flag*, Jan. 11, 1919
69 *Western Clarion*, Oct. 15, 1918
70 Chief Press Censor's File, Vol. 279-1, Chambers to Burrell, Nov. 19, 1917; and Vol. 144-A-1, Chambers to Popovich, May 27, 1918; and *British Columbia Federationist*, May 31, 1918
71 Chief Press Censor's Files, Vol. 144-A-1, Chambers to Burrell, Sept. 20, 1918
72 Ibid., Mulvey to Chambers, Sept. 24, 1918; and Vol. 279-1, Chambers to Stephenson, Oct. 26, 1918
73 Ibid., Vol. 272, Jukes to Chambers, Oct. 21, 1918; and Burrell to Chambers, Aug. 3, 1918; and Vol. 279-12, Sykes to Chambers, Oct. 20, 1918

74 Ibid., Vol. 272, Chambers to Burrell, Aug. 5, 1918; and Vol. 279-12, Chambers to Ivens, Sept. 24, 1918; and Robinson to Chambers, Oct. 5, 1918; and *British Columbia Federationist*, Sept. 20, 1918

75 Chief Press Censor's File, Vol. 279-12, Chambers to Sherwood, Oct. 26, 1918; and Vol. 272, Chambers to Burrell, Nov. 19, 1918

76 *British Columbia Federationist*, Nov. 29, 1918

77 Ibid., Nov. 8, 1918

78 PAM, Attorney General's Department Records, Court of King's Bench, 1919-20, The King vs. William Ivens et al., Vol. 3, Russell to Stephenson, Jan. 3, 1919

79 *British Columbia Federationist*, Nov. 22, 1918; and Jan. 3, 1919; Justice Dept. Records, 1918-2473, 'Alhambra Local No. 74' to Doherty, Dec. 22, 1918; and *Alberta Federation of Labor, Proceedings [of the] Sixth Annual Convention*, 35

80 Chief Press Censor's Files, Vol. 279, Chambers to Burrell, Jan. 14, 1919

81 *Western Labor News*, Jan. 24, 1919; Regina Trades Council Records, circular from Sambrook, ND; *British Columbia Federationist*, Feb. 7, 1919; Victoria Trades Council Minutes, Feb. 24, 1919; and *Alberta Federation of Labor, Proceedings [of the] Sixth Annual Convention*, 40

82 DND Records, Vol. 2543, F. 2051-2, Jukes to Davis, Jan. 29, 1919.

83 *Western Clarion*, Oct. 1, 1918; and *The Red Flag*, Dec. 28, 1918

84 *British Columbia Federationist*, Jan. 24, 1919

85 *Alberta Federation of Labor, Proceedings [of the] Sixth Annual Convention*, 35; Victoria Trades Council Minutes, Jan. 8, 1918; *Western Labor News*, Dec. 27, 1918; and DND Records, Vol. 2543, F. 2051-2, Reid to Chambers, Dec. 30, 1918

86 DND Records, Vol. 2571-2817-2, 'Re Longshoremen,' March 31, 1919; and Vol. 2543, F. 2051-1, Jukes to Davis, Dec. 17, 1918; and *British Columbia Federationist*, Dec. 6, 1918

87 *British Columbia Federationist*, Nov. 15, 1918; and *Western Labor News*, Jan. 3, 1919

88 *The Soviet*, March 8, 1919; and Cherwinski, 'Trade Union Movement in Saskatchewan,' 241

89 Bercuson, *Confrontation at Winnipeg*, 83-5

90 Ibid., 126

91 Quoted in D.C. Masters, *The Winnipeg General Strike* (Toronto, 1950), 32

92 PAM, One Big Union Records, Midgley to Robinson, Oct. 9, 1918

93 Ibid., Rees to Midgley, Nov. 24, 1918; and The King vs Ivens, Vol. 3, Russell to Knight, Jan. 3, 1919

94 The King vs Russell, Russell to Knight, Nov. 29, 1918; and Knight to Russell, Jan. 13, 1919

95 *Alberta Federation of Labor, Proceedings [of the] Sixth Annual Convention*, 32-40

96 McMillan, 'Trade Unionism in District 18,' 140

97 *British Columbia Federationist*, March 14, 1919; March 21, 1919; and March 28, 1919

98 *Origins of the OBU*, 10-11, 30

99 Ibid., 24-30, 33-6

100 Ibid., 24

101 Ibid., 46-50

102 Ibid., 11

103 *One Big Union Bulletin*, No. 1 (April, 1919)

104 *British Columbia Federationist*, March 21, 1919; April 11, 1919; and May 16, 1919; Victoria Trades Council Minutes, April 2, 1919; Interview with Pritchard, Aug. 16-18, 1971, and Phillips, *No Power Greater*, 79

105 McMillan, 'Trade Unionism in District 18,' 142; and UMW Records, District 18 Executive Board Minutes, March 29, 1919

106 *Western Labor News*, April 11, 1919; April 18, 1919; April 25, 1919; and May 9, 1919; and The King vs Ivens, Vol. 3, Russell to Midgley, March 19, 1919

107 Askin, 'Labor Unrest in Edmonton,' 64-8; and *Edmonton Free Press*, April 26, 1919; and May 10, 1919

108 DND Records, Vol. 2571-2817-2, McLean to Davis, April 23, 1919; and April 29, 1919; The King vs Ivens, Vol. 3, Midgley to Russell, April 26, 1919; and Phillips, *No Power Greater*, 80

109 The King vs Ivens, Vol. 4, Midgley to Berg, May 22, 1919; *British Columbia Federationist*, May 16, 1919; and *Labour Organizations in Canada*, 1919, 272. I am indebted to Professor David Bercuson for the OBU membership data.

110 *Manitoba Free Press*, March 6, 1919

111 Quoted in Bercuson, *Confrontation at Winnipeg*, 106

112 DND Records, Vol. 2543, F. 2051-2, Pennock to Chambers, Jan. 14, 1919

113 Ibid., Vol. 2665-3686-1, McLean to Davis, April 8, 1919

114 RCMP Records, H, typescript report of Samuel Blumenberg's deportation hearing, Vol. 4, testimony of Reames and Blumenberg and Vol. 5, testimony of Goldstein

115 Borden Papers, Vol. 104, Borden to Cahan, May 19, 1918

116 DND Records, Vol. 2543, F. 2051, Chambers to Maclean, Jan. 10, 1919

117 Chief Press Censor's Files, Vol. 272, Cahan to White, Jan. 7, 1919; and DND Records, Vol. 2543, F. 2051-1, Cahan to Doherty, Jan. 8, 1919

118 RCMP Records, B-2(c), Vol. 68, F. 18, Perry to Horrigan, Feb. 20, 1919; and

DND Records, Vol. 2543, F. 2051-2, Davis to Gwatkin, Feb. 2, 1919;
and Vol. 2544, F. 2051-1, Gwatkin to Ketchen et al., March 11, 1919

119 DND Records, Vol. 2576, F. 3042-2, Leckie to Ashton, May 5, 1919
120 Borden Papers, Vol. 112, White to Borden, April 16, 1919; and Borden to White, April 18, 1919; and April 29, 1919

CHAPTER 9

1 All earlier literature on the Winnipeg general strike has been superceded by David Jay Bercuson, *Confrontation at Winnipeg: Labour, Industrial Relations and the General Strike* (Montreal, 1974)
2 *Western Labor News*, May 20, 1919
3 *British Columbia Federationist*, June 6, 1919
4 *The Soviet*, June 10, 1919
5 Canada, *House of Commons Debates*, May 27, 1919, 2852-4
6 The King vs Russell, Johns to Midgley, May 19, 1919
7 RCMP Records, H, Vol. 2, Perry to McLean, June 10, 1919
8 *Edmonton Free Press*, June 14, 1919
9 C.J. McMillan, 'Trade Unionism in District 18, 1900-1925: A Case Study,' MBA thesis, University of Alberta, 1969, 146-55
10 *Labour Organizations in Canada*, 1919, 25-40
11 For the emergence of the Communist party see Ivan Avakumovic, *The Communist Party in Canada: A History* (Toronto, 1975), and William Rodney, *Soldiers of the International: A History of the Communist Party of Canada, 1919-1929* (Toronto, 1968).
12 In making this assertion, I did not ignore the Communist party; because of its preoccupation with the Soviet Union, its ethnic composition, and its ideology, the CP was never more than an isolated and inconsequential sect.
13 My remarks on labour parties in the twenties are based upon Kenneth McNaught, *A Prophet in Politics: A Biography of J.S. Woodsworth* (Toronto, 1959); Martin Robin, *Radical Politics and Canadian Labour 1880-1930* (Kingston, 1968); and Walter D. Young, *The Anatomy of a Party: The National CCF, 1932-61* (Toronto, 1969).

Selected bibliography

NEWSPAPERS

The Agitator, Lakebay, Wash. (1912)
American Labor Union Journal, Butte (1902-4)
Appeal to Reason, Greensburg, Ind. (1898-9)
The B.C. Workman, Victoria (1899)
British Columbia Federationist, Vancouver (1911-19)
The Bond of Brotherhood, Calgary (1903-4)
The Camp Worker, Vancouver (1919)
Canadian Forward, Toronto (1916-18)
The Canadian Socialist, Toronto and Vancouver (1902)
Citizen and Country, Toronto (1899, 1900, and 1902)
Coming Nation, Greensburg, Ind. (1899)
The Confederate, Brandon (1919)
Cotton's Weekly, Cowansville (1908-14)
The District Ledger, Fernie (1908-14 and 1918-19)
Edmonton Free Press, (1919)
The Independent, Vancouver (1900-4)
Industrial Union Bulletin, Chicago (1906-8)
Industrial Worker, Spokane (1909-13)
International Socialist Review, Chicago (1900-12)
Labor's Realm, Regina (1909-10)
Lardeau Eagle, Ferguson, BC (1900-2)
Miners' Magazine, Denver (1900-6)
The People, New York (1896-1900)
The People's Voice, Winnipeg (1894-7)
Railway Employees' Journal, San Francisco (1902-4)

The Red Flag, Vancouver (1919)
Saskatchewan Labor's Realm, Regina (1907-8)
The Socialist, Seattle (1901-3)
Solidarity, New Castle, Penn. (1910-14)
The Soviet, Edmonton (1919)
The Syndicalist, Lakebay, Wash. (1913)
The Trade Unionist, Vancouver (1908-9)
The Voice, Winnipeg (1897-1918)
The Voice of the People, New Orleans (1913-14)
Weekly People, New York (1905-6)
Western Clarion, Vancouver (1903-18)
Western Labor News, Winnipeg (1918-19)
Western Socialist, Vancouver (1902-3)
The Western Wage-Earner, Vancouver (1909-11)

MANUSCRIPT COLLECTIONS

Canada, Department of Labour Library
Clute, R.C. 'Royal Commission on Mining Conditions in British Columbia' 1899
– 'Royal Commission on Mining Conditions in British Columbia, Supplementary Report.' 1900
– 'Royal Commission on Mining Conditions in British Columbia, Evidence.' 1899
'Royal Commission on Industrial Relations, Evidence.' 1919
Glenbow Foundation
United Mine Workers of America, District 18 Records
Western Canadian Coal Operators Association Records
Miscellaneous (copies in the possession of the author)
Penner, Jacob 'Reminiscences of Early Labor-Farmer Elections'
Sheppard, Alex 's.p. of c. Notes'
Provincial Library of British Columbia
Royal Commission on Labour, 1914, Typescript Proceedings
Public Archives of British Columbia
Attorney General's Department Records
British Columbia Provincial Police Records
Public Archives of Canada.
Sir Robert L. Borden Papers
John W. Dafoe Papers
W.L. Mackenzie King Papers
Arthur Meighen Papers

Sir Wilfrid Laurier Papers
R.A. Rigg Papers
Sir Clifford Sifton Papers
James S. Woodsworth Papers
Chief Press Censor's Files, Secretary of State's Department Records
Immigration Department Records
Justice Department Records
Labour Department Records
National Defence Department Records
Royal Canadian Mounted Police Records
Public Archives of Manitoba
Attorney General's Department Records, The King vs Wm. Ivens Et. Al.
Fred Dixon Papers
William Ivens Papers
T.C. Norris Papers
One Big Union Records
Arthur Puttee Papers
Winnipeg General Strike Trials Collection, The King vs R.B. Russell
Saskatchewan Archives Board
Regina Trades and Labor Council Records
State Historical Society of Wisconsin
Socialist Labor Party of America Records
University of British Columbia
Angus MacInnis Memorial Collection
Industrial Workers of the World Records
International Union of Mine, Mill and Smelter Workers' Records
One Big Union Records
Vancouver Trades and Labor Council Records
University of Victoria
Victoria Trades and Labor Council Records
Victoria College, University of Toronto
Salem Bland Papers
Wayne State University
Industrial Workers of the World Records
E.W. Latchem Papers
H.E. McGucken Papers

ORAL SOURCES

Manitoba Museum of Man and Nature

214 Selected bibliography

Interview of Jacob Penner by Roland Penner
Public Archives of Canada
David Bercuson Collection
David Millar Collection
Public Archives of Manitoba
Interview of R.B. Russell by Lionel Orlikow
University of Toronto
Woodsworth Memorial Collection, Interviews by Paul Fox
University of Winnipeg
Interview of W.A. Pritchard by the author
Interview of Fred Tipping by the author

GOVERNMENT DOCUMENTS

CANADA, DEPARTMENT OF LABOUR. *Annual Report on Labour Organizations in Canada.* 1911-19
- *Labour Gazette.* 1900-19
CANADA. *Sessional Papers*, Vol. XXXVII, No. 36a, 1903. 'Report of the Royal Commission on Industrial Disputes in the Province of British Columbia'
- *Sessional Papers*, Vol. XXXVIII, No. 13, 1904, 'Evidence Taken Before the Royal Commission to Inquire into Industrial Disputes in the Province of British Columbia'
COATS, R.H. *Report of the Board of Inquiry into the Cost of Living.* Ottawa, 1915
MANITOBA. Royal Commission to Enquire into and Report upon the Causes and Effects of the General Strike in the City of Winnipeg, *Report.* Winnipeg, 1919

CONVENTION PROCEEDINGS

ALBERTA FEDERATION OF LABOR. *Proceedings of Annual Conventions.* 1912-14 and 1917-19
BRITISH COLUMBIA FEDERATION OF LABOR. *Proceedings of Annual Conventions.* 1911-12; 1914, and 1917-19
INDUSTRIAL WORKERS OF THE WORLD. *Proceedings of Annual Conventions,* 1905-15
The Origin of the One Big Union: A Verbatim Report of the Calgary Conference. Winnipeg, ND
TRADES AND LABOR CONGRESS OF CANADA. *Proceedings of Annual Conventions.* 1890-1919
WESTERN FEDERATION OF MINERS. *Proceedings of Annual Conventions.* 1902-08

PAMPHLETS

The Activities and Organization of the Citizen's Committee of One Thousand.
  Winnipeg, 1920
BLAKE, F. *The Proletarian in Politics.* Vancouver, ND
BUDDEN, ALF. *The Slave of the Farm.* Vancouver, ND
DESMOND, GERALD. *The Struggle for Existence.* Vancouver, ND
HARDENBURG, W.E. *What is Socialism?* Vancouver, ND
HEDLEY, JOHN N. *The Labor Trouble in Nanaimo District.* Nanaimo, ND
Labor Day Souvenir. Winnipeg, 1896
Manifesto of the Socialist Party of Canada. Third, Fourth and Fifth Editions,
  Vancouver, ND
An Open Letter on the Chinese Question to Sir Wilfrid Laurier, P.C., K.C.M.G.,
  Etc., Premier of Canada. Vancouver, 1902
OSBORNE, J.B. *The Way to Power.* Vancouver, ND
PILKINGTON, J. *Wage Worker and Farmer.* Vancouver, ND
PLACE, JACK. *The Record of J.H. Hawthornthwaite: Member for Nanaimo City*
  in the Local Legislature. Nanaimo, ND
Socialism and Unionism. Vancouver, ND
The Winnipeg General Sympathetic Strike. Winnipeg, ND

BOOKS

AITCHISON, J.H., ed. *The Political Process in Canada.* Toronto, 1963
ALLEN, RICHARD. *The Social Passion: Religion and Social Reform in Canada*
  1914-28. Toronto, 1971
ANDERSON, FRANK W. *Hillcrest Mine Disaster.* Calgary, 1969
BABCOCK, R.H. *Gompers in Canada: A Study of American Continentalism Before*
  the First World War. Toronto, 1974
BELL, DANIEL. *Marxian Socialism in the United States.* Princeton, 1967
BENNETT, WILLIAM. *Builders of British Columbia.* Vancouver, ND
BERCUSON, DAVID J. *Confrontation at Winnipeg: Labour, Industrial Relations*
  and the General Strike. Montreal, 1974
BERGEN, MYRTLE. *Tough Timber: The Loggers of B.C. – Their Story.* Toronto,
  1967
BRADWIN, EDMUND. *The Bunkhouse Man.* 2nd ed. Toronto, 1972
BRISSENDEN, PAUL. *The I.W.W.: a Study of American Syndicalism.* New York,
  1919
BUCK, TIM. *Canada and the Russian Revolution.* Toronto, 1967
– *Lenin and Canada.* Toronto, 1970

- *Thirty Years: 1922-1952: The Story of the Communist Movement in Canada.* Toronto, 1952
CLARK, S.D. *The Canadian Manufacturers' Association: A Study in Collective Bargaining and Political Pressure.* Toronto, 1939
CLEGG, H.A.; A. FOX, and A.F. THOMPSON. *A History of British Trade Unions Since 1889.* Oxford, 1964
CLEVERDON, CATHERINE LYLE. *The Woman Suffrage Movement in Canada.* Toronto, 1950 (rev. ed., Toronto, 1974)
COLE, G.D.H. *A History of Socialist Thought: Vol. III: The Second International 1889-1914.* London, 1960
CROOK, W.H. *The General Strike.* Chapel Hill, NC, 1931
CONLIN, J.R. *Bread and Roses Too: Studies of the Wobblies.* Westport, 1969
CRYSDALE, STEWART. *The Industrial Struggle and the Protestant Ethic in Canada.* Toronto, 1961
DUBOFSKY, MELVYN. *We Shall Be All: A History of the Industrial Workers of the World.* Chicago, 1969
EGHERT, DONALD DREW and S. PERSONS, eds. *Socialism and American Life.* Princeton, 1952
FERNS, H.S. and B. OSTRY. *The Age of Mackenzie King: The Rise of the Leader.* Toronto, 1955 (rev. ed., Toronto, 1976)
FONER, PHILIPS S. *History of the Labor Movement in the United States: The Industrial Workers of the World, 1905-1917.* New York, 1965
FREIDHEIM, R.L. *The Seattle General Strike.* Seattle, 1964
FRENCH, DORIS. *Faith, Sweat and Politics.* Toronto, 1962
GOMPERS, SAMUEL. *Seventy Years of Life and Labor: An Autobiography.* New York, 1943
GRAHAM, ROGER. *Arthur Meighen: The Door of Opportunity.* Toronto, 1960
GRIFFIN, HAROLD. *British Columbia: The People's Early Story.* Vancouver, 1958
HARDY, GEORGE. *Those Stormy Years.* London, 1956
Bill Haywood's Book. New York, 1929
HEAPS, LEO. *The Rebel in the House.* London, 1970
HERRESHOFF, DAVID. *American Disciples of Marx: From the Age of Jackson to the Progressive Era.* Detroit, 1967
HOFFMAN, F.L. *Fatal Accidents in Coal Mining.* Washington, 1910
HOROWITZ, GAD. *Canadian Labour in Politics.* Toronto, 1968
HOWAY, F.W.; W.N. SAGE, and H.F. ANGUS. *British Columbia and the United States.* Toronto, 1942
HUGHAN, JESSIE W. *American Socialism of the Present Day.* New York, 1912
JAMIESON, STUART. *Industrial Relations in Canada.* Toronto, 1957
- *Times of Trouble: Labour Unrest and Industrial Conflict in Canada, 1906-66.* Ottawa, 1971

JENSEN, V.H. *Heritage of Conflict: Labor Relations in the Non-ferrous Metals Industry up to 1930.* New York, 1950

KENNEDY, D.R. *The Knights of Labour in Canada.* London, Ontario, 1956

KOVACS, A.E., ed. *Readings in Canadian Labour Economics.* Toronto, 1961

LASLETT, JOHN H.M. *Labor and the Left.* New York, 1970

LAUT, AGNES C. *Am I My Brother's Keeper: A Study of British Columbia's Labour and Oriental Problems.* Toronto, 1913

LIPTON, CHARLES. *The Trade Union Movement of Canada 1827-1959.* Montreal, 1966

LOGAN, H.A. *Trade Unions in Canada.* Toronto, 1948

LYSENKO, VERA. *Men in Sheepskin Coats.* Toronto, 1947

MCBRIAR, A.M. *Fabian Socialism and English Politics, 1894-1914.* Cambridge, 1962

MC EWEN, TOM. *He Wrote for Us: The Story of Bill Bennett.* Vancouver, 1951

MC NAUGHT, KENNETH. *A Prophet in Politics: A Biography of J.S. Woodsworth.* Toronto, 1959

MASTERS, D.C. *The Winnipeg General Strike.* Toronto, 1950

MORTON, W.L. *Manitoba: A History.* Toronto, 1957

MURRAY, R.K. *The Red Scare: A Study in National Hysteria, 1919-1920.* Minneapolis, 1955

ORMSBY, MARGARET A. *British Columbia: A History.* Toronto, 1958

PARKER, CARLETON H. *The Casual Laborer and Other Essays.* New York, 1920

PELLING, HENRY. *A History of British Trade Unionism.* Harmondsworth, Middlesex, 1963

- *The Origins of the Labour Party: 1880-1900.* London, 1954

- *A Short History of the Labour Party.* London, 1965

PHILLIPS, PAUL. *No Power Greater: A Century of Labour in British Columbia.* Vancouver, 1967

QUINT, HOWARD H. *The Forging of American Socialism.* New York, 1964

REYNOLDS, L.G. *The British Immigrant: His Social and Economic Adjustment in Canada.* Toronto, 1935

ROBIN, MARTIN. *Radical Politics and Canadian Labour.* Kingston, 1968

- *The Rush for Spoils: The Company Province 1871-1933.* Toronto, 1972

ROCKER, RUDOLPH. *The London Years*, trans. J. Leftwich. London, 1956

RODNEY, WILLIAM. *Soldiers of the International: A History of the Communist Party of Canada, 1919-1929.* Toronto, 1968

SAVAGE, M.D. *Industrial Unionism in America.* New York, 1922

SHANNON, D.A. *The Socialist Party of America: A History.* Chicago, 1967

SMITH, A.E. *All My Life.* Toronto, 1949

STEEVES, D.G. *The Compassionate Rebel: Ernest E. Winch and his Times.* Vancouver, 1960

TAFT, PHILLIP. *Organized Labor in American History.* New York, 1964
THOMAS, L.G. *The Liberal Party in Alberta.* Toronto, 1959
THOMPSON, L.V. *Robert Blatchford: Portrait of an Englishman.* London, 1951
TYLER, R.L. *Rebels of the Woods: The I.W.W. in the Pacific Northwest.* Eugene, Oregon, 1967
WEINSTEIN, JAMES. *The Decline of Socialism in America: 1912-1925.* New York, 1969
WOODS, H.D., and S. OSTRY. *Labour Policy and Labour Economics in Canada.* Toronto, 1962
YOUNG, WALTER D. *The Anatomy of a Party: The National CCF, 1932-61.* Toronto, 1969
ZAKUTA, LEO. *A Protest Movement Becalmed: A Study of Change in the CCF.* Toronto, 1964
YUZYK, PAUL. *The Ukrainians in Manitoba.* Toronto, 1953

ARTICLES

ALLEN, RICHARD. 'The Social Gospel and the Reform Tradition in Canada, 1890-1928.' *Canadian Historical Review* XLIX (Dec., 1968)
AMY, W. LACY. 'Snaring the Bohunk.' *The Railroad and Current Mechanics* XVII (May, 1913)
ARTIBISE, A.F.J. 'Advertising Winnipeg: the Campaign for Immigrants and Industry, 1875-1914.' *Historical and Scientific Society of Manitoba Transactions,* Series III, No. 27 (1970-1)
– 'An Urban Environment: The Process of Growth in Winnipeg 1874-1914.' *Historical Papers* (1972)
AVERY, DONALD. 'Canadian Immigration Policy and the Foreign "Navvy." ' *Historical Papers* (1972)
BERCUSON, D.J. 'The Winnipeg General Strike, Collective Bargaining, and the One Big Union Issue.' *Canadian Historical Review* LI (June, 1970)
CHERWINSKI, W.J.C. 'Honore Joseph Jaxon, Agitator, Disturber, producer of plans to make men think, and Chronic Objector ... ' *Canadian Historical Review* XLVI (June, 1965)
DUBOFSKY, M. 'The Origins of Western Working Class Radicalism, 1890-1905.' *Labor History* VI (Spring, 1966)
FAY, E.R. 'The Early Years.' *Marxist Quarterly* (Spring, 1966)
IRELAND, R.R. 'Some Effects of Oriental Immigration on Canadian Trade Union Ideology.' *American Journal of Economics and Sociology* XIX (Jan., 1960)
JAMIESON, STUART, and PERCY GLADSTONE. 'Unionism in the Fishing Industry of BC.' *Canadian Journal of Economics and Political Science* XVI (Feb., 1950)

JOHNSON, G. 'The Harmony Industrial Association: A Pioneer Co-operative.' *Saskatchewan History* IV (Winter, 1951)

KOLISNYK, W.N. 'In Canada Since the Spring of 1898.' *Marxist Review*. (Jan.-Feb., 1961)

MC CORMACK, A.R. 'Arthur Puttee and the Liberal Party: 1899-1904.' *Canadian Historical Review* LI (June, 1970)

MC KEE, D.K. 'Daniel De Leon: A Reappraisal.' *Labor History* I (Fall, 1960)

OSTRY, BERNARD. 'Conservatives, Liberals and Labour in the 1870's.' *Canadian Historical Review* XLI (March, 1960)

– 'Conservatives, Liberals and Labour in the 1880's.' *Canadian Journal of Economics and Political Science* XXVII (May, 1961)

PENNER, JACOB. 'Recollections of the Early Socialist Movement in Winnipeg.' *Marxist Quarterly* (Summer, 1962)

REA, J.E. 'The Politics of Conscience: Winnipeg After the Strike.' *Historical Papers* (1971)

SAYWELL, J.T. 'Labour and Socialism in BC: A Survey of Historical Developments before 1903.' *British Columbia Historical Quarterly* XV (Winter, 1951)

WATT, F.M. 'The National Policy, the Workingman and Proletarian Ideas in Victorian Canada.' *Canadian Historical Review* XL (June, 1959)

WILLIAMS, C. BRIAN. 'Development of Relations between Canadian and American National Trade Union Centres – 1886-1925.' *Industrial Relations* XX (April, 1965)

WYNNE, R.E. 'American Labor Leaders and the Vancouver Anti-Oriental Riots.' *Pacific Northwest Quarterly* LVII (Winter, 1966)

THESES AND UNPUBLISHED STUDIES

ALLEN, A.R. 'Salem Bland and the Social Gospel in Canada.' MA, University of Saskatchewan, 1961

ASKIN, W.R. 'Labour Unrest in Edmonton and District and Its Coverage by the Edmonton Press: 1918-1919.' MA, University of Alberta, 1973

AVERY, DONALD. 'Dominion Control over the Recruitment and Placement of Immigrant Industrial Workers in Canada, 1890-1918.' Paper read before the Conference on Canadian Society in the Late Nineteenth Century, Montreal, 1975

BERCUSON, DAVID J. 'The Roots of the One Big Union: A Study of Western Canadian Syndicalism.' Paper read before the convention of the Canadian Historical Association, Edmonton, 1975

BOUDREAU, J.A. 'The Enemy Alien Problem in Canada, 1914-1919.' PHD, University of California, Los Angeles, 1964

CHERWINSKI, W.J.C. 'The Trade Union Movement in Saskatchewan.' PHD, University of Alberta, 1972

CHISICK, ERNIE. 'The Development of Winnipeg's Socialist Movement, 1900 to 1915.' MA, University of Manitoba, 1972

EMERY, G.N. 'Methodism on the Canadian Prairies 1896-1914: The Dynamics of an Institution in a New Environment.' PHD, University of British Columbia, 1970

FRIESEN, GERALD. 'Western Canada and the Trades and Labour Congress, 1898-1919.' Paper read before the convention of the Northern Great Plains Historical Association, Winnipeg, 1972

GRANTHAM, RONALD. 'Some Aspects of the Socialist Movement in British Columbia, 1898-1933.' MA, University of British Columbia, 1942

MC MILLAN, C.J. 'Trade Unionism in District 18, 1900-1925: A Case Study.' MBA, University of Alberta, 1969

ORLIKOW, L.G. 'A Survey of the Reform Movement in Manitoba 1910 to 1920.' MA, University of Manitoba, 1955

ORR, A.D. 'The Western Federation of Miners and the Royal Commission on Industrial Disputes in 1903 with Special Reference to the Vancouver Island Coal Miners' Strike.' MA, University of British Columbia, 1968

PENTLAND, H.C. 'Labour and the Development of Industrial Capitalism in Canada.' PHD, University of Toronto, 1969

- 'A Study of the Changing Social, Economic and Political Background of the Canadian System of Industrial Relations.' prepared for the Task Force on Labour Relations, 1968

PHILLIPS, PAUL. 'The National Policy and the Development of the Western Canadian Labour Movement.' Paper read before the Western History Conference, Calgary, 1970

RALSTON, H.K. 'The 1900 Strike of Fraser River Sockeye Salmon Fishermen.' MA, University of British Columbia, 1965

RYDER, W.S. 'Canada's Industrial Crisis of 1919.' MA, University of British Columbia, 1920

SUTCLIFFE, J.H. 'The Economic Background of the Winnipeg General Strike: Wages and Working Conditions.' MA, University of Manitoba, 1972

- and PAUL PHILLIPS. 'Real Wages and the Winnipeg General Strike: An Empirical Investigation.' 1972

THOMPSON, LORNE. 'The Rise of Labor Unionism in Alberta.' 1965

TROOP, G.R.F. 'Socialism in Canada.' MA, McGill University, 1927

UNDERHILL, H.F. 'Labour Legislation in British Columbia.' PHD, University of California, Berkeley, 1935

WARRIAN, PETER. 'The Challenge of the One Big Union Movement in Canada: 1919-1921.' MA, University of Waterloo, 1971

WEIR, JOHN. 'The Flaming Torch.' Copy in author's possession.

Index